The Moral Imagination

The Moral Imagination

The Art and Soul of Building Peace

JOHN PAUL LEDERACH

OXFORD
UNIVERSITY PRESS

OXFORD
UNIVERSITY PRESS

Oxford   New York
Auckland   Bangkok   Buenos   Aires   Cape Town   Chennai
Dares Salaam   Delhi   Hong Kong   Istanbul   Karachi   Kolkata
Kuala Lumpur   Madrid   Melbourne   Mexico City   Mumbai
Nairobi   São Paolo   Shanghai   Taipei   Tokyo   Toronto

Copyright © 2005 by Oxford University Press, Inc.

Published by Oxford University Press, Inc.
198 Madison Avenue, New York, New York 10016

www.oup.com

First issued as an Oxford University Press paperback, 2010

Library of Congress Cataloging-in-Publication Data
Lederach, John Paul.
The moral imagination: the art and soul of building peace / John Paul lederach.
p.   cm.
Includes bibliographical references and index.
ISBN 978-0-19-974758-0
1. Peace-building.   2. Pacific settlement of international disputes.
3. Conflict management.   4. Social change.   I. Title.
JZ5538.I43 2004
303.6'6—dc22   2004011794

13 12 11 10 9

Printed in the United States of America
on acid-free paper

This book is dedicated to Rose Barmasai

So we rise
Dust Dancers
Sandals to the ground
Between heat and fires.
No matter the dark
For she rises each night
Smile bouncing
Ancestor eyes lighting
The Rift Valley sky.

She, Rose.

In Memory of Rose Barmasai
March 9, 2000

John Paul Lederach

Thoughts for a Preface

For a long time I debated with myself a rather disconcerting question: For whom was I writing this book? I have always operated with the idea that an author should pick an audience, in fact a single person exemplary of that audience and write to that person. But I wanted to write a book that could be of wide interest, one that would cut across multiple disciplines and appeal to policy makers and practitioners, to people in town halls and those kneeling for Friday prayers or sitting in Sabbath or Sunday pews, to social theoreticians and conflict professionals. The more you try to speak to everyone, however, the less you speak to anyone. Since I could not find an elegant solution, I suspended the question and I just started to write.

About midway in the process of developing chapters, a sense of conversation emerged. I realized I was writing to colleagues in the professions of conflict transformation, mediation, restorative justice, and peacebuilding. I still entertain hopes that the ideas I wish to share and converse about will have a wide appeal, but my partner in the conversation is clear.

This book started as a sequel. On completion, it feels more like a prequel. Originally I set out to write a follow-up to what is probably my most well known book in the small universe where I tend to teach and work. The first pages of *Building Peace: Sustainable Reconciliation in Divided Societies* were written in early 1990, though the edition published and more broadly shared through the U.S. Institute of Peace Press did not appear until 1997. For all practical purposes, the first draft of that book was written more than fifteen years ago. Much of what follows in *The Moral Imagination* is indeed sequel in nature. The reader will find described the evolution and changes of my ideas, approaches, and revisions and specific references to how these developed since the writing of *Building Peace*. But *The Moral Imagination* is not an addendum to something else. It has become an effort to find a way back to the source of my work, the wellspring of that which lies invisible below the surface but gives life to a stream that trickles, then flows.

Building Peace could be understood principally as a book about the engineering of social change. That was not the expressed intent nor the language I used to describe it. But in all honesty that may well be a better way to situate the content. Based on experience, I sought to provide a theoretical framework to improve practical application. I have often said that the *Building Peace* framework does not suggest solutions. It poses a series of questions useful for thinking about and developing responsive initiatives and processes in settings of deep-rooted conflict. Those processes, however, must be connected to the specifics of situations and contexts. That is still true and underpins the potential usefulness of the book. Nonetheless, by its very nature, the framework lends itself to the design and engineering of peacebuilding. Therein I found a tension, present not only in the field at large as to how we move from destructive violence to constructive social engagement, but present within myself.

Through *The Moral Imagination*, I want to address that tension. In some regards, perhaps more than in any other book I have written, I discovered that taking up a conversation with my colleagues in the broadly defined conflict resolution field was in fact the carrying on of a conversation with myself as a conflict professional. Carl Rogers suggested that those things that are most personal are shared universally. I believe there is great merit to the idea, though it tends not to be practiced in formal academic writing. In the professional world of writing, we view with caution, even suspicion, the appearance of the personal, and lend a higher accent of legitimacy to models and skills, theory, well-documented case studies, and the technical application of theory that leads toward what we feel is the objectivity of conclusion and proposal. In the process, we do a disservice to our professions, to the building of theory and practice, to the public, and ultimately to ourselves. The disservice is this: When we attempt to eliminate the personal, we lose sight of ourselves, our deeper intuition, and the source of our understandings—*who we are* and *how we are* in the world. In so doing we arrive at a paradoxical destination: We believe in the knowledge we generate but not in the inherently messy and personal process by which we acquired it.

The Moral Imagination is about this messiness of innovation. I propose to explore the evolution of my understanding of peacebuilding by taking up the journey of where and how I have actually been in this world of experience that I call a vocational home. It is an effort to share what I have seen, the anecdotes and stories I have lived, and most important how ideas happened along the way that led to different, perhaps innovative ways of building social change. In this regard, as early readers of this manuscript noted, this is a book that takes a decidedly personal tack, with all of the strengths and weaknesses that accompany such an endeavor. As I wrote, I discovered that the writing was speaking to things of which I had been aware but had not fully addressed, much less embraced. On the front and back sides of peace engineering, I discovered that *The Moral Imagination* was finding its way to the art and soul of what I do.

Historically, there has been a mostly unspoken tension between two schools of thought in this field, which I have heard hinted at in a number of conferences and the occasional question from the floor to a keynote speaker: Is building peace an art or a skill? Discussions have emerged between those who believe responding to conflict and building social change is primarily a learned skill and those who see it as an art. *The Moral Imagination* weighs in with a different view: Building constructive social change in settings of deep-rooted conflict requires both. But the evolution of becoming a profession, the orientation toward technique, and the management of process in conflict resolution and peacebuilding have overshadowed, underestimated, and in too many instances forgotten the art of the creative process. This book, as has been the case with my own professional journey, is a compilation of conversations about how we might find our way back to the art of the matter.

I don't see finding the art of the matter as a minor corrective to an otherwise healthy system. It requires a worldview shift. I will propose that, as conflict professionals, we must go well beyond a sideshow, well beyond lip service to attain the art and soul of constructive change. We must envision our work as a creative act, more akin to the artistic endeavor than the technical process. This never negates skill and technique. But it does suggest that the wellspring, the source that gives life, is not found in the supporting scaffolding, the detailed knowledge of substance and process, nor the paraphernalia that accompanies any professional endeavor, be it artistic, political, economic, or social. The wellspring lies in our moral imagination, which I will define as the *capacity to imagine something rooted in the challenges of the real world yet capable of giving birth to that which does not yet exist.*

As does any author, I have my misgivings and anxieties about what I have written. They loom larger in this book than in previous ones. I feel as if I am venturing into arenas that, while rooted in my experience, have pushed me to listen to the philosophical and artistic voices within me. No book, and certainly not this book, can attend to the full range of hopes and wishes of a diverse reading community, though those are legitimate and important. While this book cuts new territory, I recognize it does so with certain shortcomings. At a later stage I am sure there will be time to reflect, learn from responses, and address the gaps that are necessarily a part of a first round of new thinking. But here are my fears.

I am sure the practitioner will ask: How exactly does this translate into practical skills? While I speak in some chapters to that question, the nature of this book does not seek to provide a technician's manual. In fact it proposes to break beyond such a view. I invite the practitioner to suspend the need for tools, answers, and techniques. If possible, let these pages flow toward the deeper question of why we do this work and what sustains us.

Researchers, theoreticians, and academics will likely wonder: Where is the empirical evidence? Where is the framework of theory? In places, I speak to some aspects of those concerns. For example, I tell four guiding stories, not case studies, to which I refer throughout the book. They are evidence of the moral imagination, but they are incomplete. Questions can be legitimately raised: Are these stories too individual, microcosms of innovation but not systemic responses? Are the settings and processes too particular, unique to a given context but not replicable? How are such stories relevant to large-scale change? All of these are legitimate questions not fully addressed in this book. My effort here is not to propose rigorous academic definitions nor whole new theories in the classical sense of the term. In fact, the inverse may be true: I wish to hold myself close to the actual messiness of ideas, processes, and change and from such a place speculate about the nature of our work and the lessons learned.

Philosophers, religious studies specialists, and ethicists are likely to inquire: How does the moral imagination relate to and add to existing schools of thought? In some chapters, I do provide references to influential writers and compare some schools of thought, but my purpose has been to find a space to reflect on the nature of imagination, social change, and breaking cycles of violence. Many chapters draw more from peripheral sources and lenses, like haiku poetry, or the study of the natural world, like spiders and spider watchers, than the fields traditionally drawn on by those who write about social change or practice conflict transformation and peacebuilding.

Simply put, I wish to share thoughts and insights I have gained along the way about the nature of how constructive social change works and what contributes to it. I believe this has much to do with the nature of imagination and the capacity to envision a canvas of human relationships. This imagination, however, must emerge from and speak to the hard realities of human affairs. This is the paradoxical nature of both imagination and transcendence: Each must have a foot in what is and a foot beyond what exists. This is necessarily a messy process, wherein one can expect the occasional if not regular foot in the mouth. That is the nature of innovation. It is the nature of pursuing change. And, as I will argue, it requires naiveté and serendipity.

Books are, of course, always constructed around thoughts, insights, and ideas. But it is perhaps rare that authors are explicit about the nature of sharing thoughts which pass from the realm of the idea, emergent often in the course of multiple conversations, to become a thing that appears on paper. Black letters starkly standing on a white page take on a significance that belies the delicate nature of their actual existence. When an idea appears on paper, we attach to it a quality of definitiveness. I should like to suggest the opposite. I want to share thoughts in a process more in line with a conversation, hopefully clearly stated, but nonetheless dynamic and incomplete by its very nature. Some of my students have commented that I never seem to present the same idea in the same way from one lecture to the next. I hope this is not a comment about conviction but a reflection of the nature of ideas and learning as an indefinite, constantly evolving process.

In the most constructive sense of the term, I propose a quarrel, a wrestling with the nature of this challenge. In this regard I align myself with Eric Hofer's intriguing statement on mass movements when he suggested that his effort was not to create an authoritative textbook. Rather, he wrote, "[I]t is a book of thoughts, and it does not shy away from half-truths so long as they seem to hint at a new approach and help to formulate new questions." Citing Bagehot, he concluded: "[T]o illustrate a principle, you must exaggerate much and you must omit much" (Hofer, 1951:60). Taking this seriously, I have intentionally framed each chapter starting with the word *on* to capture the idea that what I am writing are "thoughts on" topics like simplicity, space, time, and vocation.

These thoughts were not birthed through a neat process of family planning. Many were accidents. Formally, the scientific community refers to this as *inductive learning.* Another way to describe this is to say that surprises popped up as I was otherwise doing my work, often suggesting that not only should my work change, but my way of describing my work to others and myself should also change.

Surprises may sound ridiculous for a serious book. Some would prefer "lessons learned." Hardcore scientists might suggest "hypotheses in the pursuit of a greater peace theory." Still others may suggest these as the "cutting edge of new techniques in resolving conflict." To me, most of these were vocational surprises. Of late, I have felt more comfortable calling my thoughts "surprises" when little by little it was brought to my attention that the great scientific discoveries in human history happened more often by accident than intent. I devote a full chapter to the appearance of serendipity in everyday life as part and parcel of constructive change, and of course, practitioners and scientists alike share this aspect of everyday surprises, whether we acknowledge them or not. So it was that somebody bumped the Petri dish, and lo and behold the unintended mix held a surprise, later deemed a discovery. From Louis Pasteur to Thomas Edison, the unexpected, the not-planned-for, the mistake suddenly created whole new avenues of insight and understanding. Surprises are accidents cast in a positive light.

This is what I hope to share: some thoughts on the moral imagination, the art and soul of a vocation, and how serendipitous insights and discoveries cropped up when I was trying to find my way toward the building of peace.

Acknowledgments

This book owes much of its evolution to conversations with students and colleagues over more than a decade. I have shared drafts of chapters and the full text with my graduate students at the Joan B. Kroc Institute for International Peace Studies, University of Notre Dame, and with participants of several summer peacebuilding courses at Eastern Mennonite University. The improvement of this text from the feedback received from my students and colleagues is substantial. I should like to thank especially to my colleagues who have responded to specific chapters and ideas. These include Emmanuel Bombande, Aküm Longchari, Jarem Sawatsky, Dekha Ibrahim, Janice Jenner, Harold Miller, Herm Weaver, and Wendell Jones. For wonderful support and suggestions on the overall text, I am deeply indebted to Bernard Mayer, Chris Honeyman, Bill Hawk, Heidi Burgess, and Bill Ury. A very special thanks is due to my colleagues at the Kroc Institute for their feedback as I made my way through the main ideas and text. In particular I am grateful for the comments and insights emerging from the Research Initiative on the Resolution of Ethnic Conflict conferences, and specifically from John Darby and Scott Appleby. I had a wonderful time drawing doodles with my father, John Lederach, whose artistic hand and gift are far more adept than mine and resulted in the great graphics found in this text. The final text owes much to the wonderful editing and careful eye of Maria Krenz. I wish to extend a special note of appreciation to Cynthia Read, Theo Calderara, and Jennifer Kowing at Oxford University Press. Thanks to Happy Trails and the Acoustic Coffeehouse in Nederland, Colorado, for keeping the java flowing and the fires burning while I wrestled with putting ideas to paper. Finally, no writing project of mine reaches fruition without the patience and support of my family—Wendy, Angie and Josh—to whom I am indebted and from whom I receive energy and sustenance. Thank you.

Contents

The Moral Imagination

I

On Stating the Problem
and Thesis

Akmal Mizshakarol painted the image found on the cover of this book following the tragic events unleashed in New York and Washington D.C., on September 11, 2001. Its title is that date. Tajik by birth, his studio is located in his house at the end of a street several blocks off Rudaki Avenue, the main thoroughfare in Dushanbe. On my regular visits to Tajikistan, where I have been helping to develop a national curriculum on conflict resolution with seven universities, I sought out contemporary artists and happened upon his studio. Over the course of time and visits, we became friends.

In the spring of 2002 I found Akmal completing the first of his pieces on the tragedy that hit the United States in the fall of 2001. A year later, he completed the one you find here. For Tajiks, a visitor in anyone's home always involves a process of attending well to the guest, announced or not. At Akmal's we often first visited his studio and looked at his latest paintings, then, sooner or later, we ended up in the courtyard veranda. Caged guinea hens cackled above our heads. Roses and apple and apricot trees blessed us with their aroma and shade. Even for a short visit the table was filled with nuts, raisins, breads, and juices. Conversation ranged from daughters (advice about how to marry well) to art (the loneliness and intensity of studio work), from local to international politics. His daughters, wonderfully polite and interested, hovered, listened, and occasionally helped with translation through their nearly perfect English. They are members of the rising new generation of Tajiks, more conversant with the outside world beyond Central Asia than their parents.

Akmal was trained at the Surikov Moscow Art Institute, one of the best Russian art academies. Near the end of his studies he wandered from the norms of his Russian mentors, exploring roots in himself and in his native Tajikistan. Speaking of his now growing internationally recognized style, he once commented, "It took some time, but I found my voice. At some point, even though it is totally uncertain, you have to take the risk of following your own intuition, your own voice." All direct quotations from my friends and colleagues have been reconstructed to the best of my ability from my notes, journals, and recollections.

We talked about the painting he titled *September 11*. From first sight, I was mesmerized by the combination of the painting itself, the context in which it was made, the color choices, the faces, and the implications of such an effort. A Tajik Muslim painter sitting just north of Afghanistan had reflected through his hands a response to the events that had taken place half a world away, yet that were close to home. When I inquired about what he was thinking when he painted the canvas, Akmal, in the fine fashion of most artists responded:

> I can't comment too much. The painting is the comment. But I re-
> member that day. We watched with unbelief as the planes crashed.
> It was like we were all standing and looking at the sky. Wondering
> where it came from and what was falling into our lives. I used to
> have dreams of being on a plane, you know, one of those dreams
> where a plane is falling and you wake up just before it crashes. It
> was like this was too close to that dream.

He added: "This was the same feeling we had in our civil war. Every day, we would look toward the sky and wonder what was coming next. And hoping that we could find something better, something to stop it, something to end the bad dream."

I stood in Akmal's studio, looking at the painting. In it, five people circle in a courtyard, three women and two men looking upward, watching for what might be coming. One is obviously perplexed. Some are filled with wonder, and, it seemes to me, with a sense of looking for something beyond what is befalling them. Clearly they express concern, even anxiety. Yet the painting as a whole, maybe because of the colors chosen, engenders a hope. It is this kind of hope that links people half a world away and suggests the possibility of change, a concern not only for the tragedy that fell on some and the fear of what may befall us all, but also a concern for what we will create from and for this humanity we share. In the painting, I find a quality of transcendence, something that wishes to touch a stream of shared humanity beyond the violence. From the canvas and its creator's surrounding context I found a simple offer of mutuality and healing. I told Akmal that I wanted to use his *September 11* painting on the cover of a book I was writing because it captured so many elements of my work's title and thesis.

The academic community, unlike the artistic community, often begins its interaction with and journey into the world by stating a problem that defines both the journey and the interaction. The artistic community, it seems to me, starts with experience in the world and then creates a journey toward expressing something that captures the wholeness of that feeling in a succinct moment. The two communities share this in common: Ultimately, at some moment in time, they both rely on intuition.

While I have never been a big fan of problem stating, I have come to appreciate the art of posing a good question. The question this book poses is simple and endlessly complex: *How do we transcend the cycles of violence that bewitch our human community while still living in them?* I could call this the statement of the problem. I could suggest that it emerges from twenty-five years of experiences working in settings of protracted conflict and as such this question is the canvas of the human condition in too many parts of our globe. I have come to believe that this is *the* question that, at every step of the way, peacebuilding, this noble endeavor to break beyond the shackles of violence, must forcibly face.

Through this book I propose a thesis that I feel may be a start at answering that question: Transcending violence is forged by the capacity to generate, mobilize, and build the moral imagination. The kind of imagination to which I refer is mobilized when four disciplines and capacities are held together and practiced by those who find their way to rise above violence. Stated simply, the moral imagination requires the capacity to imagine ourselves in a web of relationships that includes our enemies; the ability to sustain a paradoxical curiosity that embraces complexity without reliance on dualistic polarity; the fundamental belief in and pursuit of the creative act; and the acceptance of the inherent risk of stepping into the mystery of the unknown that lies beyond the far too familiar landscape of violence.

The thesis that a certain kind of imagination is within reach and necessary to transcend violence requires that we explore these four disciplines in two broad directions. First, we must understand and feel the landscape of protracted violence and why it poses such deep-rooted challenges to constructive change. In other words, we must set our feet deeply into the geographies and realities of what destructive relationships produce, what legacies they leave, and what breaking their violent patterns will require. Second, we must explore the creative process itself, not as a tangential inquiry, but as the wellspring that feeds the building of peace. In other words, we must venture into the mostly uncharted territory of the artist's way as applied to social change, the canvases and poetics of human relationships, imagination and discovery, and ultimately the mystery of vocation for those who take up such a journey.

We stand before the inquiry of what makes possible movement beyond ingrained patterns of protracted, destructive conflict. Our thesis requires us to explore the survival of the artist's genius and gift in the lands of violence.

2

On Touching the Moral Imagination

Four Stories

A Story from Ghana: "I Call You Father Because I Do Not Wish to Disrespect You"

During the 1990s, northern Ghana faced the rising escalation of ethnic conflict mixed with the ever-present tense undertones of Muslim-Christian relationships. In the broader West African region, Liberia had collapsed into chaotic, violent internal warfare, spilling refugees into neighboring countries. The chaos seemed simultaneously endemic and contagious. Within a short period of time, Sierra Leone descended into cycles of bloodletting and cruelty that were unprecedented for the subregion. Nigeria, the largest and most powerful regional country, walked a fine line that barely seemed to avoid the wildfires of full-blown civil war. In such a context, the rise of intercommunal violence, and even sporadic massacres had all the signs of a parallel disaster in the northern communities of Ghana.

These were not historically isolated cycles of violence. The roots of the conflicts between several of the groups, particularly the Konkombas and Dagombas, could be easily traced back into the era of slavery.[1] The Dagombas, a group with a sustained and powerful tradition of chieftaincy, have a social and leadership structure that loaned itself to negotiation with European slave traders. They were the most powerful and dominant group in the north of the country; their allies to the south were the people of the equally strong Ashanti Empire. *Chiefly groups* retained royalty, culminating in the paramount chief, whereas groups in Ghana referred to as *nonchiefly* no longer had or were not accorded a chiefly political structure.

The Konkombas, on the other hand, were more dispersed. Principally agriculturalists, "yam growers," as they at times were denigrated and stereotyped the Konkombas did not organize around the same social and royal features. They were a nonchiefly tribe, not necessarily by their choice. High chieftaincy in this part of the world brought benefits and a comparative sense of importance that translated into superiority. For example, the chiefly groups gained advantage from collaboration with the slave trade; the nonchiefly were fated to live the great travesty of dehumanization and exploitation incarnated in this trafficking of men, women, and children. Following the period of the slave trade, the chiefly groups again benefited during the period of colonization. They received recognition and their traditional power and sense of superiority were further ingrained. The seeds of division sown during the period of slavery flourished in the period of colonial rule.

In subsequent centuries their conflicts were played out over control of land and resources. The arrival of religiously based missionary movements added more layers of division to their relationships. While some groups remained animists, the Konkombas followed Christianity, and most Dagombas, including the powerful royal houses and paramount chieftancy, became Muslim. One unexpected result was that the Christian missions, with their emphasis on education, provided schools that gave access and entry to rising social status for the Konkombas. This would eventually have an impact on the communities and politics.

As Ghana gained independence, the country moved toward democracy based on elections. Politicians with aspirations for votes understood the existing divisions and fears and often exacerbated them in order to get the support of their respective communities during election campaigns. Electoral periods became regular cycles of repeated and ever-greater violence. Even little events, like a dispute between two people in a market over a purchase, could spark an escalation into violence, as was the case with the Guinea Fowl War.

In 1995 the cycle threatened to explode again. A dispute over land claimed by both groups in a small town in the north suddenly exploded into overt violence during the electoral campaign. The killing sprees spread rapidly, spilled well beyond the locale of the original dispute, and threatened the stability of the whole northern region. The images of recent chaotic collapse in Sierra Leone and Liberia were fresh in the minds of many people. This cycle of intercommunal violence in Ghana appeared on the verge of creating yet another destructive full-blown civil war. In response, a consortium of nongovernmental organizations working in the northern region of Ghana began to push for a peacebuilding effort. A small team of African mediators, led initially by Hizkias Assefa and Emmanuel Bombande, began the process of creating space for dialogue between the representatives of the two ethnic groups. Eventually this process would find a way to avoid the escalation of violence to civil war and would even create an infrastructure for dealing with the common recurrence of crises that in the past had translated into deadly fighting. But it was not a smooth road.

In one of their early encounters those involved in the mediation observed a story that created a transformation in the process and in the relationship between these two groups and therefore changed the fundamental direction of the conflict. In the first face-to-face meeting of the two groups, the Dagomba paramount chief arrived in full regalia and with his entourage. There were designated persons who carried his staff and sat at his feet. In the opening moments of the meeting he assumed a sharp attitude of superiority. Taking the role of the paramount, he wasted no time in denigrating and verbally attacking the Konkombas. Given the traditions and rights afforded the highest chiefs, little could be done except to let the chief speak.

"Look at them," he said, addressing himself more to the mediators than to the Konkombas. "Who are they even that I should be in this room with them? They do not even have a chief. Who am I to talk to? They are a people with nothing who have just come from the fields and now attack us in our own villages. They could have at least brought an old man. But look! They are just boys born yesterday."

The atmosphere was devastating. Making matters worse, the mediators felt in a very difficult bind. Culturally, when facing a chief, there was nothing they could do to control the process. You simply cannot tell a chief to watch his mouth or follow ground rules, particularly in the presence of his entourage and his enemies. It appeared as if the whole endeavor may have been misconceived and was reaching a breaking point.

The Konkomba spokesman asked to respond. Fearing the worst, the mediators provided him space to speak. The young man turned and addressed himself to the chief of the enemy tribe:

You are perfectly right, Father, we do not have a chief. We have not had one for years. You will not even recognize the man we have chosen to be our chief. And this has been our problem. The reason we react, the reason our people go on rampages and fights resulting in all these killings and destruction arises from this fact. We do not have what you have. It really is not about the town, or the land, or that market guinea fowl. I beg you, listen to my words, Father. I am calling you Father because we do not wish to disrespect you. You are a great chief. But what is left to us? Do we have no other means but this violence to receive in return the one thing we seek, to be respected and to establish our own chief who could indeed speak with you, rather than having a young boy do it on our behalf?

The attitude, tone of voice, and use of the word *Father* spoken by the young Konkomba man apparently so affected the chief that he sat for a moment without response. When finally he spoke, he did so with a changed voice, addressing himself directly to the young man rather than to the mediators:

> I had come to put your people in your place. But now I feel only
> shame. Though I insulted your people, you still called me Father. It
> is you who speaks with wisdom, and me who has not seen the truth.
> What you have said is true. We who are chiefly have always looked
> down on you because you have no chief, but we have not under-
> stood the denigration you suffered. I beg you, my son, to forgive
> me.

At this point the younger Konkomba man stood, walked to the chief, then knelt and gripped his lower leg, a sign of deep respect. He vocalized a single and audible "Na-a," a word of affirmation and acceptance.

Those attending the session reported that the room was electrified, charged with high feeling and emotion. It was by no means the end of the problems or disagreements, but something happened in that moment that created an impact on everything that followed. The possibility of change away from century-long cycles of violence began and perhaps the seeds that avoided what could have been a full-blown Ghanaian civil war were planted in that moment.

This possibility of change continues. In March 2002, the king of the Da-gombas, Ya Na Yakubu Andani II, was killed in an internal feud between the two clans of the Dagombas, the Abudu and Andani families. As long-time adversaries of the Dagombas, the Konkombas could have been expected to take advantage of the internal strife among the Dagombas. On the contrary, they met at a grand Durban of all their youths and elders and issued an official declaration on Ghana television. First they expressed solidarity with the Da-gombas in the time of their grief and loss. Then they pleaded with the Dagom-bas to work together in finding a long-term solution to their internal chieftaincy dispute. They declared that Konkombas would not allow any of their tribesmen to undermine the Dagombas because of the internal difficulty they were ex-periencing. They concluded by suggesting that Konkombas who took advantage of the internal strife within the Dagombas to create a situation that may lead to violence would be isolated and handed over to the police.

A Story from Wajir: How a Few Women Stopped a War

The women of Wajir did not set out to stop a war.[2] They just wanted to make sure they could get food for their families. The initial idea was simple enough: Make sure that the market is safe for anyone to buy and sell.

Wajir district is located in the northeastern part of Kenya, near the Somali and Ethiopian borders. The district is made up mostly of Somali clans. Like those in other parts of the Horn of Africa, the people of Wajir have suffered the impact of numerous internal wars in neighboring Somalia and Ethiopia. With the collapse of the Somali government in 1989, increased fighting inside the country created countless refugees, who spilled over the border into Kenya. Wajir soon found itself caught up in interclan fighting, with a flow of weapons, fighting groups, and refugees who made life increasingly difficult. By 1992 the Kenya government declared Wajir to be in a state of emergency.

The 1990s were not the first time Wajir had experienced clan-based war, but it soon became one of the worst cycles of violence. Dekha, one of the key women leaders in Wajir, recalls that one night in mid-1993 shooting erupted once again near her house. She ran for her first-born child and hid for several hours under the bed while bullets crisscrossed her room. In the morning, discussing the events of the night before, her mother recalled days in 1966 when Dekha was a child and her mother held her under the bed. They were reflecting that morning and feeling sad that the violence had not come to an end. As mothers, they were tired of the violence. Dekha was so affected by her mother's statement that she determined to find a way to make Wajir a place where her daughter would enjoy a violence-free life. She found other women with similar stories. Fatuma tells how at a wedding the women worried about how they would get home and had to leave early. They lamented the rising violence, the thievery along the highways, the guns that were everywhere carried by their young boys, and the fear of abuse and rape with which young girls lived even in their home villages.

So the women quietly gathered, fewer than a dozen of them at first. "We just wanted to put our heads together," they said, "to see what we knew and could do. We decided the place to start was the market." They agreed on a basic idea. The market should be safe for any woman of any clan background to come, to sell, and to buy. Women were looking out for their children. Access and safety to the market was an immediate right that had to be assured. Since women mostly ran the market, they spread the word. They established monitors who would watch every day what was happening at the market. They would report any infractions, any abuse of someone because of her clan or geographic origin. Whenever issues emerged, a small committee of women would move quickly to resolve them. Within a short period of time, the women had created a zone of peace in the market. Their meetings and initiatives resulted in the creation of the Wajir Women's Association for Peace.

While they were working hard on the market, they soon discovered that the broader fighting still affected their lives. Sitting again, they decided to pursue direct conversations with the elders of all of the clans. Though they had access to their elders, this was not an easy thing to do. "Who are women to advise and push us?" was the response they feared they might get. So they sat and thought through their understanding of the elder system, the actual key elders, and the makeup of the Somali clans in Wajir. Using their personal connections within their own groups, they worked with concerned men and succeeded in bringing together a meeting of the elders of all the groups. They aligned themselves carefully to not push or take over the meetings. Instead they found one of the elderly men, quite respected, but who came from the smallest and therefore the least threatening of the local clans. In the meeting he became their spokesperson, talking directly to the other elders and appealing to their responsibility. "Why, really," he asked, "are we fighting? Who benefits from this? Our families are being destroyed." His words provoked long discussions. The elders, even some of those who had been promoting revenge killings, agreed to face the issues and stop the fighting. They formed the Council of Elders for Peace, which included a regular meeting group and subcommissions. They began the process of engaging the fighters in the bush and dealing with clan clashes.

The women, recognizing that this effort could be very important for Wajir, decided to take up contact with government officials from the district and eventually the national representatives in Parliament. Accompanied by some elders, they transparently described their initiative and process. They agreed to keep the officials informed and invited them to various meetings, but they asked that in return the officials not disrupt the process that was in motion. They received the blessing of the government.

Soon the question became how to engage the youth, particularly the young men who were hidden and fighting in the bush. The women and elders met with key youth in the district and formed what became known as the Youth for Peace. Together they not only went to the bush and met with fighters, they began to travel the district, giving public talks to mothers and youth. They soon discovered that a key concern was employment. Guns, fighting, and rustling had significant economic benefit. If the youth were to leave the fighting, their guns, and the bush, they would need something to occupy their time and provide income. The business community was then engaged. Initiatives for rebuilding and local jobs were offered. Together, the women from the market, the elders commissions, the Youth for Peace, the businesspeople, and local religious leaders formed the Wajir Peace and Development Committee.

Through the work of the elders, ceasefires came into place. Commissions were created to verify and help the process of disarming the clan-based factions. A process of turning over guns to local authorities was coordinated with these commissions and the district police. Emergency response teams were formed made up of elders from different clans who would travel on a moment's notice to deal with renewed fighting, rustling, or thievery.

Solidifying the rising peace, the Wajir Peace and Development Committee brought together all of the groups and held regular meetings with district and national leaders. They could not control the continued fighting in neighboring Somalia nor the influx of problems that came from outside their borders, but increasingly they found ways to protect their villages and stop the local fighting before it spiraled out of control. Key to their success was the ability to take quick action and stop the potential moments of escalation by directly engaging the people involved. Former fighters now disarmed and, back in the community, became allies of the movement. They helped to constructively engage other fighting groups, increasing the process of disarmament. When crimes were committed, their own group brought those responsible forward, and restitution was sought rather than blind protection and cycles of revenge.

Ten years later, Wajir district still faces serious problems, and the Wajir Peace and Development Committee still actively works for peace and has continued to expand. New programs include police training and work in local schools. More than twenty schools are participating and have formed the Peace Education Network, which involves peer mediation and teacher training in conflict resolution.

Poverty and unemployment remain significant challenges in Wajir. Guns still cross borders in this region. Fighting has not stopped in Somalia, and it spills into Wajir. Religious issues and the global implications emerging since September 11, 2001, with the presence of U.S. marines and the antiterrorism campaigns, have become new issues. But those involved in the Wajir Peace and Development Committee continue their strong work. The elders meet on a regular basis. There is greater cooperation among the local villages, clans, and the district officials.

And the women who stopped a war monitor a now much safer market.

A Story from Colombia: We Have Decided to Think for Ourselves

Josué, Manuel, Hector, Llanero, Simón, Oswaldo, Rosita, Excelino, Juan Roy, Miguel Angel, Sylvia, and Alejandro shared several things that forever bound them together.[3] They lived along the Carare River in an area called La India, in the jungles of Magdalena Medio in the country of Colombia. They were *campesinos*, peasants. They considered themselves ordinary folk. And they faced an extraordinary challenge: how to survive the wicked violence of numerous armed groups that traversed their lands and demanded their allegiance.

The Rio Carare is located in the heart of Magdalena Medio. It is a territory that brings together a stream of influence and people. Water flows through this thick jungle territory, and it brought *campesinos* in search of land from other parts of Colombia around the middle of the twentieth century. They came seeking refuge from the more conflicted zones of Colombia in the middle of the fifty-year-old war, the longest in the Western Hemisphere. It was at best a frontier territory with many natural dangers, a lack of any basic civil protections or law, and requiring hard work. Petroleum was discovered and now flows in this region and out to the Atlantic coast for delivery to the international community. So does the river of drug traffickers. And, of course, as is the case in many rural parts of Colombia, the river of armed groups and guns flows too.

By the late 1960s the leftist-oriented guerrilla movement FARC (Armed Revolutionary Front of Colombia) entered the territories of Carare. Military response from the national government followed and escalated. Unable to affect or eliminate the influence of the guerrilla movements in the region, landowners privately financed and secretly arranged, often in conjunction with the military, the "paras," armed groups of vigilantes from the Right, which soon gained a greater independence. Battles took place not just for the land where the early *campesinos* had made their homes and against informal war taxes but for their very allegiance. Whoever controlled the particular territory at the time controlled the laws: Whoever robs will be killed; anyone who kills someone will be killed; whoever informs anyone of our presence will be killed. As one statement put it: "[N]o one is obligated to follow our code; you always have the right to leave the territory." The law of silence prevailed: "It is prohibited to talk about the death of any friend or family member, about those who killed them or the reasons why they were killed. If you open your mouth, the rest of your family will be killed." Such were the realities faced by Josué, Hector, Manuel, and the other *campesinos* of the region.

In 1987 the situation reached its nadir. Increased fighting and larger scale massacres began to take over. In response to the guerrillas, a notoriously violent captain of the Colombian army convened more than 2,000 peasants from La India and offered them forgiveness in the form of an amnesty if they would accept his weapons and join the ranks of local militia to fight against the guerrillas. In the eyes of the captain, many of these peasants were guilty of supporting the guerrillas—if not directly participating. So the offer of forgiveness was considered an ultimatum about choosing sides in the conflict. He concluded with what he called the four choices before the *campesinos*: "You can arm yourselves and join us, you can join the guerrillas, you can leave your homes, or you can die."

The crowd was stunned. In the midst of the silence, a middle-aged *campesino*, Josué, spoke from the crowd and from his heart. His speech that day was so memorable that up until today you will find peasants in La India who can recite his response to the captain word for word even though they were not there. Garcia (1996), who did a study of this movement, offered this version of Josué's speech that day. Responding to the captain in the open meeting, he said:

> You speak of forgiveness, but what do you have to forgive us? You
> are the ones who have violated. We have killed no one. You want to
> give us millions in weapons paid for by the state, yet you will not
> facilitate even the minimum credit for our farming needs. There are
> millions for war but nothing for peace. How many men in arms are

there in Colombia? By rough calculation I would say at least 100,000, plus the police, plus 20,000 guerrillas, not to mention the Paras, the drug lords and private armies. And what has all this served? What has it fixed? Nothing. In fact Colombia is in the worst violence ever. We have arrived at the conclusion that weapons have not solved a thing and that there is not one reason to arm ourselves. We need farm credits, tools, tractors, trucks to make this little agricultural effort we try [to] make produce better. You as members of the National Army, instead of inciting us to kill each other should do your job according to the national constitution, that is, you should defend the Colombian people. Look at all these people you brought here. We all know each other. And who are you? We know that some years ago you yourself were with [the] guerrilla[s] and now you are the head of the paramilitaries. You brought people into our houses to accuse us, you lied, and you switched sides. And now you, a side switcher, you want us to follow your violent example. Captain, with all due respect, we do not plan to join your side, their side or any side. And we are not leaving this place. We are going to find our own solution. (Garcia, 1996:189).

Later that week a group of twenty *campesino* leaders decided to play the ultimate card: They would pursue civilian resistance without weapons. As one of them put it, "We decided that day to speak for ourselves." In the weeks and months that followed they organized one of the most unique and spontaneous processes of transformation Colombia had seen in fifty years.

They formed the Association of Peasant Workers of Carare (ATCC). Their first act was to break the code of silence. They developed ways of organizing and participating. Participation was open to anyone. The quota for entry was a simple commitment: Your life, not your money. This was expressed in the phrase "We shall die before we kill." They developed a series of key principles to guide their every action:

1. Faced with individualization: solidarity.
2. Faced with the Law of Silence and Secrecy: Do everything publicly. Speak loud and never hide anything.
3. Faced with fear: Sincerity and disposition to dialogue. We shall understand those who do not understand us.
4. Faced with Violence: Talk and negotiate with everyone. We do not have enemies.
5. Faced with exclusion: Find support in others. Individually we are weak, but together we are strong.
6. Faced with the need for a strategy: Transparency. We will tell every armed group exactly what we have talked about with other armed groups. And we will tell it all to the community. (Garcia, 1996:200).

And these were not just ideas. The *campesinos* created a living laboratory of immediate impact and great risk. They solidified their group by finding a core they called the "key folks," who were uniquely placed as individuals to link them with different geographic parts of La India and with the various groups. Within weeks after consultation with local villages they posted handmade signs with the title "What the People from Here Say," which included a declaration that no weapons would be allowed in their villages. They spontaneously declared their lands to be a territory of peace.

Delegations were sent to meet with the armed groups. Never conducted by a single individual and always public, each meeting with each different armed group required careful preparation and choice of who would speak. But the message remained the same: respect for the territory of peace and the *campesinos*. They approached each meeting seeking the connection with the person not the institution. The key, as several people reported it, was that they had to find a way to meet the human being, the real person. Informal and in some instances formal agreements and arrangements were reached. The association held to its promise of never giving in to weapons and never giving up on dialogue. In the public debriefing of any meeting, everyone was welcome, friend and foe alike. The doors were never shut. Transparency was carried to its fullest extent.

During the next years violence was greatly reduced, though Magdalena Medio remained and is yet today a hotbed of armed conflict. In 1990 the association won the Alternative Nobel Peace Prize for its innovative work. In 1992 the United Nations recognized the movement with the We Are the People Award. Nonetheless, the local campaign for respect and dignity came with its price. Josué and several other leaders were assassinated by unknown and yet undetermined *sicarios* (hired guns). Survivors believe the murders were due to local politicians, not the armed groups. Their legacy, however, lives on. Today in Colombia many speak of the potential of local groups to develop and build a capacity for civilian resistance as the key to building a permanent peace. As Alejandro Garcia, the history professor who extensively interviewed many of the early and subsequent participants in the association, aptly wrote: "Born in the nucleus of violence, the ATCC introduced into the logic of war a sense of uncertainty: it broke the conventional cycle of spiraling violence and developed through lived demonstration the basic idea that solutions without violence were possible" (Garcia, 1996:313).

A Story from Tajikistan: Talking Philosophy with the Warlord

The following information is based on notes from a trainer's journal, February, 2002.

We are seated in a seminar room in Dushanbe with twenty-four professors from seven universities across Tajikistan. Two small electric heaters, their coils burning bright red, keep the late February cold at bay inside the Republican Healthy Lifestyle Centre. We have the appointed cream of the crop. One or two are deans and a few others are heads of their respective disciplinary departments. From the perspective of the organizers we count ourselves lucky to have five women and a strong showing of younger scholars, though seated each day in the corner, occasionally drifting in and out of late afternoon naps, is the kind and always enthusiastic seventy-year-old head of the Department of Scientific Communism, now re-titled Political Science.

The Intertajik War lies nearly six years in their past. Our seminar on conflict resolution and peacebuilding probes into the challenges and difficulties of responding to violence and building a nation in this newly independent Central Asian country. Following the events of September 11, 2001, the schedule for our three-year initiative, aimed at helping to build the civil society, was set back a few months, as the Tajik-Afghan border and the space above this mountainous region witnessed the anti-Taliban war effort unfold. Our subject matter now seems doubly interesting and urgent.

Our Tajik University colleagues completed their higher education through the Soviet system. Most have doctoral degrees. Travel, when it happened for academic reasons, was to Russia or Eastern Europe. Of the twenty-four, four speak English with any proficiency. Our English-Tajik translation is painstakingly slow. Some would prefer Russian. Under the encouragement and guidance of the minister of education we will produce a Tajik-language text that compiles approaches to peacebuilding from different parts of the world coupled with original Tajik research on conflict and peace in this setting.

The professors become considerably more animated when the topic of the Tajikistan civil war emerges. They have a variety of opinions about what difficulties were experienced and what made the achievement of a negotiated peace possible under the guidance of a UN mandate. One participant asks my co-trainer, Randa Slim, and me, the only two non-Tajiks in the room, why so few in the international community have given careful consideration to what the Tajiks achieved in ending the war. They may well have a point. Tajikistan, as journalist Ahmed Rashid convincingly argues, is the only country in the region or the world for that matter, to have ended a brutal civil war with the "creation of a coalition government that included Islamicists, neo-communists, and clan leaders." He goes onto to note: "Islamicists lost elections, but they were *represented* in the elections, and they accepted their loss" (Rashid, 2002:241). The professors want a straight answer: Why don't people pay attention to what we have learned? Neither of us has a good answer.

During that afternoon's chai break, I have tea with the only professor in our group who knows some of the inner details of how the Tajiks negotiated while war raged and how they brought the Islamic movements into negotiation rather than isolating or trying to defeat them. He draws me to a corner with a translator to tell me the story.

"I was tasked by the government to approach and convince one of [the] warlords, a key Mullah-Commander located in the mountains, to enter negotiations," Professor Abdul begins. "This was difficult if not impossible, because this commander was considered a notorious criminal and he had killed one of my close friends." He stops while the translation conveys the personal side of this challenge.

> When I first got to the encampment, the commander said I had arrived late and it was time for prayers. So we went together and prayed. When we had finished, he said to me, "How can a communist pray?"
>
> "I am not a communist: my father was," I responded.
>
> Then he asked what I taught in the university. We soon discovered we were both interested in philosophy and Sufism. Our meeting went from an agreed twenty minutes to two and a half hours. In this part of the world you have to circle into truth through stories.

In the hallway Abdul's gold-capped teeth sparkled with a smile as he finished his idea: "You see in Sufism there is an idea that discussion has no end." His point well conveyed, the professor picked up the story again:

> I kept going to visit him. We mostly talked poetry and philosophy. Little by little I asked him about ending the war. I wanted to persuade him to take the chance on putting down his weapons. After months of visits we finally had enough trust to speak truths and it all boiled down to one concern.

Abdul stopped and leaned over, taking the voice of the warlord. "The commander said to me, 'If I put down my weapons and go to Dushanbe with you, can you guarantee my safety and life?' " The Tajik storyteller paused with the full sense of the moment. "My difficulty was that I could not guarantee his safety."

Abdul waited for the translator to finish, making sure that I understood the weight of his peacemaking dilemma, and then concluded: "So I told my philosopher warlord friend the truth, 'I cannot guarantee your safety.' "

In the hallway Professor Abdul swung his arm under mine and came to stand fully by my side to emphasize the answer he then gave the commander: "But I can guarantee this. I will go with you, side by side. And if you die, I will die."

The hallway was totally quiet.

"That day the commander agreed to meet the government. Some weeks later we came down together from the mountains. When he first met with the government commission he told them, 'I have not come because of your government. I have come for honor and respect of this professor.' "

The professor stopped. "You see, my young American friend," he tapped my arm lightly, "this is Tajik mediation."

We finished our chai and moved back to the classroom discussions on the theory of conflict and peacebuilding.

Years have passed since the end of the war. The weapons have been laid down. Things are not easy in Tajikistan, but from all accounts, the professor-mediator and the renegade warlord are alive and well, and occasionally they still talk poetry and philosophy.

The Moral of the Stories

What made these changes possible? Though working their hardest and very skilled in their trade, at the moment of the initial meetings it was not the techniques used by the mediators nor the nature and design of the process that created the shift in the Dagomba-Konkomba encounter. The inverse may be true: The process seemed to have gotten off to a bad start. It was not the technical expertise introduced by professional peacebuilders in Wajir or Magdalena Medio or by the professor-philosopher and his counterpart, the warlord. It was not the local or national political power, exigencies, the fears of a broader war, nor the influence and pressure from the international community that created the shift. It was not a particular religious tradition: the stories in fact cut across religions. It was not political, economic, or military power in any of the cases. What then, created a moment, a turning point, of such significance that it shifted whole aspects of a violent, protracted setting of conflict?

I believe it was the serendipitous appearance of the *moral imagination* in human affairs.

3

On This Moment

Turning Points

Do not remember the former things,
Or consider the things of old.
I am about to do a new thing;
Now it springs forth, do you not perceive it?

—Isaiah 43:18–19

In the first decade of the new century and millennium, we face a turning point, a unique moment with the potential to affect and redefine the ways we organize and shape our global family. The turn of centuries—and, much more, the turn of millennia—provide unique times to reflect about the grand journey of humanity. We have traversed a century filled with extraordinary changes, one that has left us even greater challenges. Through numerous decades, expectations were raised, then dashed, that we were finding our way toward a world defined less by our divisions than by our cooperation, more by our ability to meet fundamental human needs than by the outright denigration of human dignity and rights. If nothing else, the twentieth century created within us a keener understanding that humanity has the potential for constructive change within our political, economic, and technological reach and, an equal dose of realism, that we have fallen short and shown ourselves incapable of realizing our potential. If we take seriously this realizable potential and our incapacity to reach it, we are left with a singularly perplexing question that seems especially appropriate in the timeframe of the first decade of the new millennium: What collective and global legacy are we leaving for our great-great-grandchildren this century?

This is not just a challenge posed generally, or reserved for political leaders or policy makers. This is a challenge I wish to place before the burgeoning fields of conflict transformation and peacebuilding broadly defined with all of their professional applications. I count myself a practitioner within these disciplines and I believe we need a dose of realism. Ours are professions afflicted with a proclivity toward the promise of great change. It is true. Our rhetoric comes easy. If constructive social change rolled forward as easily as our words and promises pour out, world justice and peace would have surely been attained by now.

Some argue that we suffer from an exaggerated rhetoric coupled with an overly optimistic, and therefore unrealistic, understanding of how the world really works and how change can or cannot take place. Following the events of 9/11, I heard that a perplexed member serving on the board of a major foundation which had contributed to a variety of initiatives in the field of conflict resolution asked the question: "Have our investments not made any significant difference in the big picture of things?" While I do not believe in the remotest sense that blame can be laid at the feet of a particular field nor its effectiveness determined by what transpired on September 11, 2001, there is a wake-up call inherent in the events that have been transpiring in the first few years of this millennium.

The start of the 1990s was filled with hope that as a global community we were witnesses to a new era. The ideas of our field, of finding whole new ways for individuals, communities, and even nations to respond to violence and build a justpeace[1] appeared as the great dawn of this new era. Now, nearly fifteen years later, we must ask ourselves a daunting set of questions. These are not posed in reaction to doubts about our potential, doubts that frequently arise from different sources, particularly from *realpolitik* advocates. These questions beg something more important. They plead for critical reflection at the core of our professions as justice, peace, and conflict practitioners.

How does constructive social change happen? How can we be more strategic in the pursuit of this change? What carries us closer to the promise of our words? How do turning points that make a difference happen? Are we capable of participating in a turning point that will affect the whole of the human community?

Thinking about and understanding the nature of a turning point requires a capacity to locate ourselves in an expansive, not a narrow view of time. Elise Boulding suggested that such a view of time must take place within what we touch and know but never be limited to a fleeting moment that passes us by. In a provocative twist of terms she created an intriguing image: We live in a "two-hundred-year present" (Boulding, 1990:3). Her idea is not hard to calculate. Let me give a personal example to illustrate it.

I well remember conversations with my great-grandmother Lydia Miller whose hand I held in the first decade of my life. She was born in the 1860s.

The newest members of my extended family are Nona Lisa, Eliza Jane, Gracie, and Garrison, all four only a few months or years into the adventure. If they enjoy a full life, I will have held the hands of people who in old age will perhaps live to see the celebrations of 2100. Boulding suggests we calculate "the present" by subtracting the date of birth of the oldest person we have known in our lives from the projected passing-on date of the youngest person in our family. In my case, the hands that held mine date back into the nineteenth century and those I now touch will live forward into the twenty-second. This is my 200-year present. It is made up of the lives that touched me and of those I will touch. The 200-year present represents my lived history. It is in this sense of "the present" that we need to locate ourselves in order to understand the nature of the turning point.

The convergence of events in the first few years of the new century, perhaps best symbolized in the tragedy of September 11, 2001, appears to me to represent such a moment, a crystallization of a singular opportunity. The turning point in our 200-year present is pregnant with enormous potential to constructively impact affect the fundamental well-being of the human community. However, contrary to the range of scientific and political projections, this turn in humanity's journey does not rotate on which specific forms of governing political, economic, or social structures we devise. It does not spin primarily around finding answers to ever-present and pressing issues of population growth, environmental degradation, use of natural resources, or poverty. It does not find its essence in the search to understand the roots of violence, war, or terrorism, or in solutions to the same. It does not develop on the basis of learning a few good communication skills, new facilitation methodologies, or teachable techniques for resolving conflicts. Each of these is important, and many represent the core challenges we face. But they do not constitute the capacity to create a turning point that orients us toward a new and more humane horizon. The turning point of human history in this decade of the 200-year present lies with the capacity of the human community to generate and sustain the one thing uniquely gifted to our species, but which we have only on rare occasions understood or mobilized: *our moral imagination.*

At the midway point of the last century, a critical essay appeared that created a stir in the evolution of the social sciences. C. Wright Mills (1959) suggested that the endeavor taken up by the scientific community needed to embrace a deeper challenge than had been fully comprehended by his fellow scientists. Exposing the false tensions of ideologies that wished to govern political and intellectual debate and stripping bare the verbose layers of grand social theory that obscured rather than clarified, Mills made a simple argument: Structural history and personal biography are connected. He admonished academics, in particular social scientists, to take up their proper vocation. That vocation is lost, he argued, when it is distracted by the narrowness of discipline-based technical applications or becomes drunk with esoteric verbiage that avoids critical assessment of the social world. The antidote, he penned in an unforgettable phrase, is only found in those willing to engage and build "the sociological imagination."

I recognize the intellectual and cultural debt this book owes to Mills's insights and formulation of the problem. My interest is not to further develop his critique of the state of affairs within the scientific community. Nor am I oriented toward an exploration into what became of this sociological imagination, though anyone reading his book fifty years since its writing cannot help but be struck by its extraordinary relevance to contemporary academic and scientific debates and quandaries. My interest emerges initially from my own sense of vocation and the need to reflect more intentionally on the experiences I have been afforded in the past twenty-five years of international peacebuilding. Obviously, one's circle of experience influences what one observes and writes. My vocation and my circle of experience have taken me into and around the geography of violent human conflict. In those contexts I have been witness to the best and worst sides of humanity.

In other writings, I have intentionally referred several times to *vocation*. Though conflict resolution and peacebuilding have come into their own rights as professions and though I consider myself a professional working in these fields, I have always understood my entry and sustained work at the level of a vocation. Beyond profession, my concern has been to find and follow a calling, a deeper voice. In the truest sense of the word, *vocation* is that which stirs inside, calling out to be heard, calling out to be followed. Vocation is not what I do. It finds its roots in who I am and a sense of purpose I have on earth.

To follow the voice and develop work as "craftsmanship" in the social scientific sphere, argued Mills (1959), requires a sociological imagination. For those of us in the justice, peace, and conflict professions, vocation calls us back to the road that winds beyond the rest stops of techniques and day-to-day practice. It beckons us to search for our deeper purpose and possibility, found more in *who we are* than in *what we do*. For our human community to find this deeper sense of who we are, where we are situated, and where we are going requires that we locate our bearings, our compass. A compass needle functions by finding its north. The north of peacebuilding is best articulated as finding our way toward becoming and being local and global human communities characterized by respect, dignity, fairness, cooperation, and the nonviolent resolution of conflict. To understand this north, to read such a compass, requires that we recognize and develop our moral imagination far more intentionally.

This kind of imagination has a parallel with Old Testament theologian Walter Brueggemann's proposals, which are captured in the title of his book *The Prophetic Imagination*. For all intents and purposes, finding the voice of truth, ways to turn toward humanity in the fullest sense, and faithfulness to live in God the Creator's sustenance were the mainstay of the prophets' vocation. Intriguingly, Brueggemann provides a keen sense that this work is both moral and requires connection to the artist's, particularly the poet's, voice. Brueggemann describes the role of the prophet as bringing "to public expression those very hopes and yearnings that have been denied" (2001:65). It seems noteworthy that an Old Testament theologian and a midcentury sociologist dipped into the realm of imagination to describe the capacity for both connection to reality and transcendence. In both cases, it leads us to something that lies beyond yet is rooted in people's day-to-day lives and struggles.

Somewhere midstream in writing this book I gave a lecture on the topic of the moral imagination to a young seminary audience in Yangoon, Burma. In attendance that evening was my colleague Ron Kraybill, who expressed enthusiasm for the ideas and added that he was not sure where exactly but he thought he had seen a book with the title *The Moral Imagination*. My dreams of originality met the age-old adage "there is nothing new under the sun."

Since September 11, 2001, I had been calling on religious leaders and politicians alike to exercise a greater moral imagination in response to the unprovoked violence released that day. It seemed to me then and even more so as I write two years later that we, as Americans, have difficulty envisioning ourselves embroiled in a cycle of violence. The acts of 9/11 were viewed as unwarranted provocation that came out of the blue. And indeed they were. But it is also true that these acts can be equally situated not as isolated events but as part of a cycle with a history of actions, reactions, and counteractions. Only when understood in the context of a broader pattern, which in the short term can be very difficult to visualize, is it possible to see that how we choose to respond has consequences and implications in terms of a wider, historic pattern. Through our response, we choose to transcend or enter and sustain the cycle of violence. For the most part since 9/11 the leaders of the United States have chosen the route of perpetuation. In less than two years as a nation we have engaged ourselves in two land-based wars costing billions of dollars. And by all current accounts, the route of choosing violent response has not increased domestic or international security. It has succeeded in fostering the cycle.

In the late fall of 2001, I argued that we seriously consider the implications of falling prey to the cycle of violence and should pursue to our utmost the development of responses that transcend the cycle. In several essays and numerous editorials in local newspapers, I argued that this required unleashing our moral imagination and pursuing the unexpected (Lederach, 2001). I later saw the phrase emerging in a few religious magazines. But it had not occurred to me that this phrase, *the moral imagination*, had already been used as a book title. Research soon confirmed Ron's intuition and more: There was not *a* book with this title—there were dozens.

I soon found myself engrossed in a community of authors linked by the choice of *the moral imagination* as the title or subtitle of their books.[2] I found it a fascinating journey to read through the range of disciplines and perspectives. Although I have sleuthed and even read a chapter on Sherlock Holmes as an agent of moral imagination (Clausen, 1986), I have not been able to discover who may have first used this phrase or in what context. My best guess is Edmund Burke's essay on the French Revolution in which he laments the loss of elements that would "beautify and soften private society" furnished "from the wardrobe of a moral imagination, which the heart owns, and the understanding ratifies, as necessary to cover the defects of her naked shivering nature" (Burke, 1864:515–516). Brown (1999) in his excellent *The Ethos of the Cosmos* suggests in his subtitle that the genesis of the moral imagination is found in creation itself. By virtue of such a view we could, without stretching the truth or the metaphor, propose that the capacity of the moral imagination dates to time immemorial.

Relevant to our exploration however, is the inquiry of why such a range of authors and disciplines converged in using *the moral imagination* as part of the title of their books. At a first level, several categories emerge. The largest set of volumes is oriented toward the concerns and approaches of ethics and de-cisionmaking, primarily in the spheres of business and public policy (Clausen, 1986; McCollough, 1991; Johnson, 1993; Tivnan, 1995; Stevens, 1998; Wil-liams, 1998; Werhane, 1999; Brown, 1999; Fesmire, 2003). A second category explores the moral imagination in literature and the arts, drawing principally on story and narrative as providing guidance for the character development of both adults and children (Price, 1983; Clausen, 1986; Kirk, 1988; Bruce, 1998; Guroian, 1998). Still others draw on the term to promote a particular way of critiquing, provoking, and encouraging their professional disciplines to a greater sense of purpose or developing moral standards within a religious tra-dition (Babbit, 1996; Stevens, 1998; Allison, 1999; Fernandez and Huber, 2001; Newsom, 2003). A fourth group of authors suggested that this phrase captured the essence of extraordinary, ground-breaking individuals (Clausen, 1986; Kirk, 1988; Johnson, 1993; Babbit, 1996; Bruce, 1998; Fesmire, 2003). Many were well-recognized writers and visionaries like T. S. Eliot, W. H. Au-den, Toni Morrison, J.R.R. Tolkien, and Martin Luther King, Jr. Some were renowned philosophers like Immanuel Kant, Sören Kierkegaard, Hannah Arendt, and John Dewey. Other authors pointed to traditional understandings as found in Kaguru thinking (Beidelman, 1993) or the efforts against signifi-cant structural impediments to feminist Cuban writers to find their place and voice (Babbit, 1996).

Looking across these categories we can begin to locate several points of convergence. Though I was well along in my own writing and conceptualiza-tion, I suddenly found myself very much at home in the essence of what linked this set of diverse authors to the phrase *the moral imagination*. I found three keys.

First, the authors concurred that the moral imagination develops a capacity to perceive things beyond and at a deeper level than what initially meets the eye. Perhaps best captured in Guroian's term, *awakening*, the authors spoke of attentiveness to more than is immediately visible. In her discussion of George MacDonald's *The Princess and the Goblin*, Guroian described this quality of imagination as "a power of perception, a light that illuminates the mystery that is hidden beneath a visible reality: It is the power to 'see' into the very nature of things" (1998:141).

Second, no matter the particular disciplinary field, the authors landed on the term *imagination* in order to emphasize the necessity of the creative act. The subtitle of Brown's book, *The Genesis of Moral Imagination in the Bible* (1999), suggests that this kind of imagination has its essence in the very act of original creation. More frequent however were the authors who explored the "arts" not as the domain of professional artists, but rather as a frame of reference for understanding a defining characteristic of the moral imagination: the capacity to give birth to something new that in its very birthing changes our world and the way we see things. Johnson explored this most intentionally in the chapter that carried the title of his book, "Moral Imagination," commenting that though art is often perceived as having the liberty to break the rules of morality, in fact art makes moral reasoning possible. "Everyone recognizes," he writes, "that imagination is the key to these artistic acts by which new things come into existence, old things are reshaped, and our ways of seeing, hearing, feeling, thinking and so forth are transformed" (1993:212).

Third, while expressed in different ways for a variety of purposes, the authors converged in the idea that the moral imagination has a quality of transcendence. It breaks out of what appear to be narrow, shortsighted, or structurally determined dead-ends. Whether this is the capacity of a character in a fairy tale to transcend what appears as predetermined disaster or the need to open a wider range of possible actions in decisions facing the NASA space program, or a car manufacturer, or an anthropological method of study, the exercise of the moral imagination, these authors argue, breaks out into new territory and refuses to be bound by what existing views of perceived reality suggest or what prescriptive answers determine is possible. Babbit in her intriguing exploration of rationality, *Impossible Dreams*, suggested that the role of the moral imagination is to set in motion the "bringing about of possibilities that are not imaginable in current terms" (1996:174). Rather than set aside my initial attraction to the phrase, I felt reinforced by much of what I was reading in the application of the moral imagination to peacebuilding. I chose to stay with it as my title.

Some readers may feel unsettled with the use of the word *moral* in approaching the topic of conflict and peace. Contrary to the word *imagination*, it seems to carry a strong bias toward narrowing and confining boundaries. The word is not without its negative connotations and certainly has less than desirable affiliations and misuses. However, *moral*, like *vocation*, appeals to something great. As terms, they beckon us to rise toward something beyond those things that are immediately apparent and visible. The quality of this phrase I most wish to embrace reverberates in this potential to find a way to transcend, to move beyond what exists while still living in it.

However, the term clearly merits a discussion on what I do not wish to convey with the word *moral*. We typically connect moral with morality and then relegate morality to the sphere of religion. Though I come from a religious community, the moral imagination is not the commodity or exclusive realm of a particular religious belief, much less religious establishments or systems. Moreover, those religious communities, from one persuasion to another, who wish to corral and pen up morality by providing rigid boundaries that can and cannot be crossed often create the antithesis of the moral imagination: dogmas. While pretending to give life, dogmas are little more than static ideological structures. They stare at us like ossified bones in an archaeological dig, attesting to something that once was alive and gave life. Modern religious moralizing has too often translated into rigid ideas, unresponsive and ill adapted to our most pressing challenges. We fall significantly short of our God-given potential when morality becomes prescriptive dogma, creating moral stasis. The moral imagination of which I speak has little in common with such morality.

Ironically, the moral imagination does not build itself around nor is it primarily about ethics. Noble and necessary as it is in the human community, the ethical inquiry remains somewhat reductionist and analytical by its very nature. The purpose, the raison d'être of imagination, on the other hand, moves in a different sphere for it seeks and creates a space beyond the pieces that exist. Not confined by what is, or what is known, imagination is the art of creating what does not exist.

Centuries ago the apostle Paul described our world as a community wracked with unrelenting pain. "The whole creation groans," he wrote, "with labor pains until now" (Romans 8:22). The metaphor suggests that humanity lives in a time of great pain and great potential. Birth is simultaneously pain and potential, the arriving of that which could be but is not yet. I believe the human community still groans with such pain today. We seek a birth of something new, a creation that can break us out of the expected. We seek the creative act of the unexpected. This is the potential and the aspect of the moral imagination I wish to explore.

In accordance with these understandings we must not relegate the term *moral* exclusively to a religious inquiry. Our challenges require that we link its fundamental energy as practical and relevant to the political affairs and issues we face today. Politics, economics, and global structures have become so inauthentic that few of us truly believe in them. We live in this paradox: The things most omnipresent that govern our lives are the very things from which we feel distant. We hold fast to myths that what we have created to govern our lives is responsive to whom we are as human beings and to our communities. Yet at the same time these creations appear to have lives of their own independent of us, foreign to us, and distant from us. An inquiry that seeks to understand how cycles of violence can be broken and transcended is precisely one that must infuse politics, political discourse, and governing structures with a capacity for responsiveness to our human community.

In this book, I suggest and will explore the moral imagination as the capacity to imagine something rooted in the challenges of the real world yet capable of giving birth to that which does not yet exist. In reference to peacebuilding, this is the capacity to imagine and generate constructive responses and initiatives that, while rooted in the day-to-day challenges of violence, transcend and ultimately break the grips of those destructive patterns and cycles.

This exploration does not push toward finding *the answer* to our problems in a single overarching solution, like some miraculous new political, social, or economic system. It does push us toward understanding the nature of turning points and how destructive patterns are transcended. Turning points are moments pregnant with new life, which rise from what appear to be the barren grounds of destructive violence and relationships. This unexpected new life makes possible processes of constructive change in human affairs and constitutes the moral imagination without which peacebuilding cannot be understood or practiced. However, such pregnant moments do not emerge through the rote application of a technique or a recipe. They must be explored and understood in the context of something that approximates the artistic process, imbued as it is with creativity, skill, serendipity, and craftsmanship.

Turning points suggest that violence and the moral imagination point in opposite directions. As Vicenç Fisas paraphrased philosopher Bruno Bettelheim: "[V]iolence is the behavior of someone incapable of imagining other solutions to the problem at hand" (Fisas, 2002:58). Headed in the inverse direction, I will argue that the moral imagination rises with the capacity to imagine ourselves in relationship, the willingness to embrace complexity without reliance on dualistic polarity, the belief in the creative act, and acceptance of the inherent risk required to break violence and to venture on unknown paths that build constructive change. The moral imagination proposes that turning points and a journey toward a new horizon are possible, though based on perplexing paradoxes. The turning points must find a way to transcend the cycles of destructive violence while living with and being relevant to the context that produces those cycles. A horizon, though visible, is permanently just out of touch, suggesting an epic journey, the pursuit of which in peacebuilding is the forging of new ways to approach human affairs with an enemy. For our field this kind of journey is not built with a technician's manual. It requires us to explore the art and soul of social change and it starts with the need to explore the essence of peacebuilding and the heart of on-the-ground realities where violent patterns have dominated human affairs.

4

On Simplicity and Complexity

Finding the Essence of Peacebuilding

I would not give a fig for the simplicity this side of complexity,
But I would give my life for the simplicity on the other side of
complexity.
—Oliver Wendell Holmes

Man is an over-complicated organism. If he is doomed to extinction
he will die for want of simplicity.
—Ezra Pound

Peacebuilding is a complex task. It is, beyond a shadow of a doubt,
an overwhelming challenge. How, really, do we get whole societies
wrapped in histories of violence that date back generations to move
toward a newly defined horizon? It may seem odd that something
this complex begins with a discussion about simplicity. However I
want to talk about the surprise of simplicity here precisely because
the framing of the moral imagination emerged for me out of a conversation walking in the Rocky Mountains with a colleague, Wendell
Jones. As was so well put by Margaret Wheatley (2002), most social
change initiates or is shaped by a single traceable conversation. So
let me tell the story of a mountain conversation that affected this
book.

Wendell was supposedly my mentee. In early 2002 a mutual
friend and conflict resolution professional, Bernie Mayer, contacted
me. Bernie is a founder-partner in CDR Associates and they, in conjunction with Antioch College's master's program in conflict resolution, were launching a new advanced mediator mentorship initiative.

The idea was to match an experienced mediator with a mentor who was doing related work that these mediators would have interest in exploring. The mentor would be available for phone calls, occasional meetings, and grappling with the questions the mentee might have. So it was that Bernie, the matchmaker, put Wendell and me together.

Wendell has worked for the past ten years as an ombudsman at the Sandia Institute in New Mexico in the arena of disputes around the rights to intellectual knowledge as property. This is indeed a relatively new and complex field of application for conflict resolution. Wendell comes from a background in physics; at earlier stages in his professional life he directed research teams delving into cutting-edge theory in the field of applied physics. But his passion lay equally in the ebb and flow of human relationships, in personal and spiritual development. So I found myself in conversation via e-mail, phone, and then face to face during a walk in the mountains with a colleague who was my elder, had conducted "hard science" research in complexity theory, and was mediating disputes in the contested field of who owns knowledge. Our titles of mentor and mentee were, at best, an oxymoron.

We set out one morning toward the trailhead for Arapahoe Pass in the Front Range of the Rocky Mountains. On our trek we talked about life, learning, and books we were reading and writing. I told Wendell about the beginnings of this book and that I had in mind writing chapters on simplicity and complexity. He noted in response that for some time "new science" approaches were exploring and finding linkages between complexity and simplicity. As we moved toward higher altitudes on the hike he launched into a story of one research endeavor, an early contributor to complexity theory and application. Essentially, scientists had posed the challenge of whether a computer could emulate a complex natural system. The story caught my attention to such a degree that it recreated the framework for this whole chapter.

Wendell gave examples of the types of challenges people took up. For example, they inquired whether a computer could find a way to imitate the action and the flow of a flock of birds or a school of fish. I immediately related to the bird image. In the fall of each year around the farms on the rolling hills of the Shenandoah Valley I had often watched these sky-painting flocks. Thousands of blackbirds would move together, merging then extending, dropping then rising. The patterns they created in the sky made you stop in your tracks to watch. Simultaneously, without a commander in chief, individual birds moved with a whole flock in a way that was coordinated yet unpredictable. You never knew what the next movement would be, what shape the flock would take, or what any individual bird might do. It was mesmerizing, moving beauty. Could a computer capture this? If yes, what would it take?

The answer was not complexity. It was what poet Oliver Wendell Holmes might have meant by "simplicity on the other side of complexity." The programmers needed to understand the essence, the core rules, that set in motion the resulting visual beauty. What they created, starting back in the late 1980s, were generic simulated flocking creatures emerging from the zeros and ones of numeric computer language in a program they called BOIDS. The program was based on discovering a few simple rules that could be written into a computer program to guide complex group behavior. For example, in nontechnical vernacular, they created rules like these: Steer to avoid crowding. Steer toward the average heading of local flockmates.

When these rules were put into numeric commands a dynamic rendition of flocking was emulated on the computer screen. From simplicity came the complexity of beauty. No pattern was predictable, but patterns emerged. You can never predict exactly what a flock of birds will do when a telephone pole appears in their way: Will they split, rise, go left, go right? The beauty lay in the creative act, the unpredictable, unexpected response created anew during each flight and moment. Permanently dynamic, permanently adaptive, they flow as a flock in response to the stimuli that emerge. All this complexity of movement and artful pattern boiled down to a few basic, simple rules. At the base of complexity was simplicity.

I remember coming down that mountain trail listening to this story and at one point I commented to Wendell: "You know what I have not done. I have never asked: What are the three to four most basic elements that comprise peacebuilding? I wonder what the BOIDS of peacebuilding would be?"

What I had clear was this. Peacebuilding is an enormously complex endeavor in unbelievably complex, dynamic, and more often than not destructive settings of violence. I had often thought about and suggested that a peacebuilder must embrace complexity, not ignore or run from it. "Complexify before you simplify," I would often say in class. To simplify, as I saw it, was the second tier of activity. Once the full complexity is understood, you can then make a choice about what particular thing to do in a given setting. You then recognize that this one activity and process is in a complex system that has multiple actors pushing processes at multiple levels at the same time.

This was in fact my working definition of complexity: multiple actors, pursuing a multiplicity of actions and initiatives, at numerous levels of social relationships in an interdependent setting at the same time. Complexity emerges from multiplicity, interdependency, and simultaneity. In many regards this is *the* great challenge of peacebuilding: how to build creative responses to patterns of self-perpetuating violence in a complex system made up of multiple actors, with activities that are happening at the same time. What I had not fully contemplated was the idea that rather than focus directly on the complexity, it would be useful to locate a core set of patterns and dynamics that generate the complexity. In other words, simplicity precedes complexity. This required me to think about simplicity as a source of energy rather than as the choice of reductionism. It was, as I will describe in a later chapter, a lesson in the haiku attitude.

The thought provided a reorientation as I was writing this book. I posed for myself a slightly different question than the one posed by the technical approach of BOIDS on the computer. Rather than seek the "rules" of simplicity, I became curious about what constitutes the core "essences" of peacebuilding. These I came to see as a small set of disciplines, or practices, out of which the complexity of peacebuilding emerges in all of its beauty. Put in a slightly different way, I asked myself about essence in this way: What disciplines, *if they were not present*, would make peacebuilding impossible? On exploration I discovered that when held together and practiced, these disciplines form the moral imagination that make peacebuilding possible. The essence is found in four disciplines, each of which requires imagination. They are relationship, paradoxical curiosity, creativity, and risk.

The Centrality of Relationships

At the cutting edge of fields from nuclear physics and biology to systems theory and organizational development, relationships are seen as the central organizing concept of theory and practice. According to science, as Margaret Wheatley has noted time and again, "nothing in the universe exists as an isolated or independent entity. Everything takes the form of relationships, be it subatomic particles sharing energy or ecosystems sharing food. In the web of life, nothing living lives alone" (Wheatley, 2002:89). In reference to our inquiry, the centrality of relationship accrues special meaning, for it is both the context in which cycles of violence happen and the generative energy from which transcendence of those same cycles bursts forth. Time and again, where in small or large ways the shackles of violence are broken, we find a singular tap root that gives life to the moral imagination: the capacity of individuals and communities to imagine themselves in a web of relationship even with their enemies.

This kind of imagination is accompanied by and produces several key disciplines. First and foremost, where cycles of violence are overcome, people demonstrate a capacity to envision and give birth to that which already exists, a wider set of interdependent relationships. This is akin to the aesthetic and artistic process. Art is what the human hand touches, shapes, and creates and in turn what touches our deeper sense of being, our experience. The artistic process has this dialectic nature: It arises from human experience and then shapes, gives expression and meaning to, that experience. Peacebuilding has this same artistic quality. It must experience, envision, and give birth to the web of relationships. Literally, people in settings of violence experience and see the web of patterns and connections in which they are embroiled. They see that individuals, communities, and networks, along with their activities and actions, are linked and contribute to patterns that may give rise to destructive or constructive actions. Faced with the experience of violence, the choice of response that gives rise to the moral imagination requires the acknowledgment of interdependency. The perpetration of violence, more than anything else, requires a deep, implicit belief that desired change can be achieved independently of the web of relationships. Breaking violence requires that people embrace a more fundamental truth: Who we have been, are, and will be emerges and shapes itself in a context of relational interdependency. As will be discussed later, the essence of peacebuilding requires us to explore in much greater detail the inner makeup of creativity as embedded in understanding the dynamics and potentials of networking—the arts of web making and web watching.

A second and equally important discipline that emerges from the centrality of relationship is found in an act of simple humility and self-recognition. People don't just take notice of the web. They situate and recognize themselves as part of the pattern. Patterns of violence are never superseded without acts that have a confessional quality at their base. Spontaneous or intentionally planned, these acts emerge from a voice that says in the simplest of terms: "I am part of this pattern. My choices and behaviors affect it." While the justification of violent response has many tributaries, the moral imagination that rises beyond violence has but two: taking personal responsibility and acknowledging relational mutuality.

Peacebuilding requires a vision of relationship. Stated bluntly, if there is no capacity to imagine the canvas of mutual relationships and situate oneself as part of that historic and ever-evolving web, peacebuilding collapses. The centrality of relationship provides the context and potential for breaking violence, for it brings people into the pregnant moments of the moral imagination: the space of recognition that ultimately the quality of our life is dependent on the quality of life of others. It recognizes that the well-being of our grandchildren is directly tied to the well-being of our enemy's grandchildren.

The Practice of Paradoxical Curiosity

Cycles of violence are often driven by tenacious requirements to reduce complex history into dualistic polarities that attempt to both describe and contain social reality in artificial ways. People, communities, and most specifically choices about ways they will respond to situations and express views of the conflict are forced into either-or categories: We are right. They are wrong. We were violated. They are the violators. We are liberators. They are oppressors. Our intentions are good. Theirs are bad. History and the truth of history is most fully comprehended by our view. Their view of history is biased, incomplete, maliciously untruthful, and ideologically driven. You are with us or against us.

People who display a moral imagination that rises above the cycles of violence in which they live also rise above dualistic polarities. That is, the moral imagination is built on a quality of interaction with reality that respects complexity and refuses to fall into forced containers of dualism and either-or categories. As such, this kind of imagination is infused with a paradoxical curiosity.

Paradox is a word that has long been appropriated in philosophy, theology, and the social sciences. With its origins in Greek (*paradoxos*), paradox combines the words *para* and *doxa* and is generally taken to mean "contrary to common belief." There is however a nuance that accompanies the root etymology that suggests that *para* refers to something that is outside or beyond common belief as opposed to something that is an outright contradiction of what is perceived to be true. The concept of a paradox suggests that truth lies in but also beyond what is initially perceived. The gift of paradox provides an intriguing capacity: It holds together seemingly contradictory truths in order to locate a greater truth.

Curiosity suggests attentiveness and continuous inquiry about things and their meaning. Etymologically, it rises from the Latin *curiosus* which is formed on the word *cura*, literally meaning "to take care of" and having to do with both "cure" and "care," as in spiritual and physical healing. From this we get terms like *caregiver* and *curator*. In its negative form, curiosity pushes toward exaggerated inquisitiveness best seen perhaps in the snooping detectives or overly interested neighbors who poke around too much in the affairs of others. In its most constructive and positive expression, however, curiosity builds a quality of careful inquiry that reaches beyond accepted meaning. It wishes to go deeper and in fact is excited by those things that are not immediately understood.

When the two terms are combined, we have *paradoxical curiosity*, which approaches social realities with an abiding respect for complexity, a refusal to fall prey to the pressures of forced dualistic categories of truth, and an inquisitiveness about what may hold together seemingly contradictory social energies in a greater whole. This is not primarily a thrust toward finding the common ground based on a narrowly shared denominator. Paradoxical curiosity seeks something beyond what is visible, something that holds apparently contradictory and even violently opposed social energies together. By its very nature therefore this quality of perspective, this stance vis-à-vis others, even enemies, is built fundamentally on a capacity to mobilize the imagination.

Rather than moving to immediate conclusions, paradoxical curiosity suspends judgment in favor of exploring presented contradictions, at face and at heart value, for the possibility that there exists a value beyond what is currently known that supersedes the contradiction. *Face value* is the simple and direct way that things appear and are presented. In settings of violence, it is the context as it is in all of its ugliness and difficulties. It is the way people say things are, with all of the contradictions that arise as one listens to different sides of suffering humanity. Paradoxical curiosity starts with a commitment to accept people at face value. *Heart value* goes beyond the presentation of appearance and ventures into the way these things are perceived and interpreted by people. It explores where meaning is rooted. It seeks to find the home of meaning in the experience of people. Face value and heart value suppose a paradox. Inherent in what is and how it is presented are found the resources that make possible things and understandings that do not yet exist. This is the paradox of accepting at face value what exists and taking up the journey toward heart value of where it came from and where it might lead.

To suspend judgment and explore face and heart value in settings of conflict require a capacity to develop and live with a high degree of ambiguity. On the one hand, we must accept the realness of appearance, the way things appear to be. We must on the other hand explore the realness of lived experience, how perceptions and meanings have emerged and how they might point to realities of both what is now apparent and the invisible that lies beyond what is presented as conclusive. To suspend judgment is not to relinquish opinion or the capacity to assess. It is fundamentally a force to mobilize the imagination and lift the relationships and understandings of relationships in a violent context to a new level. Suspending judgment refuses to force complex social histories and constructed realities into artificial dualistic categories in favor of the seeking of understanding that breaks the hold of social polarization. Far from being paralyzed by complexity, paradoxical curiosity as a quality of the moral imagination relies on complexity as a friend not an enemy, for from complexity emerges untold new angles, opportunities, and unexpected potentialities that surpass, replace, and break the shackles of historic and current relational patterns of repeated violence.

Serendipitous as they may be, the four guiding stories of this book suggest paradoxical curiosity. A young man treated his elder, the enemy chief, as a father, thereby creating a wiser and inherently more fatherly response. Women mobilized the patriarchy to give rise to a safe market where men were incited to be men and make peace and women were truth keepers and peace preservers. A group of peasants appealed to the truth of the rhetoric of violent actors to move them beyond violence. A professor-poet offered only his own vulnerability to provide security to a poet-warlord.

Paradoxical curiosity stimulates and provokes the moral imagination. It is a discipline that, in settings of deep-rooted violence filled with social polarization, views complexity as a friend and refuses to fall into the historic traps of dualistic divisions, which drive the cycles of violence. Paradoxical curiosity sustains a permanent inquisitiveness that vigilantly explores the world of possibilities beyond the immediate arguments and narrow definitions of reality, whose shores are only attainable by taking the arguments seriously while refusing to be bound by their visions. In this regard, paradoxical curiosity is indeed the *cura* that attends to and takes care of the health of greater humanity.

Provide Space for the Creative Act

The moral imagination takes form and expression through an act. While we might initially think of the space where *moral* and *imagination* meet as a conceptual exercise, in reality we cannot know this kind of imagination outside of concrete human action. Theologically this notion is found in the Word that becomes flesh, the moment when potentiality moves from the realm of possibility to the world of the tangible. In other words, the moral imagination finds its clearest expression in the appearance of the creative act.

In his subtitle, Matthew Fox (2002) calls *creativity* the place "where the divine and the human meet." There is, once again, inherent to our exploration, a quality of paradox that accompanies the process, for the creative act simultaneously has an element of the transcendent and the mundane. In other words, creativity moves beyond what exists toward something new and unexpected while rising from and speaking to the everyday. This is in fact the role of the artist and why it is that imagination and art are at the edge of society. Artists tend to be, as we shall explore in subsequent chapters, people who live on the thresholds of the communities they inhabit, from whence the pulse of their lifework emerges and to which they speak. However, by being on the edge they also pose a threat for they push the edges of what is thought to be real and possible. As Brueggemann suggests, "[E]very totalitarian regime is frightened of the artist. It is the vocation of the prophet to keep alive the ministry of imagination, to keep on conjuring and proposing futures alternative to the single one the king wants to urge as the only thinkable one" (2001:40).

Therefore, another key discipline that gives rise to the moral imagination is the provision of space for the creative act to emerge. Providing space requires a predisposition, a kind of attitude and perspective that opens up, even invokes, the spirit and belief that creativity is humanly possible. Fundamentally, this requires a belief that the creative act and response are permanently within reach and, most important, are always accessible, even in settings where violence dominates and through its oppressive swath creates its greatest lie: that the lands it inhabits are barren. Artists shatter this lie, for they live in barrenness as if new life, birth, is always possible. Though not foretold or initially clear, people who display a deep quality of moral imagination in these settings of violence demonstrate a capacity to live in a personal and social space that gives birth to the unexpected. Having much in common, the survival of both creativity and imagination require this quality of living. They embrace the possibility that there exist untold possibilities capable at any moment to move beyond the narrow parameters of what is commonly accepted and perceived as the narrow and rigidly defined range of choices.

In this book I will explore this quality of providing for and expecting the unexpected. It is a quality better known in the world of art and artists than in the worlds of social technique and management expertise, though our task is not to pit these worlds against each other. What I wish to explore here is not the question of whether technicians or artists are better or more needed, but to understand the epistemological and ontological qualities that differentiate and connect technique and imagination. Creativity and imagination, the artist giving birth to something new, propose to us avenues of inquiry and ideas about change that require us to think about how we know the world, how we are in the world, and most important, what in the world is possible. What we will find time and again in those turning points and moments where something moves beyond the grip of violence is the vision and belief that the future is not the slave of the past and the birth of something new is possible.

The Willingness to Risk

The final discipline at the essence of the moral imagination can be described simply but requires heart and soul and defies prescription: the willingness to take a risk. *To risk* is to step into the unknown without any guarantee of success or even safety. Risk by its very nature is mysterious. It is mystery lived, for it ventures into lands that are not controlled or charted. People living in settings of deep-rooted conflict are faced with an extraordinary irony. Violence is known; peace is the mystery. By its very nature, therefore, peacebuilding requires a journey guided by the imagination of risk.

To fully understand the moral imagination we will need to explore the geographies of violence that are known and the nature of risk and vocation, which permits the rise of an imagination that carries people toward a new, though mysterious, and often unexpected shore. This means in concrete terms that we must understand both the deeper implications of risk and the longer-term sustenance of vocation. Vocation, as we shall see, requires us to explore the promptings of the inner voice and provides a center for this most difficult journey to break out from the historic grasp of violence.

Conclusion

Combined, these simple disciplines form the conditions that make the moral imagination and peacebuilding possible. The guiding stories in chapter 2 from Ghana, Wajir, Colombia, and Tajikistan provide windows into moments when this imagination was sparked. In each and every story the four elements were present. Though invoked by what may seem to be the time and space of serendipity, each context tells the story of a journey, people seeking a way to respond at a given moment to historic patterns of animosity and violence. In each story the journey involved a turning point, the movement toward a new horizon in order to redefine both the moment and the relationship. Time and again the process was defined by the capacity of the actors to imagine themselves in relationship, a willingness to embrace complexity and not frame their challenge as a dualistic polarity, acts of enormous creativity, and a willingness to risk. The results were complex initiatives of building peace defined by moments that created and then sustained constructive change.

We turn our attention next to the context in which this journey must be initiated, the hard realities of living in settings of violence and the lessons we can learn—ironically—from pessimism and from those who survive without losing sight of what poet Seamus Heaney calls the "farther shore."

5

On Peace Accords

Image of a Line in Time

the trick of finding what you didn't lose
(existing's tricky: but to live's a gift)
the teachable imposture of always
arriving at the place you never left

—e. e. cummings

Since 1990, the date that marked the opening of the globally rede-
fined post-Soviet era, more than eighty partial or complete peace accords have been penned (Darby and MacGinty, 2003).[1] The simple
act of former enemies placing their names side by side on a piece of
paper represented the culmination of negotiations to supposedly end
what were years, if not decades, of violence and war. I say "supposedly" because ending war and cycles of violence, especially in settings of deep-rooted conflict, have proven to be complex tasks indeed. Dozens of those accords have collapsed into renewed fighting
and renewed rounds of negotiation.

We are growing in our capacity to think about and develop
mechanisms for supporting the processes that reduce and even stop
open fighting. We are, however, still in our infancy in reference to
shaping and sustaining a positive justpeace, the rebuilding of genuine community in areas that have suffered from great division and
violence. The difficulties of attaining a durable peace in contexts of
protracted violence suggest we know more about how to end something painful and damaging to everyone but less about how to build
something desired. When we do build after a war, we think first and
foremost about physical infrastructure: buildings, roads, bridges,

and schools. To fully understand and reweave the social fabric of relationships torn apart by decades and generations of hatred remain significant challenges. These challenges have roots in a question that is, to use a Pauline image, seen as if looking through a thick glass darkly. The question goes to the heart of the moral imagination: How exactly do we transcend cycles of violence? How do we create genuine constructive change in and with the human community?

One place to look for insights and lessons about these questions is precisely where many of us are least likely to look: in the rough terrains and geographies of violent, protracted conflict. My surprise has been this: People who face the worst situations of human degradation, violence, and abuse often see the challenge of genuine constructive change with piercing vision. Maybe it is because for these people survival to a large degree depends on gut intuition, a sense of what things mean and who people really are beyond their words. Maybe it is due to their hard-earned calluses of caution and prevention layered after decades of pain, injustice, and violence.

Before exploring this further it is useful to ask what exactly is meant by the phrase *constructive social change*. I would propose a simple definition that emerges from these settings of protracted conflict. It might best be understood with the metaphor of a continental divide. Such a divide defines how water flows: On one side, the water flows toward a shore on the far reaches of the continent; on the other side of the divide, it flows toward the opposite shore. In social conflict these two distant shores are fear and love. These may seem unfamiliar as academic terms, but these exact concepts were proposed years ago by economist Kenneth Boulding in several of his seminal treatises (for example, Boulding, 1985, 1989). The question at each moment of violent conflict and its sustained cycle is this: Which way will the water flow that defines our relationship, toward the shore of fear or that of love?

When the water flows toward fear, the relationship is defined by recrimination and blame, self-justification and protection, violence and the desire for victory over the other. When the water flows toward love, it is defined by openness and accountability, self-reflection and vulnerability, mutual respect, dignity, and the proactive engagement of the other. Unlike the image of the continental divide, which has a fixed location, the great challenge of social realities defined by violence is the dynamic and constantly moving nature of relationships. As such, the waters of fear and love can move back and forth, in small and larger quantities, given the particular nature of the relationship at a given moment. But herein we find a working definition of *constructive social change*: the pursuit of moving relationships from those defined by fear, mutual recrimination, and violence toward those characterized by love, mutual respect, and proactive engagement. Constructive social change seeks to change the flow of human interaction in social conflict from cycles of destructive relational violence toward cycles of relational dignity and respectful engagement. The flows of fear destroy. Those of love edify. That is the challenge: how to move from that which destroys toward that which builds. I call this *constructive social change.*

However, if patterns of destruction are repeated over and over again across generations, which is the nature of what we call deep-rooted or protracted conflict, how do we know that a change process is genuine? This is the doubt that many people express about "the promises of peace" in settings of deep violence. Over my years of working in these settings I have come to know that if you want to learn something of what genuine change means you must listen carefully to the voices of people who have suffered greatly and are slow with their belief that things are in fact moving in a constructive direction. People living through the worst cycles of violence have much to teach us about authenticity in human affairs. Unlike many of us, their lives depend on it. And what we find is that they are, generally speaking, pessimistic. Their pessimism, I have come to understand, is a gift not an obstacle. However, before exploring this grounded pessimism, we need first to look more closely at what all of these peace agreements are about and how this phase, known as *post-accord*, poses a challenge for genuine change.

Peace Agreements: The Line in Time

As e. e. cummings suggested in the poem quoted above, "the trick of finding what you didn't lose" is "arriving at the place you never left." The irony of this concept has much to do with the field of peacebuilding. Practitioners and academics seem to have a need for the analytical project, the breaking of complex reality into pieces, the creation of categories, and the pursuit of knowledge by taxonomy. Thus it was that at some point social conflict came to be seen as a linear progression of phases. In the case of sustained, organized violence, otherwise known as war, the rise and descent of violent conflict became a single, wave-like timeline. On this wave, categories were located, indicating what should be done when by whom in response to escalating conflict and the building of peace. At the highest point of the wave, we usually find the agreement, a single line in time. It is followed by the phase known as the "posts": post-agreement, post-accord, post-violence, and sometimes the greatest oxymoron of them all, post-conflict.

Over the last years my professional academic shelf and files have filled with an increasing volume of useful studies and treatises on how peace is attained and supported after war. Post-accord peacebuilding has become a category of specialization. Some authors and researchers focus on the technical aspects, like how troops are demobilized, refugees are repatriated, or basic institutions, like police forces, are retooled in the period that follows a war (Darby and MacGinty, 2003; Call and Stanley, 2003; Leatherman, 2003). There are books on truth commissions and on war crime tribunals (Villa-Vicencio and Verwoerd, 2000; Hayner, 2003). There are also a rising number of books on the politics of reconciliation and forgiveness (Helmich and Peterson, 2001; De Gruchy, 2003). Each of these brings useful insights, sharpens our understandings of the challenge, and describes processes attempted, at times prescribed, to suggest corrections to meet identified needs. This increased explicit study is important and represents an effort to grow in our abilities to build constructive change processes.

Reading this growing literature I have been struck by a single prevailing—though mostly unconscious—image of violent conflict and correspondingly of peacebuilding as the rising then falling line of escalation. Doodle 1 captures this image in a way I might draw it in class.[2] Images, as we know from Boulding (1984) and Lakoff and Johnson (2003), are powerful not just because they *convey* meaning but more important because they *create* meaning. For the purpose of study and category creation, conflict-as-escalation has several characteristics.

The doodle captures the image of a single line in time, very much like a slow-rising bell curve with a sharper descent on the end. Though it suggests that conflict evolves over time, the impression it leaves is of conflict in an eye blink. We easily lose a sense of time in this particular picture. For example, if we take the period of actual open fighting and warfare in a dozen of the most prominent contemporary internal conflicts, from Sudan to Colombia, Liberia to Aceh, the time reference is across decades if not generations. The rise of conflict happens over long periods of time, but the images of the peace accord and the post-accord are often seen in much shorter periods.

Typically in this visual depiction, categories of tasks, activities, or roles can be drawn that provide a kind of lexicon of conflict and peace. Advocate roles are typically placed early on, in periods of latent conflict, and may have the role of surfacing issues that need to be addressed. Prevention finds its home in the rising escalation of potential violence. Negotiation emerges when the conflict is more highly escalated or seeking to deescalate. The "agreement," often seen as the result of negotiation, is not a category but a discrete moment in time, a line in itself. And then, of course, we arrive at the post-accord category, the way down out of escalation.

Let us take a moment to explore the significance, promise, and challenge posed by the image created with the word *agreement*. What is the agreement? It is of course the signed document. But even the person in the street in settings of armed conflict will say, "No, it is not the paper." So, beyond the paper, what is the agreement? I find time and again that the prevailing image of agreement is the notion of solution. "The sides to the conflict have reached an agreement" means they have found a solution. Agreement creates the expectation that the conflict has ended. This assumes of course that the agreement represents substantive solutions to specific problems and that we can in some way characterize the agreement as solutions that are to be sustained. This is how the

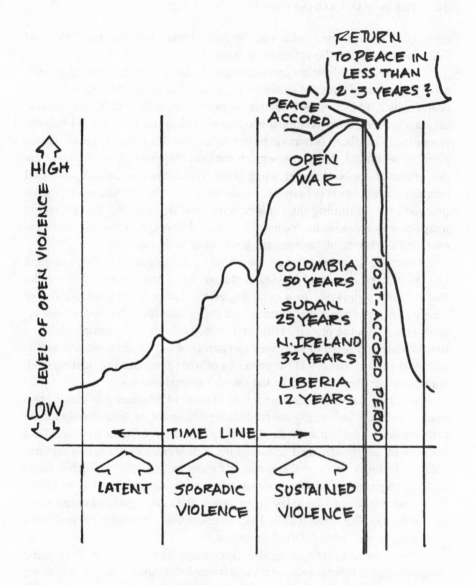

DOODLE ONE
CONFLICT AS A LINE IMAGE

contending groups, the media, and the professionals talk about it: "We must find a way to sustain the agreements reached."

On closer consideration agreements that end a conflict are hard to find. Most peace accords are not solutions in content but proposed negotiated processes, which if followed, will change the expression of the conflict and provide avenues for redefining relationships. Mayer (2000) has even argued that the resolution of conflict has many expressions and depths, from cognitive to emotional to behavioral, and that any given solution may only attend to part of the deeper-rooted needs. However, when peace accords are broached in protracted conflicts nobody wants to be quite so blunt as to say, "The agreement represents processes for continuing the conflict under new definitions." The prevailing image creates a significant meaning structure that suggests that the conflict is over, and the image of "agreement" lends itself to that desire.

Returning now to our image, the conflict as an escalation and deescalation line poses a certain way of looking at change and a particular level of conflict that is being addressed. To a large degree the image focuses on the rise of violence, an agreement that stops it, and the deescalation that follows the accord. This places the primary emphasis on negotiation of the symptomatic, or more visible and often destructive expressions of the conflict, but not on the relational context that lies at the epicenter of what generates the fighting (Lederach, 2003a). This seems to be the case for several reasons.

First, negotiation on the immediate content of disputes provides a pragmatic handle for addressing the conflict. In settings of protracted violence the complexities of dealing with the deeper epicenter are difficult and have long histories of deeply damaged relationships with seemingly unending recriminations. To break this cycle, negotiations move to find what is doable, focus on those steps and solutions, especially where violence can be halted, and defer the deeper transformation to later timeframes. Political negotiated pragmatism carries the day. The result is touted as a solution, when it roughly approximates an "arrangement" with deferred processes.

Second, more than anything else, agreements have been aimed at stopping the shooting and killing, a necessary and laudable humanitarian goal. However, this only represents the tip of the iceberg and is episodic in nature, even if the episodes of violence have multiple-year or even multiple-decade parameters. There are of course multiple assumptions about change that accompany the process. When shooting stops, space is created to change other things. Confidence is built little by little as negotiators propose little things upon which opposing sides can agree. Or the assumption of the "thingification" of peace and war occurs; in other words, wartime violence creates specific goals on which to focus in terms of solutions, like ceasefires, the exchange of prisoners, territorial protection or retreat, or the reduction of troops. Mostly this means that peace through negotiation results in agreements created through "things" that can be quantified.

Not explicit in either the metaphor of agreement or the image of the line is the actual nature of social and human change. Both may hide important elements of change concerning the relational epicenter of the conflict. They tend to hide the reality that the conflict has not ended. The conflict has been placed within a newly defined context where it can be pursued by other, hopefully nonviolent means. We attach and expect agreements to provide more than they can, especially around the idea that with peace accords the negotiation process is over. In fact the inverse is true. Peace agreements create a social and political space where negotiations represent an ongoing platform. In this sense, negotiations are not a short-term exceptional endeavor. In reality, peace accords mean that a whole new range of negotiations, often more arduous and difficult, are just beginning. This suggests that to sustain the change processes engendered by an accord, people in settings of violence must shift from a temporary effort to negotiate an agreement that ends the violent expression of conflict to a context-based, permanent, and dynamic platform capable of non-violently generating solutions to ongoing episodes of conflict, which they will experience in the ebb and flow of their social, political, and economic lives.

Such a viewpoint suggests we would do well to switch our metaphors and images. Sustaining peaceful transformation in settings of deep-rooted violence requires a long-term view that focuses as much on the people in the setting of conflict building durable and flexible processes as it does on specific solutions. We move away from an image of a single rising bell curve, the line in time with an agreement as its product. We move toward the image of a transformative platform: ongoing social and relational spaces, in other words, people in relationship who generate responsive initiatives for constructive change. This strategy is not driven by the concern of how to end the immediate and most pressing symptoms of the conflict, but rather focuses on how to create and sustain a platform capable of generating adaptive change processes that address both the episodic expression of the conflict and the epicenter of the conflictive relational context. An image that approximates this understanding can be found in the moving sidewalks in many modern airports. To the moving sidewalk, we add a trampoline. The sidewalk continuously moves across time, and the trampoline has the capacity to launch new ideas in response to unexpected and emerging problems. As such, a platform is responsive to day-to-day issues that arise in the ebb and flow of conflict while it sustains a clear vision of the longer-term change needed in the destructive relational patterns. The creation of such a platform, I would submit, is one of the fundamental building blocks for supporting constructive social change over time.

Framing the challenge as building dynamic platforms requires two things. First, we must recognize the need to think about the post-agreement phase not exclusively as a distinct temporal time period, but also as systemically connected to the broader processes of change embedded within the web of relationships in a given context. This suggests that we are not dealing with a single process of change proposed and controlled by those few people who negotiate mostly military and political arrangements and who are signatories to the peace accord. Constructive social change and peacebuilding itself promote and must harness multiple processes of change, which cut across the levels and populations affected by the conflict (Lederach, 1997). The broader context pushes us to reflect before, during, and after negotiations between contending groups about the nature of platforms that create and sustain constructive processes of change and about the building of relationships, not just processes that produce the content of negotiated settlements.

Second, the image of platforms requires that we recognize agreements for what they are: social and political antacids, temporary acid reducers that creates an exit for symptomatic problems and an opportunity to create a way to work on repeated patterns and cycles of destructive relationships. Platforms are much more akin to immune systems that stay the course and provide the movement toward long-term health. The big picture is less about how the antacid calms the churning pain and more about how it creates a social moment wherein deeper change can be pursued in the relational context.

What do these observations suggest to us about the moral imagination and constructive social change? First, genuine change is located at a deeper level in the complex web of the social and relational histories embedded in the context of the conflict. The moral imagination must find ways to connect and mobilize this web of relationships in and around the change that takes place in the context. The guts of change can be invoked by—but are not located in—a few good words on paper. Constructive change must build responsive processes that address the deep challenges rooted in the relational context. Second, authenticity requires the building and sustaining of platforms with the capacity to generate the constructive engagement of people in a dynamic and evolving situation that continuously tosses up new challenges.

Consider for a moment the important shifts in thinking, with the inherent ironies and paradoxes, that might accompany changing the guiding image of agreement as representing a final and complete solution to one that sees it as building a platform to promote ongoing change. Three come immediately to mind.

First, platforms are built by supporting the constructive engagement of people who have been historically divided and who are or may remain in significant levels of conflict. Solutions to any short-term issues that arise on the way do not make conflicts go away. The key to understanding and building such platforms emphasizes the sustaining of relationship and engagement in the presence of continued conflict, historic differences, experienced pain, and perceptions of injustice.

Second, relational platforms to produce change are more important than the individual solutions they create. In other words, platforms that create responsive processes must be permanent and continuously adaptive.

Third, solutions that meet particular demands in temporally discrete time-frames provide answers to pressing problems, but are ephemeral rather than permanent. Solutions create a way out, an exit from an episodic issue. This clearly alleviates systemic anxiety at any given moment, but must not be mistaken for the capacity to generate processes and solutions in an ongoing way. Agreements may solve a specific problem. Platforms, however, generate processes that produce solutions and potentially transform the epicenter of relationships in context.

For the most part, the prevailing images of negotiations, settlements, and agreements operate in the exact opposite ways. Negotiations are commonly seen as temporary efforts to create solutions. We then believe that those solutions must be sustained. The platform that created the solution is understood as a kind of scaffold, useful for a short period, but ultimately irrelevant, and therefore it disappears. The solution is seen as permanent. However, in the end, if we accept this view, we pay a price: The very things that we most need to sustain—relational platforms for the adaptive and continued generation of solutions—are either not created or are dropped. This accounts for one key aspect of what we might call the *authenticity gap* when it comes to peace processes. People are led to believe that the key to changing the situation lies in some kind of miraculous solution. Intuitively, they do not believe the signed paper will make that much difference. And their intuition is correct. Signed papers do not make a difference, and the agreements collapse unless the deeper processes of genuine engagement are created.

Conclusion

In sum, this discussion of what we find as we look from the professional lenses outside of the conflict provides an initial insight into the challenge of creating genuine change. The first step toward authenticity is to understand and publicly recognize that the engagement of deep issues and of people, sustained dialogue, is hard work and does not end with a ceasefire or the signing of a paper. Authentic engagement recognizes that conflict remains. Dialogue is permanent and requires platforms that make such engagement at multiple levels of the affected society possible and continuous. In the stories of the moral imagination in this book, both the Wajir initiative and the peasants' efforts in Magdalena Medio were built around creating and sustaining such platforms. Genuine constructive change requires engagement of the other. And this is not just a challenge for leaders—we must encompass and encourage a wide public sphere of genuine human engagement.

6

On the Gift of Pessimism

Insights from the Geographies of Violence

Are your wonders known in darkness,
Or your saving help in the land of forgetfulness?

—Psalms 88:12

Journal entry from April 2002.
    I have been reading Psalm 88 during my regular visits
in Colombia over this past year. I do not find it an easy
read, but the impact of the words seem[s] doubly heavy
given the paradoxes of the context: In this beautiful Andean
country I have found myself spending a good bit of time
over coffee and suppers with Catholic priests and lay workers struggling with their vocation in armed conflict zones of
the country. One confessed he hates to hear the phone ring
or a knock at the door in the early morning because inevitably he has to go identify corpses, more often than not from
his Parish. Another said in a three-month period he was
conducting two to three burials and ninth-day Eucharist[s]
per week. His worst days, he noted, are when the body has
been mutilated, or when it is a father or a mother, and the
surviving family members are in front row attendance at
the Mass. "What blessing do you even give," he mumbled a
number of times, "when you have to look an eight-year-old
in the eye and explain why his mother was butchered?" I
get physically tired just listening to the stories. I cannot
imagine what it must feel like to be this thirty-year-old
priest.

The Psalmist asks what help is possible in a land of forgetfulness. I sometimes feel that my journeys to Colombia over the past
fifteen years are to a place where memory is short, though I hasten
to add that forgetfulness is not exactly the absence of memory. The
plague of forgetfulness resides in the presence of intentional dele-
tion, choosing not to see what is visible or focus on what is known.
We are told that selective memory represents a psychological defense mechanism that makes survival possible. And literally survival
is the name of the game in Colombia. However, the cost of such de-
fensive and collective protection is the cheapening of hope, for the
rightful antonym of forgetfulness is not memory. It is hard-won, collective, and sustained hope, the belief that things can be different.
Forgetfulness requires, more than anything else that we live and respond to current circumstances by a series of myths, half-truths,
and outright lies, and correspondingly we lower our expectations of
[a] new tomorrow.

So to be honest, I am struggling with the plague [of] forgetfulness for in my past visits to Colombia I have found myself fighting
hopelessness. Maybe I have been impacted by the combination of
pessimisms that float about the country like a viral flu. The day I
arrived on this last visit the leading presidential candidate was car
bombed, escaping death in the midst of his campaign and adding
fuel to his already strong rhetoric that total war is the only way to
pull the country back to peace and democracy. Even taxi drivers
seem to have arrived at a thoroughly discussed and complete consensus. One commented, "We are tired of the sweet candy of peace
through negotiation, dangled like a caramel just out of reach. We
don't believe it any more."

"What don't we believe?" I kept finding myself asking. "And
how did people get so sick of negotiations that war seems a more
promising option?"

As the reader likely noted in earlier chapters, I am uneasy with the growing
technique-oriented view of change in settings of violence that seems to dominate much of professional conflict resolution approaches. What gnaws at me
is not something that comes from the intellectual engagement about empirical
evidence and approaches related to post-accord peacebuilding, nor the extraordinary efforts of people to make a difference through the practices of conflict
resolution, negotiation, and political mediation. The gnawing sensation
emerges from what I increasingly hear and feel as I work with people who are
from these settings, more often than not, in my case, at the level of local
communities. What I find are three prevalent feelings: suspicion, indifference,
and distance. The meaning that I attach to the combination of these feelings

finds expression in the idea that viewed from the ground by the people most affected by peace decisions and logistics, there exists a profound gap of authenticity in how peace and post-accord change processes operate and shape their future. By their experience, something does not ring true between the rhetoric and the actualization of peace.

The informal "taxi survey" that I conduct on every trip and almost anywhere I travel usually comes filled with on-the-ground assessments, not always scientific, but more often than not they are windows into reality. The view of this particular taxi driver, bore the mark of what formal survey research would surely have affirmed: At a popular level in Colombia, like many other places, people live with a profound deficit of authenticity when the subject of peace is broached.

"Colombia?" Some of you may be thinking. "I thought you were going to discuss lessons from 'post-agreement' settings. Colombia is still at war." If that statement was phrased as a true-or-false question on an undergraduate exam the answer would be "True. And False." True: Colombia is a country at war internally, and negotiations between the government and the major guerrilla movements have collapsed on numerous occasions. At this writing, negotiations are off and the fighting has escalated. And false: Colombia has a history of negotiated agreements between armed groups that weaves in and out of the past fifty years of open warfare. And false: Colombia has wars, not *a* war. And false: The very conceptualization of our category "post-agreement" may well be a heuristic device of academics and politicians so nefarious in nature that it constructs a taken-for-granted version of social reality powerful enough to obscure what actually exists: complex processes of change that defy neat chronological categorizations. To quote the psalmist and as noted in the preceding chapter, post-accord may incarnate forgetfulness, because the category subtly requires us to think in lines rather than circles, in causes and effects rather than in systems.

I do not want to belabor my argument with the category of post-agreement because even though I believe it obscures certain realities, I also believe it provides a useful lens for looking at discrete moments within larger processes of conflict transformation. However, caution is needed, and it is found among the people living in these settings where peace is being "implemented." Those folks suggest that we approach the category of post-accord with a great deal of care and a critical eye. We must not embrace this time period so wholeheartedly that we sacrifice the capacity to envision the broader context of conflict cycles or blur the important lessons that this particular phase can provide us about the nature of social change.

Their insight, I believe, is birthed from the struggle to traverse and survive the geography of violence. Such a land teaches you lessons. I have lived in such settings during several short periods of my life, but not nearly to the extent of my teachers, community people whose daily trek is across this terrain.

Over the years I have picked up these cautions from people living in violence. In different settings I have often heard people repeat the following:

1. Change to move away from violence does not come easy. Anybody that says it does has not lived here.
2. Change does not come quickly. Be suspicious of anybody with a quick-fix solution. It is usually a trap.
3. The more things change, the more they remain exactly the same. Just ask my granddad. And it is what I teach my grandchildren. Never judge a change by months or a year. At a minimum, judge the change by decades if not generations.
4. Words are cheap. Don't believe promises. Don't accept offers. Don't expect a piece of paper signed by politicians to change your life.
5. To survive violence, create walls and retrench. Plan to do it for a long time. Don't give your walls up easily. You will likely live to regret it.

Their pessimism, or what we might call a well-grounded realism, suggests that the subject of post-agreement must address certain questions: How do we view desired social change in the context of long-term social and economic divisions? What do we expect from and how do we view the quality and building of the public sphere when it has been decimated by violence or, as is the case in many settings, never really existed? How is trust restored in public institutions and in leaders who are supposed to serve? How exactly does a whole society move from cycles of division and violence to respectful engagement in a way that the change is experienced as genuine?

These questions lead to two key concerns directly relevant to the purpose of this book: What do people who live in settings that are moving from war to peace teach us about the challenge of understanding the nature of genuine constructive social change? And in turn, what do these insights and challenges suggest to us about the nature and place of the moral imagination in human affairs? Several insights and lessons learned emerge from interaction with people in these settings.

The Gift of Pessimism

First, in deep-rooted conflict, people locate themselves and change and gauge authenticity within an expansive view of time and an intuitive sense of complexity. These create a cautious approach to promises that constructive social change will happen in a short period of time, independent of the historical context in which the violence has evolved. In short, there is a pervading ethos of pessimism. This does not mean that desired changes are not hoped for or possible, even in the short term. But pessimism provides a point of departure for understanding the nature of change. Very simply it says this: Gauging whether the change process is genuine requires serious engagement with the complexity of the situation and a long-term view. If simple answers are reached as if complexity did not exist, then just as Oliver Wendell Holmes suggests, they are not worth a fig. People living in settings of violence often give a warning: If the proposed changes lack a serious account of complexity or a long-term commitment, then the proposed changes are dangerous. The legacy of the setting and their lived experience inculcates a high degree of respect for the regenerative capacity of violence, repeated patterns, and shifting ground filled with traps.

We must however understand the nature and contribution of this variety of pessimism. We are not talking here of an attitude born of cynicism, an embittered attitude and predisposition to believe the worst of everything and everyone, a fault-finding par excellence. Pessimism born of cynicism is a luxurious avoidance of engagement. This is not the pessimism that arises in settings where people have learned to negotiate life in the hard terrains of violence. The surprising insight from these lands is that survival requires the horizon of hope coupled with indifference toward the impact of violence. Indifference does not mean that people don't care. Theirs is not the indifference of apathy. It is the indifference of the heroic but everyday journey. They do not allow repeated cycles of violence to kill their passion for life or derail their daily journey. They keep walking the terrain in spite of the violence. This requires a selective indifference: These particular events that are out of my control will not restrict or destroy my life. When these events are repeated over and again, across decades and generations, it creates the pessimism of survival. The space where selective indifference and hope meet gives birth to an extraordinary irony: Pessimism is a gift for survival.

The pessimism of which we speak arises from hard-won experience as a guide that tests the quality of engagement. This pessimism is a gift, not a bad attitude, lack of engagement, or bitterness gone wickedly off track. It is a terrain-based understanding of the social setting. What it seeks to engage is a deep understanding of human affairs, the true nature of how change happens, and the necessity of integrity as a condition for surviving manipulation and mendacity. As such, this pessimism provides not an early-warning but a continuous-warning system. In essence, this kind of pessimism represents a grounded realism.

Grounded realism constantly explores and questions what constitutes genuine change. For people who have lived for long periods in settings of violence, change poses this challenge: How do we create something that does not yet exist in a context where our legacy and lived history are alive and lie before us? Pessimism suggests that the birth of constructive change develops in the womb of engaging complex historical relationships, not avoiding them. To be gauged authentic, that change can neither be ahistorical nor superficially utopian. The birth of the genuine requires the embrace of complexity and the commitment to nurture birth and growth through thick and thin. For our inquiry into the moral imagination this means that transcendence is not avoidance or flight from what is, but rather it is a deep rootedness in the reality of what has existed while seeking new ways to move beyond the grips of those patterns. Transcendence and imagination respond to historical patterns but are not bound by them.

A second gift of pessimism recognizes that the authenticity of change is not organically located in campaigns, images, and words used publicly by national leaders. Though these affect and can catalyze, for good or bad, they do not constitute what people understand as the integrity of change. Authenticity is seeded in the soils of shared perception about the quality and nature of the public sphere. In other words, authenticity of social change is ultimately tested in real-life relationships at the level where people have the greatest access and where they perceive they are most directly affected: in their respective communities.

To draw on a subfield of anthropology, social change is viewed with an inherent sense of proxemics. Traditionally, *proxemics* is the study of the actual physical space that people view as necessary to set between themselves and others in order to feel comfortable. Applied to our inquiry, one way to understand how change is viewed is to study the space that people feel is necessary to perceive and experience a change process as genuine. I find rather consistently that people judge change by what can be *felt* and *touched* and by what *touches their lives*. This of course poses a major challenge for national-level processes. When national leaders and campaigns are successful, it is because people feel touched and feel they can touch what is happening. From the view of proxemics, the distance between people and the processes of change has been reduced because they feel directly connected to it. When things happen, locally or nationally, and people do not have a sense of touch and feel, the distance expands and they feel removed and remote. Correspondingly, the processes are perceived as foreign and unconnected, creating a sense of imposition or, worse, apathy. In the vernacular: "Stuff happens to us. We are not shaping what happens." This is why a prevalent feeling about peace processes is that they are distant from us. They happen out there.

Another way to describe this is through the metaphor of voice. The most prevalent statement I hear in settings of post-accord processes is the oft-repeated phrase, "We don't have a voice in the decisions that affect us." Metaphorically, *voice* constitutes a social geography mapped and measured by the distance needed to create a sense of engagement. More literally, voice is about meaningful conversation and power. *Meaningful conversation* suggests mutuality, understanding, and accessibility. *Power* suggests that the conversation makes a difference: Our voices are heard and have some impact on the direction of the process and the decisions made.

Conversation has the unique quality of providing a meaningful space of participation and interchange. In conversation, I gain entry into another's thoughts and feelings. I share my thoughts and feelings. Together we have a sense of mutuality. The proxemics of conversation and voice is one of direct access and contact. In the many direct interactions I have had with people in settings of deep conflict, I consistently hear that authenticity finds its birth in this sense of proximity. We might call this the *social distance of direct conversation*, the actual physical space that permits people to feel they are participants in, not just observers and recipients of, the process. Participation does not mean control, but it does create the clear perception that voice counts and is accounted for. This suggests a relational and spatial understanding. Voice creates access, a distance akin to conversation measured by actual speaking and hearing, and a deeper sense that participation in the conversation actually mattered.

If this is indeed the case, then we recognize what a significant challenge and paradox the proxemics of voice poses for peacebuilding: How do whole societies move from violent social division to respectful engagement when the fundamental building block for social change is measured in the distance of an accessible conversation? This is not a new paradox. C. Wright Mills (1959) suggested that the challenge of his academic discipline was to understand this type of social geography. As he put it, the very vocation of sociology was to study and understand the space that connects personal biography and social structure. People in settings of great violence astutely recognize that distance and apathy go hand in hand. When the change processes are molded and shaped without engagement, in other words, without voice or accessible conversation, then the process is held at a distance, and a sense of apathy and manipulated change emerges and grows.

The third lesson of pessimism emerges in what we might call the ultimate *litmus test of authenticity*: Did behavior actually change? At an immediate level this often involves the daily assessment of words in relation to actions. In settings of deep conflict, words and promises do not constitute an adequate measure that genuine change has taken place. People's actions, attitudes, responses, and behavior do.

Inherent in this litmus test is time, a wait-and-see approach to judging what the supposed changes really mean by seeing how they translate into real-life behavior. The biblical phrase "you shall know them by their fruit" captures this understanding. Fruit does not emerge in a single day, nor is it isolated from a context of soils, roots, and climate. It takes time, and it involves repeated testing, iterations that are continuously watched and tasted. While words are received with caution in order to test them in the laboratory of life and actual responses, people's actions and behaviors constitute an immediate test of authenticity on a one-time basis. In settings of deep-rooted conflict, judging change is a reiterative process, accumulated and built slowly over time, and one that is easily destroyed with a single wrong move or action. While behaviors that are seen to constitute genuine constructive change are judged with great caution, those behaviors that reinforce preexisting perceptions that change is not likely to happen or last are judged rapidly and severely.

Equally important in this understanding is the direct reintroduction of real-life people into the equation. Much of what is seen as constituting genuine change in these settings involves changes in the social structures and institutions. Yet institutional changes are always judged by the concrete actions of the people who represent them. For example, a local police force can engage itself in a systemwide initiative to improve its image and relationship with the community it serves. This involves structural and personal processes of change. The department may come up with a great theme that captures the changes it wants: "Serving the Community with Respect for the Law." Taking the very best scenario, it could well be that the leadership and the individual employees are committed to the change and the new goals, that they even have the training and preparation to carry out the long-term goals. The test of authenticity of this change, however, will not lie at the level of the words spoken by the leaders or written on the side of the patrol cars, the distribution of the brochures announcing the program and the new guidelines, or the budget that paid for the training, which demonstrates the system's commitment to the change. Ultimately the authenticity litmus test will ride on how people experience the behavior of police officers in real-life situations. The great paradox is this: To be authentic, constructive social change must be broadly structural but it is tested by the minutia and immediacy of people's behavior, including individual actions, which are perceived to represent the proposed change. Authenticity involves a long waiting period until people believe the change is real, but judgment of inauthenticity is continuous and immediate.

The Moral Imagination, Pessimism, and Constructive Change

The preceding discussion suggests that people from geographies of violence pose three challenging paradoxes to the testing of constructive change. First, their pessimism puts forward the dilemma of transcendence: Giving birth to something new must embrace a history that is present and alive. Second, the paradox of the public sphere suggests that while change is perceived and understood to be broadly social, national, even global, for people affected by the conflict, the authenticity of the change is tested in the public arena of greatest accessibility and proximity: the local community. Finally, the paradox of behavior suggests that change is structural yet gauged by personal and individual actions. Consider for a moment what these challenges pose for our exploration of the moral imagination.

Grounded realism and constructive pessimism require a type of imagination capable of transcending violence while engaging the immediate and historical challenges that continue to produce it. For something to be genuine it needs to reach beyond what is and yet submit itself to continuous testing. Authenticity says that change must move forward by engaging the past, without backtracking into the land of forgetfulness or condemning communities to repeat what has gone before. The real challenge of authenticity and the moral imagination is how to transcend what has been and is now, while still living in it. For the moral imagination to make a journey across this terrain it will need to address complexity and support change over time. And it will need to find ways to sustain broad strategic changes while paying close attention to the details of the little things, the ways that social change translates into changed attitudes and behaviors. Processes and solutions for peace that circumvent these fundamental requirements—complexity and long-term commitment—discover sooner or later, that the proposed changes are rarely genuine or durable.

Perhaps most important in reference to the building of and sustaining of peace, the moral imagination must take seriously the demands of authenticity as a quality built and tested in an accessible public sphere. By all accounts our track record of strategic engagement of the public sphere in peace processes is weak, if it exists at all (Barnes, 2002). We rely almost exclusively on forms of representational leadership, at best with a due process of finding representatives designated by people whose voices are to be heard, and, at worst and unfortunately more often than not, by some pragmatic equation of the political and military power of key leaders. In other words *realpolitik* has dominated not only how politics has been traditionally defined in the era of nation-states but how building peace itself is conceptualized. It has however shown itself incapable of sustaining the constructive change it publicly announces.

Realpolitik proposes a peacebuilding methodology. Rooted in the history of nation-state building and power politics, the methodology contributes several useful and necessary tools, particularly the capacity to assess which set of people can deliver pain or destroy processes. In other words, *realpolitik* assesses change and the validity of change according to the power defined by military and economic influences. As a lens it brings into focus people and processes wielding such power. The same methodology, however, makes a leap of faith not supported by the evidence found in recent peace processes that those who appear under the lens of *realpolitik* criteria are therefore the ones who should define the parameters of peace negotiations and who will safeguard its proper implementation.

The case may in fact be worse than just stated. A taken-for-granted *realpolitik* methodology obscures two important characteristics when lifted from a lens that helps assess existing power relationships to one that defines the parameters of peace. First, *realpolitik* is blind to the existence of social spaces, relationships, ideas, and processes that do not fit its preexisting definition of what counts. Therefore, for the most part, worse than miscalculating, it completely misses some of the most significant elements of social process capable of generating new relational patterns and structures. As we will explore, it is often those very elements that have shown a capacity to create and sustain the moral imagination that underpins greater authenticity in promoting constructive change. Second, *realpolitik* has the abysmal record of destroying rather than building the very thing most needed for sustaining the platforms capable of delivering a dynamic justpeace: public confidence and authentic public engagement.

Let me return for a moment to the prevalent feelings expressed by people in the street living in settings of deep-rooted conflict in a post-accord phase: suspicion, indifference, and distance. These feelings have much to do with the authenticity gap. They are rooted in a common perception held by many living and traversing the geographies of sustained violence and are captured in phrases commonly heard in the streets: "The 'peace process' is something that happened to us, just like the war happened to us." This feeling suggests that we have been hijacked by a view that peace is primarily within the purview and parameters of a small number of economically and militarily powerful and visible people. The peace process expands to include more people when those in charge of implementing the accords need them, mostly in post-accord situations. But we have not evolved a capacity to envision—much less practice—peace in the public sphere.

Constructive pessimism suggests that the most significant weakness in sustaining platforms for genuine change is the lack of authentic engagement of the public sphere. In other words, our least-developed capacities are the practical mechanisms for how people, whole communities, are provided access and are engaged in the change process and how that engagement creates a sense of ownership, participation, and genuine commitment. We have a significant gap of imagination about this type of engagement, and in consequence peace processes display a profound deficit of public authenticity, which shows up most often in the post-agreement phase.

Conclusion

If we have listened carefully to the voices that speak from settings of deep violence, they reiterate what we have explored in this chapter: To sustain constructive change, the moral imagination will need to address the challenges posed by the paradoxes of what makes change genuine.

Pessimism does not merely identify the presence of distrust. Cycles of violence and decades of division certainly create a lack of trust, and the change processes of peace are largely aimed at restoring trust. We can take a lack of trust as a given early, often, and throughout the change processes moving from war to peace. The key gift is this: Constructive pessimism teaches us that distrust is needed as a reality check to assure that change is not superficial, Pollyanna-ish, or disguising other intentions. Distrust assures us that we are not dipping into and promoting a cheap hope; it keeps us authentic.

In seeking constructive change our challenge is rarely a lack of well-intended, well-articulated ideas, proposals, designs, and even agreements. In fact I am always struck by the extraordinary insights, visions, and even inspirational speeches that seem to abound on both sides in settings of protracted conflict. Everyone is for peace and usually has eloquent ways of stating it. But words, even when well stated, do not in themselves create a sense of authenticity. The opposite is usually true: People distrust words and claim they want to see action, the litmus test of behavior. Peacebuilding has too often taken the challenge of building trust primarily at the technical level of verification: to see in action that a proposed idea was carried out. Useful as it may be, logistical verification of political actions does not constitute authenticity of change.

If we are to invoke and support constructive change processes, we must do so by embracing several paradoxes. Processes increase authenticity when they initiate from and take seriously the historical challenges of a given setting, no matter how bad, yet are not paralyzed or bound by predetermined outcomes that such a setting has created. This is the gift of pessimism, a grounded realism that keeps things close to the hard reality that must be changed. Authenticity of process must transcend historical patterns but remain close to the people, so close that they feel the process is within the reach of their voices. This is the gift of proxemics and voice to authenticity. They require that processes not just be words or proposals that drift beyond the touch of those they affect. Authenticity requires accessibility, connection, and mutuality as means toward transcendence.

Our challenge encompasses but goes well beyond the technical aspects of change. We must find ways to create spaces and processes pregnant with the moral imagination. The pursuit of authenticity in human affairs requires the practice of a discipline that can, without fear, pose these type of questions in every sphere of human activity: How can we transcend destructive relational patterns and cycles of violence while still living in the context that produced them? How can we build broad processes of social change while creating genuine spaces of accessible public engagement? How can we foster structural change that translates into visible action?

Authenticity asks for transcendence and grounded realism, accessibility and broad vision, strategic capacity and immediate behavior. In turn, these require the disciplines of the moral imagination in the public sphere. Consider the four disciplines identified earlier in regards to what we have just discussed about the settings of protracted violence.

The moral imagination understands relationships as the center and horizon of the human community. It therefore develops a vocation based on an unconditional commitment to build authentic relationships. In practical terms for deeply divided societies, this view requires the capacity to imagine a relationship with the other that transcends the cycles of violence while the other and the patterns of violence are still present. To put it bluntly, the moral imagination has a capacity, even in moments of greatest pain, to understand that the welfare of my community is directly related to the welfare of your community.

The moral imagination refuses to frame life's challenges, problems, and issues as dualistic polarities. Its fundamental approach holds multiple and even competing and contradictory needs and perspectives together at the same time. It is built on a capacity to imagine that it is possible to hold multiple realities and world views simultaneously as parts of a greater whole without losing one's identity and viewpoint and without needing to impose or force one's view on the other. It pursues complexity as a friend rather an enemy.

The moral imagination believes and acts on the basis that the unexpected is possible. It operates with the view that the creative act is always within human potential, but creativity requires moving beyond the parameters of what is visible, what currently exists, or what is taken as given. The moral imagination does not just think outside the box; it is willing to take the risk to live outside the box.

As described initially by Mills and explored in this chapter, the moral imagination must situate itself between biography and social structure, between the local and the national. This place is the accessible public sphere. The moral imagination can be encouraged and promoted by leadership, but it is not the property or exclusive responsibility of leaders. It is also the vocation of communities. The accessible public sphere engages a level where people feel they still have a voice and can actually touch processes of change. Too often the public sphere and its institutions are seen as lands beyond touch. People feel that what happens out there affects their lives, but they have no sense of access and connection. They feel a loss of voice and a distance. Imagination is the capacity to create connection between the local and the public. Being moral is the substance of seeing oneself in the bigger picture of relationships and of keeping people, not humanly created structures, at the center of public life.

So how do people living in the geographies of violence remember and change? As was so clearly stated in the psalmist's reflections, it is not by creating a land of forgetfulness. Social amnesia may be useful for political pragmatism, but it is a recipe for weak communities incapable of true identity and correspondingly genuine relationships. The land of forgetfulness creates communities without vocation. The challenge of linking memory and vision lies primarily with the vocation of the moral imagination, which can only be exercised in that place that lies between the local and the public, between personal biography and the shaping of responsive social structures.

Perhaps the greatest mystery of peace is that authenticity of change is not located in what can be quantified and controlled. It is rooted in the courage of people and communities to be and live vulnerably in the face of fear and threat, and ultimately to find therein that human security is not tied primarily to the quantity or size of weapons, the height or thickness of the wall that separates them, nor to the power of imposition or control. The mystery of peace is located in the nature and quality of relationships developed with those most feared.

To invoke this mystery and creativity we must turn our attention to resources and processes in arenas that to date have been mostly seen as peripheral to the core of professional peacebuilding and conflict resolution. The journey will take us into the surprising land of the moral imagination and will require that we explore things not typically part of our technical skill manuals. We are required to explore the uncharted waters of the art and soul of social change.

7

On Aesthetics

The Art of Social Change

One Autumn day when Bashó and one of his ten disciples, Kikaku, were going through a rice field, Kikaku composed a haiku on a red dragonfly that caught his fancy. And he showed the following haiku to Bashó:

Take a pair of wings
From a dragonfly, you would
Make a pepper pod.

   "No," said Bashó, "that is not a haiku. You kill the dragonfly. If you want to compose a haiku and give life to it, you must say:

Add a pair of wings
To a pepper pod, you would
Make a dragonfly.

—Kenneth Yasuda, *The Japanese Haiku*

When I was younger, many more years ago than I care to think about, I wrote poetry. It was not earth-shaking verse. The only thing it shook was probably my own heart and head, though during my early college days I did have several accepted for publication in some obscure poetry journal that no longer exists. Then came the years of earnest study, intellectual inquiry, and the pursuit of professionalism. Poetry fell by the wayside. I stopped writing poetry, by my account, for just short of twenty years. In the early 1990s, most likely because my life was filled with too much activity, poetry crept back into some margins of notes and got scribbled onto napkins and eventually into travel journals I had started to keep. I have often wondered what it was about higher education and becoming a professional that took the poetry out of me.

By the time I reached a sabbatical year in 1998, I decided to meet once a week with a poet-teacher whom I asked to help me work on and understand what I was doing with "this stuff that pops out." He was kind and patient, but did not waste much time getting to the point. The whole of his advice I still have scribbled on the top edge of a poem I was working on the particular morning he gave it. "You are writing poetry," he said, "as if you are producing a book." He went to his shelf and pulled down a book called *The Portable Jack Kerouac*, a copy of which now sits on my poetry shelf, and turned to page 483 (Charters, 1995). Under the chapter heading "Belief & Technique for Modern Prose" was a list of Kerouac's thirty essentials. The teacher's finger stopped at number 22, and he read: "Dont [sic] think of words when you stop but to see picture better."[1]

During that sabbatical, I, a peacebuilder who had spent most of his professional life working with deep-rooted conflicts and violence, now took up the joy of coffee shop doodles, the utter frustration of shifting one small word for another, and the occasional "Whoa, where did that come from?" that is the experience of writing poetry. I was in for a complete surprise. Rather than being a personal diversion to feed my spirit, which is what I thought I was doing on sabbatical, poetry became a pathway to peacebuilding. In my classes and teaching, usually at some point when we are all feeling overwhelmed with the complexity of studying a seemingly impossible violent conflict, I go to the blackboard and write in large letters: "Dont think of words when you stop but to see picture better." And then I say, "The hardest challenge of peacebuilding is to see the essence. If you do nothing else, take time to get a picture, an image. When you see the picture better, you will have achieved a synthesis. The key to complexity is finding the elegant beauty of simplicity."

From that period, during which I let poetry back into my life, I have taken up certain pleasurable disciplines. For example, several times a year when I face longer trips to troubled regions of the world, I have a little ritual. I go to a bookstore, head for the poetry section, and give myself the gift of a new volume. Yeats or Hughes, Rumi or Neruda, I often sit late at night when I can't sleep and read the black-on-white mini-canvasses of life. I write poetry regularly, though I have not yet ventured to publish any of it. I pay attention to the little "pops" of words that seem to capture something that is happening on the trip. On rare occasions, I read what I write in the classroom and training seminars. I feel as if I am literally finding my way across an uncharted sea. At times the parallels are remarkable, for the process of paying attention to poetry, listening to a voice that seems to come from nowhere in the midst of turbulent inner seas, is very much like sorting through the storms of protracted conflicts.

During our last session of that sabbatical year, I showed my poet-teacher some of the new things I was writing. Paraphrased in my memory, his comment was the observation, "Your short poems seem to work. The long ones need work." He was, as usual, keen in his observation. I noticed that I even liked shorter poems better than longer ones. If I read a really long poem I have to stop and take it in doses. It is as if something calls out for the shorter synthesis.

One day in the middle of the Summer Peacebuilding Institute at Eastern Mennonite University, Mary Ann Cejka, a seasoned social researcher masquerading as a student, led our opening classroom reflection to start the day. "Today," she said, "we are going to write haiku." She explained the simple rules and structure of haiku. For about fifteen minutes we all wrote structurally correct but artistically challenged haiku. Though I had read and knew about this form of poetry, something caught my attention that morning and sparked my adventure with haiku.

Bashó, the famous Japanese master of Haiku, once remarked, "[H]e who creates three to five haiku poems in a lifetime is a haiku poet. He who attains to ten, is a haiku master" (Yasuda, 2000:25). In the past few years I have tried my hand at haiku. Just like Mary Ann, I even teach it as an exercise in my peacebuilding classes. I am relieved that perhaps in the course of the next twenty years I may "attain" one haiku. So far I have found this form of poetry a most intriguing challenge. Haiku, if you let it, will take you on a journey through difficult terrain in search of a place with great promise but where it is hardly possible to live except in short, extraordinary moments. It is the place where simplicity and complexity meet. I happen to believe that this is also the place where the heart of peacebuilding pounds a steady but not often perceived rhythm and where the source of the moral imagination finds inspiration.

While there exist a historical evolution and a number of variations, traditional haiku traces to Japan and has very simple guidelines or rules of thumb. The structure of a haiku is created in three lines and the syllables of each line are counted. The most commonly accepted standard requires that the first line have five syllables, the second seven, and the third five. Five-seven-five, in seventeen syllables, the haiku must capture the fullness of a human experience. For those wishing to see a haiku, the two poems quoted from Yasuda that open this chapter are both in five-seven-five format. A haiku must capture in a few words the complex fullness of a moment, a setting, or as the poets themselves are fond of saying, an experience. I have come to see the haiku challenge as a metaphor. The practice of haiku is this: to embrace complexity through simplicity. I believe this is a core practice of peacebuilding, both discipline and art, but before we explore that understanding, let us be clearer about the nature of haiku by turning to experts and haiku poets themselves.

Kenneth Yasuda, in what is probably the most accessible book for the uninitiated, *The Japanese Haiku*, suggests that this discipline of poetry is best understood as attitude and moment. Haiku *attitude* is the discipline of preparation, a predisposition for touching and being touched by the aesthetic, in other words, to perceive and be touched by beauty. Haiku requires a state of readiness for such perception, in both its writing and its reading. As such, haiku poets talk of humility and sincerity as the two guiding values that underpin their work as they face life and seek to see the true nature of things. Asó, a poet and theorist, wrote of the master, Bashó, that he had "found the way of art in the common modes of living" (Yasuda, 2000:18).

The Haiku *moment*, Yasuda suggests, happens with the appearance of resonance. Something resonates deeply. It connects. What it connects is the eternity of truth with the immediacy of experience. He calls this "ah-ness," which I might render in my experience as the "ah-hah" moment, the "I see exactly what you mean." Theorists about poetry quote poets who quote poets, so in this regard, it is not long until Ezra Pound appears and weighs in with similar observations and is cited by the haiku theorists. "Image" he wrote, "is that which presents an intellectual and emotional complex in an instant of time." He continued, "[I]t is better to present one Image in a lifetime than to produce voluminous work" (Pound, 1913:200). Following this idea, Yasuda (2000:25) concludes, "[T]he haiku moment results . . . in a new insight or vision which the haiku poet must render as an organic whole."

The origin of the length of haiku appears to be that of a breath-length. It explores the complexity of what is experienced in the timeframe of what can be pronounced easily in a single breath. As such, haiku poets connect the core of their art to gut intuition. Yasuda explains this with the idea of the ah-ness. Including a citation from well-known theorist Otsuji, he states, "[T]here is here no time or place explicitly for reflection, for judgments, or for the observer's feelings. There is only the speaking, impassioned object, with its 'extraordinary powers to set up echoes in the reader's mind.' " (Yasuda, 2000:31). The core of the practice of haiku is to find your way to intuition unfettered by logic, explanation, or even emotion.

Intuition is a funny thing. Most of us don't trust it. In fact, most training about conflict resolution and peacebuilding seems to be built on skills that reduce, circumvent, or ignore intuition. But if you have ever talked at length with good practitioners about how they know what they should or should not do next, or even more if you talk with people working on peacebuilding who are from the setting of violence, you will hear that what they circumvent are the rules of proper procedure. What they follow is their gut.

With its emphasis on aesthetics, haiku suggests that lived experience and intuition are related. "The nature of things is grasped in clear intuition," Yasuda writes. "The world, in the haiku moment stands revealed for what it is." (2000: 62). Asó, the gifted haiku poet, wrote of his work, "[I]t is not the art of passion; it is an art that attempts to grasp the intimations of things or the atmosphere arising from the tension of emotion rather than the emotion itself. Consequently it is the art of synthesis rather than analysis, of intimation rather than realism" (Yasuda 2000:63). This suggests something we have been slow to fully embrace in the field of peacebuilding: Knowing and understanding conflict does not take place exclusively, nor perhaps primarily, through processes of cognitive analysis, the breaking down of complexity into manageable pieces. Knowledge and, perhaps more important, understanding and deep insight are achieved through aesthetics and ways of knowing that see the whole rather than the parts, a capacity and pathway that rely on intuition more than cognition.

Etymologically, the word *aesthetic* traces to Greek and is defined as "being sharp in the senses." Haiku is after this quality of sharpness. It connects intuition, observation, and experience. Not a feeling like emotion, intuition constitutes the sense of something. Sense touches. It sees and experiences things as a whole, not as pieces. Sense creates meaning. It puts things together and holds them there. By its very nature, intuition synthesizes. This kind of intuition is an "essential," as Kerouac stated, precisely because it "sees picture better."

This may well be why my short poems got closer to aesthetics than my long ones. They were finding their way down the slippery slope toward intuition. I say "toward" because the trail is long, and I have yet to write my haiku, much less the one image of which Pound speaks. But the discipline of writing poetry and haiku more specifically has brought me closer to the art, and the art has brought me closer to the discipline of touching intuition as a resource rather than considering it a distracting disturbance.

This kind of discussion is not prevalent in much of the technical, skill-based, and process-oriented writing common in the field of peacebuilding. Yet I have found that transformative moments in conflict are many times those filled with a haiku-like quality that floods a particular process or space. We might call them the moments of the aesthetic imagination, a place where suddenly, out of complexity and historic difficulty, the clarity of great insight makes an unexpected appearance in the form of an image or in a way of putting something that can only be described as artistic. Take the young Konkomba man in our opening story, who in a moment of great tension, in a short phrase with the use of the image "father" captured the sense of historical conflict but in such a way that it created whole new meaning. His few words penetrated historically yet transcended in the immediate. The same happened with the Wajir women. In the grounded simplicity of creating a safe market, they found the imagination through which the whole of the situation could be addressed.

These are not moments defined by the analytical endeavor. They are deeply intuitive—short, sweet, and synthetic to the core. What they synthesize are the complexities of experience and the challenges of addressing deep human dilemmas. When they happen, it is almost as if you are gazing at a piece of art, listening to a piece of music, or hearing a line of a poem that, as Osutji put it, "echoes in your head" (Yasuda, 2000:31). These are moments when all involved feel a collective ah-hah.

I have participated and conducted a lot of training programs on conflict resolution, particularly around the process and skills of mediation. In all of them at some point we teach the necessity of developing listening skills. These often involve the skill of paraphrasing, of finding a way to feed back to the speaker what has been said. There is of course a technical side to this process, but it is not the technique that creates listening. In fact the inverse is true. Many people are put off by the technology of listening. I have increasingly come to believe that listening is not about technique or paraphrasing but about aesthetics. Listening, if understood from this direction, is akin to the haiku attitude and the haiku moment. Listening is the discipline and art of capturing the complexity of history in the simplicity of deep intuition. It is attending to a sharp sense of what things mean.

When I look back across personal experiences of mediating or accompanying people struggling in settings of deep violence and loss, I can recognize this. In those places people are anxious, angry, and fearful for the loss of life— literally and metaphorically—and listening requires the discipline of very few words and enormous patience to penetrate the great clouds of ambiguity while living in them. People talk at and then around things, and they go around and around again. So many things are said and then repeated. Whole timeframes are anachronistically leap-frogged, one over the top of the other and back again. Anger, bitterness, regret, sadness, loss, and misunderstanding are all mixed in a bundle of messages made up of words and images, spoken and unspoken. In the midst of that very human mess, listening is the art of connecting and finding the essence. More often than not the spring that bubbles from intuition flows toward this kind of deep listening. In those settings a mediator with too many words does not hear the bubbling. A mediator incapable of touching intuition misses the flow. But when a participant or mediator captures the complexity of the experience in a few words, it is as if a haiku has been written, a small canvas painted, the notes of melody floated. And there is an organic sense of "ah-hah. That is it." Listening, in that instant, becomes a haiku moment built from a haiku attitude. Picture is clear. Image emerges.

The challenge for invoking the moral imagination as a peacebuilder is not found in perfecting or applying the techniques or the skills of a process. My feeling, is that we have overemphasized the technical aspects and political content to the detriment of the art of giving birth to and keeping a process creatively alive. In so doing we have missed the core of what creates and sustains constructive social change. The corrective is not to throw the baby out with the bathwater. It is to seek the genuine connection of discipline and art, the integration of skill and aesthetics.

We work with a profession that has sought to deal with the social challenges of complexity almost exclusively through the improvement of processes by means of the technology of change. But we have neglected and poorly attended to the aesthetics of change, the art of life. This is where moral imagination comes into play. It attends to intuition. It listens for what Yeats called the "heart's core" (Yeats, 1993:28). This kind of imagination captures the depth of the challenge and at the same time casts light on the way forward. As aesthetics, the moral imagination seeks to connect with the deep intuition that creates the capacity to penetrate and transcend the challenges of violent conflict. Recognizing and nurturing this capacity is the ingredient that forges and sustains authentic constructive change.

How do we practice the aesthetics of peacebuilding? Like art itself, there is no single technique by which it can be pursued and at the same time it cannot be created without discipline. Let me share a few simple things I have found useful in my practice.

Whenever I find myself in the middle of a tense conversation, working with or between groups involved in a serious conflict, and the situation seems endlessly complex, I ask myself a simple question: If you were to capture the heart of this thing in a sentence of fewer than eight words, what would you say? This is the haiku attitude and moment. Can I find the image? Remember, haiku is not reductionism. The discipline is not to reduce complexity to facts. Haiku is synthesis. It captures the complexity of an organic whole by reaching its simplest composition. It sees things in the heart. When you capture the heart of complex experience, you have arrived at insight and often at ways forward. The discipline is to hold complexity and simplicity together. The art is to capture both in an ah-hah image.

I listen for poetry in conversation. I can be talking with a warlord, a commander, a taxi driver, or a housewife, but I listen for the poetry. I have for some years made an effort to keep a journal. Among other things in the journal I collect phrases, thoughts, statements, and conversations that popped out of my travels and encounters with people struggling to make their way through human conflict. I often take these pieces of conversations and let them breathe in black and white on paper. These don't always succeed, but what I have found is this: There is a poetry to conflict embedded in everyday conversation. Sometimes a single conversational poem captures the complexity of a whole situation.[2]

I watch spoken images. In common parlance these might be referred to as metaphors, which in everyday conversation they are, and more commonly we say that we *listen* for metaphors. I prefer to *watch* metaphors. What I have found in many settings of conflict is this: People rarely talk about conflict analytically, unless they feel they are compelled or required to do so in the formality of explaining the mess they are in to a specialist who is analyzing their conflict. People talk in images. Much literature has attended to the importance of metaphor for creating and shaping reality and experience. But less has been discussed about the aesthetics of metaphor. I have come to treat metaphor as if it were a canvas. Metaphor is a creative act. The spontaneous way it is formulated brings something new into the world. This something new interacts with the world and has a life. It creates an image of what the experience of living in the world is like. When I watch a metaphor, I take care not to approach it with instrumentalist purposes in mind. I approach it as a creation. The metaphor—like a movie, a painting, or a poem—invites inter-action, probing, and echoes. Sometimes I find that rather than moving quickly to understand the metaphor, it is much better to sit with it for a while. Let it roll around in your head and heart. I write metaphors down on anything I have handy, a dinner receipt, the stub of a ticket, and I carry them in my pockets. At some point I go back and take a more careful look, a second listen. In conflict conversations I don't just listen for metaphors, I watch them. They take on lives of their own and they speak to the conflict, to the problems, and to the ways forward. Metaphors are like a living museum of conflict resources. They usually lead me toward an aesthetic appreciation of the context, the process, and the challenges of change.

I doodle. I would not call it drawing; doodle is a more accurate description. This typically happens in the middle of conversations with people. As a peace-builder I spend a lot of time talking with people, more often than not around an informal table, at lunches, hotel and airport snack shops, during mid-afternoon tea and late evening coffee. Some of the most significant conversa-tions with Basques, Irish, Somalis, Filipinos, Colombians, and East and West Africans have happened around an informal table. The histories shared and the problems discussed are long and complex. I can't sit for very long and listen well unless I have a pencil or a pen in hand and some piece of paper, often a napkin or the back of a paper placemat. I rarely take notes. I generally find that note taking distracts from listening. I doodle and maybe jot an oc-casional word or phrase that pops out of the conversation.

What I doodle are images that the talk invokes. I try to let the many words that I am hearing make their way from my head through my heart to my hand. As I listen I keep asking myself these questions: What does this thing they are describing look and feel like? What is at the heart of the matter? Where is this thing going? Where would they like it to go? What is getting in the way? How are people, groups, and activities linked? What pictures are they painting with their words? What is missing from the pictures? Questions like these are end-less, but they all have a graphic, organic side to them. They lend themselves to doodles. I draw what I feel and hear. Many times they are circles and lines, although sometimes an actual picture crops up. I show people the doodle. They add to the picture. If we don't have pen and paper, I arrange sugar, salt, pepper, ketchup jars, coffee cups, and silverware on the table—anything to get a picture of the space, the relationships, the process, and the change that people are struggling to describe and create. What I find is this: If I can see it, I can understand it better. If I can understand it, I can find ways to shape and nudge it. "Dont think of words when you stop but to see picture better" emerges on the napkin or the table.

I once thought I would write a book titled *The Napkin Doodles* in which I would explore this feature of my work. The idea was that I would use actual napkins, placemats, and dinner receipts from the conversations as illustrations in the book. My problem turned out to be that I have very few of my original napkin doodles. It is not that I have misplaced or thrown them away. Nine times out of ten, the person with whom I am speaking will say at the end of the conversation, "Would you mind if I kept that napkin?"

Conclusion

The aesthetics of social change proposes a simple idea: Building adaptive and responsive processes requires a creative act, which at its core is more art than technique. The creative act brings into existence processes that have not existed before. To sustain themselves over time, processes of change need constant innovation. As the study and practice around social change in violent contexts have evolved, we have pushed for acceptance and legitimacy mostly by making the case that these fields are professional. Professional excellence increasingly has emphasized the technology, the technique and the skills of process management as tools that legitimate and make possible training, replication, and dissemination. This is not bad, but it also is not the only source of knowledge, understanding, and sustenance. In the process of professionalization we too often have lost a sense of the art, the creative act that underpins the birth and growth of personal and social change. I fear we see ourselves to be—and have therefore become—more technicians than artists. By virtue of this shift of perception our approaches have become too cookie-cutter-like, too reliant on what proper technique suggests as a frame of reference, and as a result our processes are too rigid and fragile.

We need to envision ourselves as artists. We need a return to aesthetics, to what Mills called the place of imagination in science that creates a "playfulness of mind . . . a truly fierce drive to make sense of the world which the technician as such usually lacks" (Mills, 1959:211). Time and again, social change that sticks and makes a difference has behind it the artist's intuition: the complexity of human experience captured in a simple image and in a way that moves individuals and whole societies. The true genius of the moral imagination is the ability to touch the art and soul of the matter.

The challenge of peacebuilding and the moral imagination is precisely what Bashó posed for his disciple as he described the challenge of haiku: How do we compose and give life to that which we create? Aesthetics helps those who attempt to move from cycles of violence to new relationships and those of us who wish to support such movement to see ourselves for whom we are: artists bringing to life and keeping alive something that has not existed. As artists, aesthetics requires certain disciplines from us. Be attentive to image. Listen for the core. Trust and follow intuition. Watch metaphor. Avoid clutter and busy-ness. See picture better. Find the elegant beauty where complexity meets simplicity. Imagine the canvas of social change.

8

On Space

Life in the Web

Spiders are not little automatons making the same thing over and over. They're flexible. And they're not stupidly flexible; they're smart flexible.

—Bill Eberhard, quoted in "Deadly Silk"

In the poem "The Second Coming," W. B. Yeats (1996) penned several well-known lines which have become points of reference and even titles to subsequent books. Often used to reflect the difficulty of holding together the flow of human history, the poem refers to the tragic inevitability that our world falls apart, that our desired social realities splinter into a thousand pieces. The question posed in this chapter comes full circle to that which is not spoken in the poem: What center holds things together? I have a simple answer in reference to building constructive social change: the invisible web of relationships.

When relationships collapse, the center of social change does not hold. And correspondingly, rebuilding what has fallen apart is centrally the process of rebuilding relational spaces that hold things together. Paradoxical by their very nature, relational spaces create social energy that is simultaneously centripetal and centrifugal. But rather than anarchy, which is like exploding into a million pieces, peacebuilding understands that relationships create and emanate social energy and are places to which energy returns for a sense of purpose and direction. In our physical world on the grandest scale, this is the place of the sun, that extraordinary and nearly uncontainable planetary body that sends out life-giving energy and around which the planets of our galaxy rotate and are held within a certain order. In our social world, a family typically has this characteristic. It sends us out into the world, yet we return to it for a sense of identity, direction, and purpose. Faith communities, chosen families, and even geographic locations provide a sense of identity and also have this centrifugal/centripetal capacity. In each of these examples, there exists a force that pushes out and pulls in, and in so doing creates a "center that holds."

Over the years I have come to intuit more than scientifically prove, to feel more than quantify, that the center of building sustainable justice and peace is the quality and nature of people's relationships. A key to constructive social change lies in that which makes social fabric, relationships, and relational spaces. This web requires a much closer look.

My understanding of the centrality of relationships began during the years of living and working in Central America. I was involved in multiple peace-building initiatives, from grassroots community training on conflict resolution to higher-level conciliation efforts to end a war, from the practice of mediation to ethnographic research and theory building on approaches to conflict and its transformation in a variety of cultural contexts. Over the course of six years, roughly from the time of my first visit in 1984 until 1990, the experiences and learning gained from these efforts changed my lenses. What I saw around social conflict and how I brought it into focus changed both my theories and my practice. For the first time I was with people whose natural everyday understanding provided a lens through which they saw conflict and response to conflict as embedded in relational spaces, networks, and connections.

The development of these new lenses stands out in the evolution of my book titles. When I first went to Central America I was asked to help develop a series of pilot workshops on conflict resolution. In 1984 I wrote a small manual that I carried down to these workshops and shared with early participants. A year later it was published under the title *La Regulación del Conflicto Social: Un Enfoque Práctico*, or in English, *The Management of Social Conflict: A Practical Focus* (Lederach, 1986). By 1992, through a Guatemalan publisher, a second and totally revamped version of the manual appeared: *Enredos, Pleitos y Problemas* (Lederach, 1992). That book is now in its fourth edition. The Spanish title does not translate easily into English. Literally, it would be something like *Tangled Nets, Fights and Problems*. Somewhere between 1984 and 1992 the book's focus moved from "management" to "tangled nets." The shift is worth exploring.

The three terms in the title—*enredo, pleito, problema*—are the most well known folk synonyms for *conflict* in everyday language in Central America. It would be as if we pulled three common ways of saying *conflict* in English like "Geez, what a *mess*. We have really got ourselves in a *bind* here. This has turned into a complete *disaster*." We might on rarer occasion say, "We've gotten ourselves into a conflict."

What did the shift in titles suggest? It was on the one hand a move to capture a more commonly understood language. In other words, the title change lifted to greater prominence the everyday expressions about conflict while the technospeak of the conflict field diminished. At a deeper level, however, hidden in the opening words, the title put "who" at the center of the "how." As I described in my doctoral dissertation (Lederach, 1988), this "who" lens gave enormous insight into a much wider world view of conflict.

The Spanish term *enredo*, a tangled net if you will, is a fishing metaphor at its roots. *Red* means "net," like a fishing net. It is also the term for "network." To be *enredado* is to be tangled, caught in a net. *Enredo* is one of the most common expressions across Latin America for describing everyday conflicts. The metaphor however is highly connected to a sense of relationship and relational spaces. A net, when tangled or torn, is carefully untangled or stitched back together. Yet, when the process of putting things back in order is complete, the weaving of the whole remains a fabric of lines, connections, and knots. As a metaphor, *enredo* sees conflict itself and the way to think about the response to conflict as an unfolding social dynamic embedded in a web of relationships. The "solution" is conceptualized as working the net; the resource and challenge are to shape a way out of the mess through relational connections. When people in everyday settings where I was working had a conflict, their first thought was not "what is the solution?" It was "who do I know who knows the person with whom I have the problem who can help create a way out?" The question "who?" came first. The question "what?" followed. To put it another way, solutions emerged from relational resources, connections, and obligations.

I consistently found this to be true in my mediation work from one level to the next in Central America. The people with whom I was working had a natural inclination to think "who" first and often. And it makes common sense. You can have the perfect substantive solution to a problem, but if you do not have the right people in place and connected in the right way, that solution collapses. On the other hand, if you have the right people in place and connected, both processes and solutions can be generated. *Enredo*, I came to discover, was the art of *know-who*.

The exploration into this surprising aspect of peacebuilding created an important lens that reoriented how I thought about the development of conflict response processes, but it posed a perplexing challenge. What exactly does it mean to have a relationship-centric approach to constructive social change? I have come to believe that the answer lies with how we approach and understand relational spaces in a given geography, the fabric of human community broadly defined as the crisscrossing connections of people, their lives, activities, organizational modalities, and even patterns of conflict. I believe there are skills that accompany a spatial approach to change, but they are less like the technology of conducting good communication than the development of, and discipline to use, appropriate lenses, which bring things into focus. The art of know-who, the essence of the *enredo* approach, lies in what we look for and what we bring into focus. To see and locate change in both a physical and social geography entails careful observation for that which is present but not always immediately visible: the web of relationships. This approach asks us to look at relationships through the lenses of social crossroads, connections, and inter-dependence.

I took yet another step on the journey toward a spatial understanding of change a few years later. I discovered, somewhat inadvertently, that networking was much more than meets the eye. Social webs exist, but to see them you must take up the guideposts of a perspective that has rarely entered the field of peacebuilding or the design of social change: arachnology, the study of spiders and their webs. The key, I found, was learning lessons from both the web makers and the web watchers (web watchers are discussed in chapter 10).

The Web Makers

My interest in spiders and webs has a history. In the early 1990s I started a text on peacebuilding that eventually was published as a book titled *Building Peace: Sustainable Reconciliation in Divided Societies* (Lederach, 1997). As I have found with other texts, by the time the book reached the public thinking, my ideas had evolved, but what was written remained hard on the page. I found this particularly true around one of my main descriptive and theoretical proposals (Lederach, 1997:39), or, more accurately stated, around the search for a proper and appropriate name for the theory that accompanied one of the approaches found in the pyramid of peacebuilding found in the book *Building Peace* (See doodle 2 below).

Over the years I used a pyramid with three distinct levels to describe leadership and approaches to peacebuilding. The pinnacle of the pyramid descriptively represented the most visible leadership and the fewest people. I called efforts to build peace from that level the "top-down" approach. The base of the pyramid, representing the greatest number of people affected by the conflict and also the level of the local communities spread across the geography under study, I referred to as "bottom-up" approaches to peacebuilding. The middle section of the pyramid did not have a neat or easy title. By far I found it the hardest to describe. My experience and observation suggested an approach that looked carefully at small sets of people who move between the grassroots and the highest level of leadership, who have some independence of activity, and who create processes that support or linked the other two levels. I opted for the rather odd-sounding term, the "middle-out" approach to peacebuilding.

Through lectures I increasingly became uncomfortable with this middle-out title, in large part because students, who were like continuous laboratories of questions and feedback, kept raising issues with the term and even the diagram. At a given point I suddenly recognized something that had been there all along but that I had not seen. Typically I would explain the middle-out approach by drawing a diagram of the pyramid and then inserting the lines that described the idea of vertical and horizontal integration.

For those who have not read the earlier book, *vertical capacity* explores and looks at relational spaces that link people up and down in the society. *Vertical spaces* are those that connect the leadership of local communities with people who are guiding the higher-level processes. *Horizontal capacity* on the other hand refers to relationships among people and groups that cut across the identity divisions that may exist in a given location, be those ethnic, religious, racial,

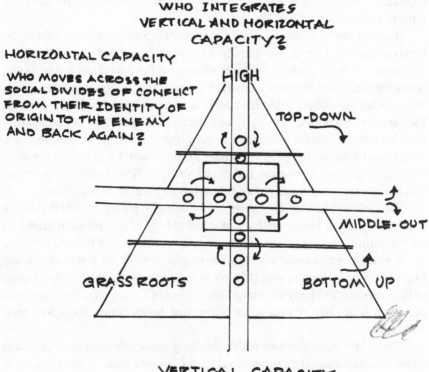

WHO INTEGRATES VERTICAL AND HORIZONTAL CAPACITY?

HORIZONTAL CAPACITY
WHO MOVES ACROSS THE SOCIAL DIVIDES OF CONFLICT FROM THEIR IDENTITY OF ORIGIN TO THE ENEMY AND BACK AGAIN?

HIGH

TOP-DOWN

MIDDLE-OUT

GRASS ROOTS

BOTTOM UP

VERTICAL CAPACITY
WHO MOVES AND CONNECTS HIGHEST LEVEL OF NEGOTIATION WITH GRASSROOTS COMMUNITIES?

DOODLE TWO
PYRAMID OF APPROACHES TO PEACEBUILDING

or linguistic. *Integration* is the space where vertical and horizontal linkages come together, at the center of things. What became obvious was that much of this effort was not "outward" bound, in the sense that the descriptor "middle-out" seemed to create. This was not about leaving the location where the conflict was happening in order find answers to the challenges outside of it. In fact, the middle-out approach was the inverse. It was about finding resources based on relationships, connectors, and social spaces within the setting that had a capacity to generate processes of change.

One day in a lecture I just decided to change the name. As I remember that classroom session, off the top of my head I said, "Calling this the middle-out approach is a misnomer. This approach is about explicit strategic networking, one that creates a web of relationships and activities that cover the setting." On the newsprint drawing, instead of writing "middle-out," I wrote "the web approach." What stuck was the word *web*, and since that time I have used this term in replacement of "middle-out."

At about the same time I had an everyday encounter with learning at the hands of my son. I mean that literally. As I recall the moment, we were sitting one evening watching television. Josh, who was at the time about ten years old, was a big fan of the Discovery Channel. In particular he loved animal shows. At an earlier age, what caught his attention were the shows about big animals like lions or anacondas, or the guy who nearly gets eaten by a crocodile every time he ventures into a river. One evening the Discovery channel projected images and a discussion of how a spider makes a web. I don't recall the story in its entirety, or even if we watched the whole show. What caught my attention was the slow-motion images of an orb web under construction.

The "orb weavers," as they were called that night, are the spiders that weave the most common image we have of a web. Many of you probably have had an opportunity at some point in time to see the marvel of a full orb web. For me it has happened more often in the tropics, usually on a morning when humidity is high, leaving visibly heavy dew. The sunlight catches the strands of this creation. Suddenly an extraordinary piece of art appears. The orb stands out in all of its beauty in a space where just hours before there had been nothing.

The spider starts the web with a few long strands hooked to strategically chosen locations and then it floats out across an open space, always linking in the center. Something stuck with me from that image. Through the good luck of channel surfing with a ten-year-old and the brilliance of the Discovery channel, by the next round of lectures I was introducing the idea of the web approach as a social theory for peacebuilding.

Then in August of 2001, my *National Geographic* arrived in the mail. The second article was titled "Deadly Silk" (Conniff, 2001:30–45). I read, and then reread the article. I was captivated by how much the language, description, and understanding of web weaving paralleled much of what I had been describing about strategic networking as an approach to peacebuilding. Spiders and webs became a passion. Even as I write this chapter I am watching a spider that somehow made its way between the window screen and the pane, and in that safe narrow space is weaving a small piece of art and life.

Philosopher and ecologist David Abram tells the story of his unexpected encounters with webs. On the island of Bali he found himself caught in a cave by torrential rains and was forced to spend the night. In the light of the moon and glistening of the humidity he suddenly discovered a spider at the mouth of the cave making a web, strand by strand. As his eyes sharpened and his gaze widened, the discovery multiplied. There was not just one spider but dozens of them. As he put it, "[S]uddenly I realized there were *many* overlapping webs coming into being, radiating out at different rhythms from myriad centers." He concluded, "I had the distinct impression that I was watching the universe being born, galaxy upon galaxy" (Abram, 1996:18–19). The next morning, after a fitful night of sleep, he awoke to find that not a single web remained from the evening's activity. Occupying space and web making, I have come to understand, is a continuous and extraordinarily dynamic process. Contrary to popular image, space and connections are never static.

Originally the silk strands that spiders spew in several varieties from the built-in technology of their spigots were used to travel and hide or disguise themselves. As Conniff (2001:43) put it, spiders practice the art of "hiding in plain sight" for "life in the web" means "hanging your butt in the breeze." Travel and invisibility remain core features of their lives. Webs may be woven across the same or slightly different spaces as many as five times a day. However, the greatest capacity of spiders, I have come to believe, is their intuition about space, their knack for seeing and understanding the nature of their environment, the contours and potentialities of a given place. Spiders must think strategically about space, how to cover it and how to create cross-linkages that stitch locations together into a net. And they must do this time and again, always at considerable risk and vulnerability to themselves.

Following the trail of the strategies taken up by orb weavers is a lesson in the art of spatial thinking. The very language used to describe the web-making process is, in and of itself, a lexicon of building networks for strategic social change, which can be easily superimposed over what now appears in comparison as a static and monotonously uninteresting pyramid of peacebuilding, which I drew in my book. Follow for a few paragraphs a paraphrased version of scientists' descriptions of web making (Crompton, 1951; Conniff, 2001). I have provided a series of doodles, like those I might draw in class to explain this to students.

Frame A: The web begins as the spider bridges a given space, laying down a dragline, then crisscrossing strands to create a *simple star*. The star anchors itself by attaching a few threads to distinct, often opposite places around the space, but all unite at an intersection called the *hub*. The hub, visually, is the

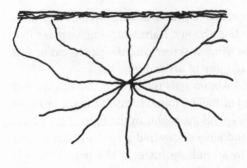

A. START A WEB;
1. SET OUTER ANCHOR POINTS
2. CROSS AT HUB

B. STRENGTHEN;
1. OUTER CIRCLES AND CONCENTRIC CIRCLES
2. ADD RADII

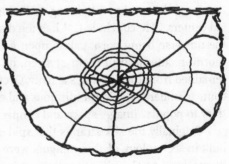

C. SOLIDIFY;
1. MORE CIRCLES
2. FILL IN GAPS
3. ALWAYS BUILD AND REINFORCE HUBS

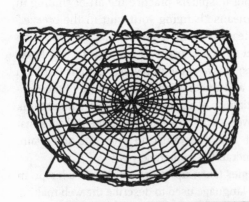

DOODLE THREE
THE WEB PROCESS

place where the initial threads meet together as the spider moves from different strategic points in its surroundings. Through the outer anchor and inner center points, the core essence of the web frame is created.

Frame B: A second set of strands completes the frame by linking together the anchor points along the outer edges, creating an *outer circle*. Then the spider moves from those points back to the center, strengthening the hub's connection to the outer circle through a series of *radii*. The radii look very much like wheel spokes from hub to frame. The center expanded out, the anchor edges connected, the web now takes visible though skeletal shape. The result of this effort creates a whole series of intersections across the web. These connections and crisscrossing intersections cover the space, while keeping a strong central hub. The goal is to create a web that has a capacity to receive blows and even structural damage to one part without those points of damage destroying the rest of the web. The structure of the web combines interdependent connections with localized independence. Strength is built by creating coordination at the hub without centralization.

Frame C: To this outer wheel frame and hub, *auxiliary spirals* are added. These strands are tougher, thicker, and stickier. The spirals encircle the hub, creating a series of smaller to larger concentric circles that imitate the form that the hub and the outer frame have taken. There now exists a whole series of circles from the smaller inner hub all the way to the largest outer edge.

Finally, the spaces remaining between the concentric circles are filled with *elastic capture threads*. Interestingly, elasticity is a strategy of resilience. The strands of some spiders have built-in beads that unreel when something heavy hits the web, permitting the whole web to give but not break. Filling in the spaces between the concentric circles is accomplished through *continuous movement*, working toward the center then reversing back toward the outer frame. The last piece of work takes the spider back toward the center, where "it rebuilds the hub and settles there to await a meal" (Conniff, 2001:36).

This whole endeavor of making a web requires a deep commitment to innovation and flexibility. The end result and the process of creating the end result are characterized by a capacity to adapt to shifting contours, ever-changing environments, and unexpected intrusions. A web, therefore, can never be thought of as permanent, fixed, or rigid. The spider's genius lies in its ability to adapt, reshape, and remake its web of connections within the realities presented in a given space.

Erroneously we often think of creatures, like spiders, as operating purely by rote instinct, as if instinct is devoid of creativity. In fact, the building of a web, as many as five times a day, is a continuous act of strategic and imaginative spatial response. This idea is captured beautifully in the essay *The Spell of the Sensuous*, by Abram:

> However complex are the inherited "programs," patterns or pre-dispositions they must still be adapted to the immediate situation in which the spider finds itself. However determinate one's genetic inheritance, it must still, as it were, be woven into the present, an activity that necessarily involves both a receptivity to the specific shapes and textures of that present and a spontaneous creativity in

adjusting one's self (and one's inheritance) to those contours. (1996: 50)

What is the relevance of these spiders and web making to peacebuilding? The answer lies in understanding that constructive change, perhaps more than anything else, is the art of strategically and imaginatively weaving relational webs across social spaces within settings of protracted violent conflict. With constructive social change in mind, consider for a moment how biologist Bill Eberhard explains what spiders must accomplish in the weaving of a web:

> You have an essentially blind animal with a limited nervous system building a complicated structure in an unpredictable environment. The spider makes what for a human being would be very complex calculations: "How big is the open space? How much silk do I have? What attachment points are available?" As Abram suggested, spiders are not programmed machines. They are responsive and creative. As Eberhard says, "spiders are not automotons." He refers to their creativity as flexibility. "They're flexible. And they're not stupidly flexible, they're smart flexible." (Conniff, 2001:36).

The relevance? Sustaining constructive change in settings of violence, I have increasingly come to believe, requires asking precisely this: How do we build a strategic structure of connections in an unpredictable environment, a structure that understands and adapts continuously to the contours of a dynamic social geography and can find the attachment points that will make the process stick? Constructing social change is the art of seeing and building webs. The soul of sustaining change requires the craftsmanship of a spider. We must learn to be "smart flexible" about web building.

Peacebuilding, like web making, is the process of creating "complicated structures in an unpredictable environment." However, the key to such complexity is found once again in the art of simplicity. Consider three principles of application that emerge from orb weaving that we can apply to the building of constructive social change in settings of conflict and violence.

Understand the Social Geography

Web making is hypersensitive to the contours of space and connections. Key in this process is the capacity to locate strategic anchor points that link different but necessarily interdependent constituencies, processes, and geographic localities if change is to be generated and sustained. Specifically, those building social change must intentionally seek to link people who are not like-minded and not like-situated in the context. Peacebuilders, no matter their location or persuasion, must eliminate the erroneous notion that change can happen independently of people who are not of common mind and are not located in similar social, political, or economic space. This is true of high-level diplomats as much as local community workers. Interdependence is. Period. Constructive change and peace are not built by attempting to win converts to one side or another, or by forcing one or the other's hand. Web making suggests that the net of change is put together by recognizing and building relational spaces that have not existed or that must be strengthened to create a whole that, like the spider's web, makes things stick. These are the fundamental skills of know-who and know-where.

Always Think Intersections

Watch for and build hubs where the cross-linking relational spaces connect the not-like-minded and not-like-situated. Like the star hub in the web, the center holds, but it is not a centralized hub that controls. Nor is this a center built on finding moderates on a political spectrum. Remember, we are thinking social spaces and watching for where things meet, even when those meeting places are seemingly unimportant. Think spaces of relationships and localities where relationships intersect. Those are the spaces that create multiple coordinated and independent connections that build strength. A spider returns most often to places of hublike activities. In peacebuilding, relational centers that hold, create, and sustain connections are key. A relationship-centric approach must see spaces of intersection, both those that exist and those that can be created. These are the hubs, the heart that throbs the rhythms of change.

Be Smart Flexible

Smart flexible is the ability to adapt to, respond to, and take advantage of emerging and context-based challenges. Scientists call spiders "actors of continuous movement." Peacebuilding can learn from spiders that web making is the art of creating platforms to generate creative responses more than creating the solution itself. A platform represents the ongoing capacity to generate processes, ideas, and solutions. In building social change, we have too often worked on the opposite idea. This is particularly true of mediated, high-level negotiations. We build a platform that produces a solution and then deconstruct the platform, assuming the solution has permanency. Experience suggests the opposite. Solutions are ephemeral. Permanency is found in adaptive platforms capable of continuous response. In peacebuilding, a platform is best understood in the idea of relational spaces, the ability to keep sets of people in creative interaction. The lesson from orb weavers is simply this: Platforms, understanding and sustaining relational spaces, must adapt and be smart flexible in reference to the changing environment and continuously rising issues, obstacles, and difficulties. The permanence of change requires the permanence of creative adaptation.

Conclusion

Of the many things discussed in this chapter, three ideas help to integrate the web of life for peacebuilding.

Think, feel, and follow relationships. Relationships are at the heart of social change. Relationships require that we understand how and where things connect and how this web of connections occupies the social space where processes of change are birthed and hope to live. The key for peacebuilding is to remember that change, if it is to be sparked and then sustained, must link and bring into relationship sets of people, processes, and activities that are not like-situated nor of similar persuasion. The challenge of our failures is that we have been unable to understand the interdependence of different sets of people and processes and recognize how they may interact constructively. We have, in essence, thought too much about "process management" and "solution generation" and too little about social spaces and the nature of interdependent and strategic relationships. This is the key role of the moral imagination: to envision the canvas that makes visible the relational spaces and the web of life where social change is located.

Develop a capacity to see and think strategically about social spaces. These are the actual places of life where unusual relationships cross and interact. This means we must develop a capacity to recognize and build the locus of social change. Markets, hospitals, schools, street corners, cattle dips, transportation service centers, youth soccer clubs—the list is interminable and different in every context. Think social spaces where people cross in natural ways, in necessary and often unnoticed ways. These are the locus resources, the "strategic where" of a geography. This is thinking web, finding the location where relationships and platforms hold potential for affecting the whole.

Be smart flexible. Processes of constructive social change and the platforms that support them can take big lessons from the natural world. The key to sustainability is not massive strength or greater force—whatever the nature of that force may be. It is adaptability: the capacity to recognize and then flexibly adapt processes of response that shift in form and shape while sustaining their core purpose of creating life. The challenge before the moral imagination at every step is how to create and respond to shifting environments without losing sight of the horizon of the desired change. Our greatest weakness is to lock onto a particular form or process, which blinds us to both the possibility of innovation and the horizon of desired change.

Peacebuilding lives in an unpredictable environment. The challenge is how to transcend what exists while creating innovative responses to the needs the real world presents. Such transcendence arises from relational spaces, understanding connections, and being smart flexible.

9

On Mass and Movement

The Theory of the Critical Yeast

That which counts can rarely be counted.

—Albert Einstein

The lessons of the spider teach us about strategically approaching space and about the nature of building webs.[1] When applied to social processes, however, the web approach may fly in the face of one commonly accepted notion of what creates shifts and change in societies. Movements for social change often tend to conceptualize their challenge as a battlefield whose success is measured by the number of people who have joined "their side."

Side-taking, unfortunately, seems to accompany social battlefields and therefore accepts the premise that change is inherently a dualistic struggle. While many of us in the peace movement feel a deep sense of discomfort with politicians who frame our challenges in this manner, for example, as issues that force a choice between the "good guys" and "the evil empires," we have often fallen prey to the trap of replicating that which we abhor. We, and here I refer to our broad community under the title of *the peace movement*, tend to frame the processes of change we wish to promote as the challenge of gaining the upper hand of influence in the public sphere. Thus we conceptualize social change as linked primarily to raising public awareness of a greater truth and then measuring how many of our compatriots within the public sphere have moved toward the awareness of what we believe in and how many are willing to act on it. This yardstick of success boils down to a numbers game: how many voted for a certain idea or how many people came to the street in protest against a particular issue or proposal. At a popular level, social change advocates often understand their goal as creating the numbers that count, what in everyday coinage has come to be called "arriving at the critical mass."

The age of the mass media has certainly added to this phenomenon. In less than a sound byte, the success of social change is measured in a single statistic. A protest march is reported and interpreted by friend and foe alike as if it were a ball game recounted by a sportscaster. If the numbers are high, it means the movement and issues are serious. If the numbers are low, it has not become a political concern worthy of attention. You will often hear reporters say, "There does not appear to be a critical mass of public opinion that will sway this administration from its proposed goal." In response, the challenge is laid: Those who want the change must create the mass.

In this framing of the change process there is an important dynamic that is often overlooked: Social change that depends heavily on the magnetic attraction of shared opposition creates social energy that can generate large numbers in discrete time frames but has difficulty sustaining the longer-term change. Social movements rise and fall as visible *moments* rather than as *sustained processes*. This seems related to two important observations about how change happens.

First, social movements find that it is easier, and in many cases more popular, to articulate to what they are opposed rather than what they wish to build. Change is seen as linear: Raise awareness first, then promote action by increased numbers of people to stop something, and finally, once that thing is stopped, develop action to build something different. Awareness and action have at times gone together and created extraordinary moments of change— from local communities stopping a new proposed highway, to whole societies achieving the recognition of civil and human rights, to nations overthrowing oppressive regimes. It has rather consistently been during the third part of the theory—developing action to build something—where we run into difficulties and where the change processes seem to collapse.

Second, framing the process as one that must create like-minded communities produces a narrow view of change wherein little thought or work is given to the broader nature of who and what will need to change and how they will be engaged in such a process. In other words, the very way the issues and process are framed undermines the fundamental web of understanding that change must strategically build linkages and coordination with and across not-like-minded and not-like-situated relational spaces. Unlike a linear change theory, the web approach suggests that multiple processes at different levels and social spaces take place *at the same time*. The web approach does not think in terms of us versus them, but rather about the nature of the change sought and how multiple sets of interdependent processes will link people and places to move the whole of the system toward those changes. In pragmatic terms the web approach asks early and often: Who has to find a way to be connected to whom?

Nonetheless, there is a certain truth to the frame of reference that convincing large numbers of people to get on board with an idea is the key to social change. Awareness of information and the willingness to act on what one believes are indeed part and parcel of the larger challenge of how societies as a whole change and move toward new ways of relating and organizing their lives together. In settings of protracted conflict and violence, movement away from fear, division, and violence toward new modalities of interaction requires awareness, action, and broad processes of change. In this sense, numbers are important. However, it is equally important for us to look deeper at how we think this shift happens. Numbers count. But experience in settings of deep division suggests that what lies invisible behind the numbers counts more. In social change it is not necessarily the amount of participants that authenticates a social shift. It is the quality of the platform that sustains the shifting process that matters. Ironically, the focus on numbers has created a misunderstanding and misapplication of the concept of critical mass.

The Critical Mass

As a sociologist, I studied with professors who were interested in the emergence, dynamics, and impact of social movements. Prominent in our discussions was how a movement creates and then reaches the juncture that generates what is commonly referred to as the critical mass. Critical mass is a cross-over term that has moved from the physical sciences to sociology, political science, and communication theory. Its origins can be traced to nuclear physics and the study of chain reactions of fission. Criticality in fission, the origin of the critical mass, merits our attention.

For our purposes, the technical details are probably less important than the meaning and original formulation of a critical mass. Fission happens as a reaction. Scientists studying this phenomenon in order to harness its power were interested in knowing whether it would be possible for a reaction not just to run its course, but to create, inherent to its very nature, subsequent reactions. In other words they asked this question: Could a reaction create a multiplier effect capable of reproducing subsequent reactions exponentially greater in number but generated on their own, independent of the original reaction? If understood in social terms, these scientists were inquiring into the nature of sustainability.

In the nuclear physics of fission, critical mass can be articulated in the specificity of numeric equations. In layperson's terms, if one-third of the neutrons in a reaction sequence create fission, then the reaction dies out as a single iteration. However, if roughly two-thirds of the neutrons cause the fission, then subsequent reactions are created that reproduce themselves. It was in this idea of "reproducing themselves" that the term *critical mass* was used. Nuclear physicists call this *criticality*. The key is the idea that a self-sustained process is generated, meaning that one reaction can reproduce itself exponentially, independent of the original cause.

The idea of the critical mass floated over into the social sciences given its natural applications to a wide variety of topics. People asked: How do social ideas make their way from inception to becoming widely accepted by society? The point at which enough people believe it and the social ethos changes is the point of a critical mass. The shift from neutrons to people, from atomic chambers to social contexts, raised intriguing challenges. But in the process of applying the concept of the critical mass, we actually may have missed the original key insight. Creating self-sustained processes of social change is not just about numbers in a sequential formula. The critical mass in fact was asking what initial, even small, things made exponentially greater things possible. In nuclear physics, the focus was on the quality of the catalyst, not the numbers that followed.

A recent popular level application of this idea can be found in Malcolm Gladwell's *The Tipping Point*. He talks about the critical mass of creating a social epidemic, drawing most of his examples from the field of marketing and business. While he states that the tipping point is the critical mass, the key in social settings is not found in the image of a standardized notion of large numbers but as he states in his subtitle, "how little things make a difference" (Gladwell, 2002). In fact, in several of his examples he watches social epidemics rise from the standpoint of strategic relational connections. This conclusion paralleled an idea that had popped up for me years ago in peacebuilding.

While common in strategies of many peace movements attempting to change settings of protracted conflict from cycles of violence toward dialogue and nonviolence, the critical mass image left me feeling discouraged in many places where I was working. The attention always seemed to be on how to generate large impact and numbers in the society or, if you will, on how to get people to move into the streets. In the last few years there have been some extraordinary examples of this, notably the overthrow of Slobodan Milosevic in Serbia and the recent parallel events that removed Eduard Shevardnadze from office in Georgia. However, in the vast majority of places we define as settings of protracted violence—like Northern Ireland, Somalia, Liberia, Colombia—there did not appear to be a critical mass on the horizon. The cycles of violence in most of these settings were decade-long if not generational. It was the forces of violence that seemed to have the critical mass. Even at times when moments of larger social participation emerged in reaction against violence, times when it felt as if a critical mass of change demanding a shift to end the violence might happen, these moments turned out to be ephemeral and short-lived. In some cases they were even counterproductive, for in the aftermath, when little or nothing changed, people believed even less that change was possible. The number of people in the streets captured the media's attention but were incapable of generating a sustained process of social change.

However, when I paid careful attention to the times when I believed significant change processes actually happened and were sustained in spite of the violence, I came to the conclusion that these did not happen with a strategy of focusing on counting the numbers and on whether they amounted to a critical mass. In fact the inverse was true. Focus on quantity distracted from focus on quality and on the space needed to generate and sustain change.

One day, by my recollection during an extended conversation with Somalis around an afternoon tea in the lobby of the Sheraton Hotel in Djibouti in 1991, an alternative popped out. We were perplexed with what would make possible a shift to overcome the paralysis people felt when faced with the power of the warlords. Some commented that what was needed was a critical mass of opposition. Some argued for a force greater than the warlords, an outside intervention of military might that would set it all straight. On the spur of the moment I made the comment, "It seems to me that the key to changing this thing is getting a small set of the right people involved at the right places. What's missing is not the critical mass. The missing ingredient is the *critical yeast.*"

Tongue-in-cheek, the metaphor stuck. Just like spiders, I have ever since been intrigued with the idea of finding and building social yeast. I use the concept extensively in training. I find it compelling. The critical or what I sometimes call the strategic yeast is built from a bread-baking image rather than one of nuclear physics. It is a metaphor that asks the "who" rather than the "how many" question: Who, though not like-minded or like-situated in this context of conflict, would have a capacity, if they were mixed and held together, to make other things grow exponentially, beyond their numbers?

Whenever I present the idea in the format of a seminar or workshop I always ask who in the group bakes bread and then I ask them to describe what they do. While the process and secrets vary, there is a commonsense understanding to bread baking that cuts across almost any cultural setting. The elements of the process are, as I indicate in the classroom, suggestive of how we can think about social change. From more than nearly a decade of working with the metaphor, here are the common observations about yeast, bread baking, and social change. Remember, we are looking into the "who" question as a social strategy. I have garnered five principles.[2]

1. The most common ingredients for baking bread are flour, salt, water, yeast, and sugar. Of all of the ingredients, flour is the largest, the mass. Among the smallest is yeast. There is only one that makes the rest grow: yeast. Smallness has nothing to do with the size of poten-

tial change. What you look for is the quality of what happens if certain sets of people get mixed. The principle of yeast is this: A few strategically connected people have greater potential for creating the social growth of an idea or process than large numbers of people who think alike. When social change fails, look first to the nature of who was engaged and what gaps exist in the connections among different sets of people.

2. Yeast, to do its thing, must first move from the jar or the foil packet and into a process, initially of its own growth, and then into the wider mass. Sitting on a shelf or never being removed from the package, yeast has only potential but no real capacity to affect any kind of growth. Mixed directly and quickly into the mass, yeast dies and does not work. This leads to our third principle.

3. Initially, yeast needs a small amount of moisture and warmth to grow. In early or preparatory growth, yeast will be stronger and more resilient if it has a dash of sugar and if it is not placed in glaring sunlight, that is, if it is located a bit out of the way and covered. The core steps for building initial growth are mixing the dry ingredient of yeast with water, sweetening it a bit, and placing it in a somewhat warm environment. Following the same principles, social change requires careful attention to the way people in their environment mix in relational spaces that provide a warm, initially somewhat separate, and therefore safe space to bring together what has not usually been brought together with enough sweetness to make the space conducive for the growth of those merged.

4. The yeast must then be thoroughly mixed into the mass. This is no minor process. In bread baking, it is called kneading. It is intentional and requires a good bit of muscle. Further, bread bakers rarely accept the first signs of growth as legitimate. To be authentic, growth must find a source that rises, again and again, in spite of everything that pushes it down. Yeast is defined principally by this capacity to be resilient. In social change, the critical yeast must find a way to sustain the purpose of whom they are as yeast yet be mixed back into the full mass such that in spite of ups and downs, they are characterized as displaying the capacity to generate growth.

5. Don't forget to preheat the oven. Bread baking and critical yeast are multitasking par excellence. While one set of things is set in motion in one place, attention is always given to the horizon of what is coming and will be needed in another. What is being done now simultaneously must connect with other things that will need to be attended to and kept present, not as a linear sequence of first A and then B, but as a simultaneous understanding of interdependent though different processes. In this sense social change requires a keen sense of

relational spaces even when those are not in direct physical proximity. Based on relational spaces, critical yeast constantly moves across a range of different processes and connections.

In this image the largest ingredient, flour, is an analogy for the critical mass. However, the smallest ingredient, yeast, is the only one with a capacity to help the other ingredients grow. If we follow the analogy, yeast needs moisture, warmth, and to be mixed in order to make the other ingredients grow. The place where the critical mass and the critical yeast meet in reference to social change is not in the number of people involved but rather in creating the quality of the platform that makes exponential growth strong and possible, and then in finding ways to sustain that platform.

I often follow this with another metaphor for social change. I tell the story of my first encounter with a siphon. During the period our family lived in Costa Rica, I was involved in a community initiative in the Pacific port town of Puntarenas. Once a week I would travel over the mountain passes from San Jose to the coast for our meetings. They usually ended in the late evening and I would make the trek back, usually arriving home about midnight. One evening, my fuel gauge was not functioning properly, and I ran out of gas on a remote mountain pass. There was little traffic at that hour of night and so I waited by the car, hoping against hope that whoever came by might stop and that whoever stopped might be a good person with creative ideas. Such a person did stop and our challenge was how to get a little gas from his vehicle to mine without a pump. It was the first time I needed to make a siphon really work.

I tell this little story in workshops and then say, "We are going to look at the physics of a siphon and apply those to social change." I frame the challenge of the siphon as this: How can we move liquid from one place to another with what is naturally available, that is, without electricity or a motor? And then we walk through almost everyone's commonsense knowledge of a siphon.

The end of a tube or hose is introduced into one container of liquid. Light pressure by inhaling at the opposite end of the tube is applied, but not too much, and this end of the tube is held lower than the other. When the liquid reaches the halfway point and begins its descent, the tube is introduced to the other container. The liquid flows on its own, due to the forces of gravity, independent of the originating pressure or influence. The principles have commonality with the yeast metaphor and raise a similar range of intriguing applicable questions.

First, with a siphon, you do not concentrate on moving all of the liquid. You focus on getting a small portion to move against gravity until momentum and then the power of gravity brings the rest. In social change application, it raises this question: Who, in a setting of conflict or related to a process of change, if they were able to move *together* against gravity, would as their momentum built, bring a much wider set of people with them? The key, once again, is in the little things, not in large numbers. The key is the capacity to locate the strategic set of people that who could create such momentum. Who they are *in relationship* creates the capacity to pull.

Gravity is both an obstacle and a resource. Careful attention must be given to how this small set of people moves against the gravity, but they are also chosen for their capacity, for who they are and how they are connected in the setting, to create an exponential use of setting-based forces.

The role of outside influence and pressure, as can be seen in the metaphor, is that of astute support. The key to sustaining the movement or the change is having a deep setting-based capacity, for the ability to sustain the movement lies with the existing resources, not with the introduction of artificial influence. Catalysts and support can come from outside, but the sustenance of change is built by keen observation of available and existing resources, space, and connections.

Webs, Yeast, Siphons, and Mediation

One way to characterize the moral imagination found in the stories of the Wajir women and the Colombian peasants was their capacity to see, understand, and mobilize relational spaces. They were masters of web making for social change, spiderlike in their capacity to imagine the contours of the space and to imagine themselves in relationship with challenging sets of people who were not like-minded and -situated and were extremely dangerous and antithetical to their desires for change. As agents of social change, their imagination took advantage of the existing context in order to transcend it. An intriguing curiosity was the nature of their role. They were simultaneously advocates and conciliators. They did not engage in mediation per se, yet their imagination of relationship and space created a mediative quality that affected the setting without a mediator. This supports the growing awareness, as proposed most recently by Bernard Mayer (2004), that the professional field of conflict resolution has too narrowly defined the nature of our role as we think about building constructive social change.

Though I have worked at international peacebuilding and conflict transformation for more than twenty years, I continuously find myself faced with an intriguing challenge: how to explain to people what I do. I sometimes have nurse, accountant, and bricklayer envy. When somebody at a construction site says, "I am a bricklayer," nobody asks for more information. It is enough. But when I say, "I work in support of conciliation processes," it is rarely sufficient to give people a sense of what I do. If I say, "I am a mediator," then there is an immediate connection and image. But what follows is a second typical question: "Which conflicts have you mediated?" And once again I find myself in a quandary. Truth be known, though I have been involved in supporting dozens of initiatives, I have only served as a mediator in several specific inter-national conflicts at the highest level of the political process, and even in those I was part of a team where I had a secondary, supporting role. Yet, if I endeavor to explain the actual heart of the experience of what I do, people soon have a lost and perplexed look on their faces. The image of "a mediator" and the work that a mediator must do in international conflicts is specific and clear in many minds, but it does not match my experience nor my understanding of what is most needed in settings of protracted conflict. I believe the image—the meta-phor of a mediator—is actually misleading and misguided, and it has a lot to do with the nature of change and our discussion about space, webs, yeast, and siphons. Serious understanding of space and webs suggests that we should reconsider the nature, purpose, and construction of mediation in protracted conflict.

The web approach requires what I would call an *imaginative mediative capacity*. I note that my computer program spell-check does not like the use of the word *mediative*. Apparently this is not an accepted adjective in the English language. But I use it intentionally, having bumped across the term with col-leagues in Northern Ireland who were trying to find ways to describe the kind of social responses they hoped to infuse in the groups that were conducting a wide variety of tasks in cross-community work, from housing to health. These people saw much of their work not as mediators in the classic sense but as helping particular institutions within the wider society build "mediative" be-havior (Lederach, 2002). Hence, the birth of a term I find useful and descrip-tive.

Mediative capacity requires us to think about social spaces for constructive change processes that have intermediary impact. Mediation on the other hand typically is more narrowly defined as a task conducted by a person or team at the level of political negotiation, which is aimed at finalizing an agreement. Honeyman (1990) and Mitchell (2003) argued some years back that we would be wise to think about mediation as a process requiring multiple roles and activities rather than as an activity conducted by a single person. This points us in the direction of understanding the conflict setting as a system, a web of relationships and processes. When applied to mediation, the web approach proposes we broaden the concept to include the development of social capacity to constructively affect the strategic points of relationship within the weblike system. But what does "mediative capacity in social spaces that promote and build constructive change processes that have intermediary impact" mean? Let me offer a definition that in many regards represents the significant shift in view that accompanies a web approach.

Mediative suggests a quality of relational interaction rather than the spec-ificity of a role. The term underscores attitudes, skills, and disciplines that include engagement of the diverse perspectives about a conflict and a capacity to watch for and build opportunities that increase creative and responsive processes and solutions around conflicts. Common to this kind of interaction is a capacity to build relationships and to address specific issues. In Northern Ireland mediative attitudes and behavior were aimed not at introducing a mediator, but rather at finding spaces of natural and necessary cross-community interaction, for example, in public housing or health, that could increase a constructive capacity in interpersonal and social skills.

Capacity is understanding, ability, and discipline. It suggests skill and will, and involves both practice and attitude. For our purposes here, *capacity* is empowerment at its most primordial essence: "I am able and committed."

Social spaces suggests that in settings where conflict has created sharp and historic divisions—more often than not along lines of collective identities—every set of social relationships has a connection to and is defined by these divisions. This means conflict at a social level has a wide impact. However in these settings we also find that in the social life of communities besieged by violence, people still create places of interaction for purely functional reasons. In other words, people from different sides of the divide interact on a daily basis out of necessity for one reason or another. From schools to hospitals, from markets to housing and transportation, the web of life in conflict settings creates spaces of interaction wherein there are, by necessity, points of relationship across the lines of conflict. These points of relationship are what we could call *social spaces*.

Ironically, however, in its typical application, mediation is conceived as a socially narrow process of action carried out by a person (or small team) who moves or facilitates direct dialogue between well-defined actors representing particular interests and groups. This is especially true of the highest level of political and military leadership. Here those in the role of mediator seek a common definition of the issues, propose processes for addressing those issues, and most important as the measure of success, nurture agreements between leaders on ways to move forward on those issues. A space is created through the relationship with the mediator for new, different, and hopefully more constructive interaction between these political adversaries. While this represents a transformative space that nudges adversaries toward change, the process is by definition exclusionary. It is based on the words, exchanges, perceptions, and dialogue of those who are connected to and through the intermediary space (Gopin, 2001). This mediation process can be communicated and connected to a wider affected population, but it remains an exclusionary space by its very nature.

Social spaces broaden and deepen the purpose of transformative intermediary design and action. By *broader* I mean the many sectors and points of interdependent interaction between social collectives affected by the division, which go well beyond what is usually included in a political negotiation. *Deeper* proposes that there are many people, relationships, and actions that need constructive, transformed, and sustained interaction well beyond a handful of key

leaders who sit at the highest level of visibility and political or military responsibility. I am not suggesting that political negotiation is not necessary. A web
approach, however, does argue that political negotiation is not the primary nor
the exclusive measure of the mediative capacity of a conflict-ridden society to
promote the broader change processes that must take place. Sustained change,
this approach posits, lies with the capacity to mobilize the web.

Change processes create a different horizon as the lens and goal of action.
Whereas, typically, political mediation is considered in reference to specific
agreements between leaders, change processes engage the challenge of how
societies, communities as a whole, initiate and sustain a journey of
relationship-oriented transformation. As such, they suggest that the measure
of success pertains less to the specifics of content and substantive outcome
than to the quality of platforms and relational capacities that sustain processes
over time, through the thick and thin, the ebb and flow of how societies move
from interactions defined primarily by division and violence toward coexis-
tence, cooperation, and constructive interdependence.

Intermediary impact has traditionally been understood as the level of success that the mediator's action has had on people's perceptions and understandings of each other in the conflict, the specific results produced by the
process measured by the agreements reached. Mediative capacity uses a different lens, one that brings into focus change processes in strategically chosen
relational and social spaces wherein increased capacity to interact constructively across the lines of conflict in those spaces creates and sustains movement
in the society as a whole. The emphasis of the impact is on the strategic component, wherein the web is constructively affected because significant change
happens in a specific set of social spaces and relationships, which brings about
a broader transformation in the whole.

In summary, the perspective of mediative capacity focuses attention on
introducing a quality of interaction into a strategic set of social spaces within
the web of systemic relationships in order to promote constructive change
processes in the conflict-affected setting as a whole.

Returning to our stories, this was precisely the role of the women in Wajir.
Not mediators per se, they were more akin to social change strategists using
strategic mediative behavior with a keen sense of relational space. With spiderlike creativity and instinctive imagination, the women engaged their environment, locating connections among strategic groups and finding imaginative
ways to get people moving within and between among those spaces, people
who were not like them in their initial thinking nor situated in similar gender,
status, economic, or political positions. In many instances, they recognized
and then rebuilt the spaces, linking elders with district commissioners, women
with police, youth with widows, markets with cattle rustlers. The forces that
perpetuated the war, that is, the forces of gravity against which they had to get
people to move, were in many instances turned toward constructive momen-

tum. Former fighters engaged elders to stop promoting clan fighting. Smaller clan elders appealed to the moral imperative of change in discussions with larger clan elders. Women created the space for men to meet, and some women even became elders. The Wajir Peace and Development Committee imbued each interaction and social space with this mediative attitude, from the markets where they created a network of people who assured access and respect, to how they engaged the traditional role of clan elders to move both individuals and the institution of eldership from one that incited war to one that nudged toward peace.

This was also the role of the peasants' movement in Rio Carare. They understood and envisioned themselves in a web of destructive patterns and relationships. They made the web clear and then imagined the spaces and steps necessary to redefine the setting. They approached the key individuals and groups whom they considered to be the connectors and decision makers. Their process of advocacy was permeated with a capacity for dialogue to create a mediative impact. They sought a change in the attitude and structures that promoted the war and formulated their strategy by finding where they had points of access, creating in the process new spaces, including one that even came to be called a *zone of respect and mutuality*. This was not the elimination of relationship. It was the redefinition of relationship, context, and the web of connections.

The results described in these settings of deep-rooted conflict suggest that people who come from different sides and locations within the space of the conflict transformed it by infusing the relational spaces with a new quality of interaction. It was the relational web that provided the point of access and the platform of change. These approaches created a different quality of interaction, significantly moving the cycle of conflict from one defined by blame, reactivity, division, and violence toward one of constructive dialogue. But rarely was it a negotiation of the type we have in mind when we speak of a mediation effort. The focus was not on producing agreements and solutions as the primary goal, though along the way agreements, informal and formal, emerged. The focus promoted relational spaces through which constructive, nonviolent change processes were initiated and sustained. In short, the web approach, as articulated in these radically different settings, captured the full essence of the four disciplines that build the moral imagination: the capacity to imagine relationship, the insusal to fall into dualistic polarities, the creative act, and the willingness to risk. In each instance, at the level affecting a whole group, a community, even a region, our stories describe actions that transcended historical patterns of violence while still living in them.

When I reflect back on my peacebuilding experience, the most significant components that shaped processes, made a difference, and held up over longer periods of time consistently were those where a small but strategically connected set of people worked for change with an instinctive knack for web thinking. The conciliation work in Nicaragua that helped shape the end of the war between the East Coast and the Sandinistas was a relational, web-based understanding of process. The work in Northern Ireland among former paramilitaries and cross-community groups, the infrastructure that helped to keep the process alive when all else seemed doomed, was built on hundreds of invisible, unmentioned sets of contacts, conversations, and coordinated processes, which understood and strategically built relational spaces. In both cases fewer than a dozen people made the key links and held the mostly informal processes of relational space-building together.

Let's look more closely at one specific context. In the early 1990s, I worked in support of the Life and Peace Institute's (Uppsala, Sweden) efforts to support peace initiatives in Somalia (Lederach, 1997; Heinrich, 1997; Paffenholz, 2003). Among the tracks contemplated in support of local and international peace efforts was one focused on the role of women and their mostly market-based associations. Many casual observers and more than a few professionals in international relations tended to consider this effort to be interesting, but peripheral to the actual forging of political peace agreements among faction leaders. It was, at best, seen as politically correct in order to create some kind of gender representation, but was largely considered as irrelevant in an otherwise patriarchal, nomadic society. Missed by these lenses however was the capacity to understand the potential of social webs, the anthropology of mediative capacity in the society, a capacity that requires us to look at resources that are natural, in place, and effective but often overlooked because they do not enter the scope of what is seen typically by professional, mostly Western expectations. In this case, given women's location in the society through cross-clan marriages and their responsibilities for their families, women's association had unique characteristics providing extraordinary resources.

1. In terms of the cross-clan fighting, women through marriage experienced the war differently than men: Their fathers and brothers were often fighting their husbands and sons. In the long Somali tradition, women could travel from their clan of marriage to their clan of origin with greater safety and often were the informal diplomats opening the process of ceasefires and elders' conferences (Farah, 1993).

2. Women's responsibility for assuring the day-to-day survival of their families meant they were often located in the marketplaces, where they interacted with women of other clans. Markets became a de facto point of communication, exchange, and contact. Many conflicts started in markets, and many of the peace initiatives were ultimately related to the people, often women, who pursued ending the violence in order to get on with life as located in the market.

3. In markets, women often carried the money. In a country where central governance and central banking collapsed, the economy was

driven to informal mechanisms, and by default into the hands of those who worked extensively in the markets.

While not appearing in the chapter outlines of textbooks that are studied in formal diplomacy, in Somalia women were anthropologically resourceful for initiating ceasefires, sociologically located in the social boundary frontiers between fighting groups in the markets, and economically central in the ebb and flow of substantive resources. A web approach looks precisely for that kind of social space, one that has natural potential for mediative capacity and impact. In my opinion, while much of it has gone unnoticed in the long history of the Somali conflict, women have played a far more innovative, constructive, and transformative role in peacebuilding than the sum total of the formal peace conferences of militia leaders. If we look at a country beset by more than a decade of violence and still unable to reconstitute a central government, many would legitimately ask, "But what good did it do?" My sense is the opposite. The miracle is that Somali society has not descended into worse chaos given the conditions that have had to be faced, particularly in Mogadishu and much of the south. While difficult to document fully, the prevention of even greater chaos and the processes that have reconstituted some order have been accomplished by the work of those who needed to survive and found a way to do so in spite of the odds.

Conclusion

In its everyday application, critical mass is understood as a strategy of making things happen by mobilizing large numbers to effect a desired change. Driven by political, business, and military concepts, we seem to have an image that this kind of strategic thinking translates into maximizing output. Success is measured in numbers and wins.

Constructive social change requires a different image of strategy. We need to generate a greater quality of process with the available, often few, resources. In peacebuilding, when we think strategy, we should think about what gives life and what keeps things alive. In the simplest terms, to be *strategic* requires that we create something beyond what exists from what is available but has exponential potential. In reference to social change, it means we must develop a capacity to recognize and build the locus of potential for change.

In sustaining peace, the critical yeast suggests that the measuring stick is not a question of quantity, as in the number of people. It is a question of the quality of relational spaces, intersections, and interactions that affect a social process beyond the numbers involved. To think quality requires that we think about the spaces, connections, and platforms that hold potential for affecting the whole.

IO

On Web Watching

Finding the Soul of Place

Whenever I quiet the persistent chatter of words within my head, I find this silent or wordless dance always already going on—this improvised duet between my animal body and the fluid, breathing landscape that it inhabits.

—David Abram, *The Spell of the Sensuous*

Web making assumes a purpose in our peacebuilding activity: We wish to put in place something that will help to mold and shape constructive social change in a given setting. The key to sparking that change and making that change it stick requires imagination, new ways of thinking, and developing processes that weave relationships and connections and that create the social spaces that form the invisible fabric of human community within and beyond the geography of violence. However, prior to such strategic development of processes a related but quite different form of imagination must be honed. This is a critical but often overlooked component of peacebuilding: the craft of watching webs.

When I first read the *National Geographic* article discussed in earlier chapters, I was not only struck not only by the process of how spiders construct webs, but was captivated by the peculiar nature and disciplines of the scientists whose lives are given to the study of webs and the micro-universe of spiders. With complete surprise I discovered that much of what I have done in the designing and shaping of peacebuilding over the past decades could be described as web watching. Many of my now-lost napkin doodles were nothing more nor less than listening and then drawing the web of connections that exists in a setting, trying to imagine and make visible the fabric that underpins violence and, potentially, peace.

Arachnophiles

Conniff (2001) suggests that web watchers, I guess we might call them arach-nophiles, comprise an unusual community made up of a unique brand of person. Their world involves hours, days, and full careers watching carefully for nearly invisible connections in spaces no larger than a backyard, a few bushes, or an open grass field. Spider webs are made up of hundreds, even thousands of silk strands. I have noted in my personal experience that more often than not I feel a part of a spider's web before I can see it. I found this was also the case for the professionals. Web watchers rarely see the whole of the arachnid's net. It is not immediately visible. As a consequence, these stalk-ers of spider weavings move gingerly across a space, locating initially only a piece, a strand, and then their journey begins, a journey with the goal of fol-lowing connections and making visible the whole.

Many spider webs are so difficult to see that web watchers carry an old sock filled with cornstarch. When they locate a strand or two, they sprinkle the starch lightly over the area to uncover the linkages. With the help of gravity and a bit of breeze, the web appears under a blanket of powder. In their case, as one of them explained, they do this in order to "figure out which lines are connected to which and which plants are connected, so you can see how to move around it without disturbing it" (Conniff, 2001:35). Respect for what is naturally in place accompanies their every step.

Conniff, like Abram, calls web watching a journey into a micro-universe. Curiously, to traverse this universe, web watchers practice the "zen of going nowhere." "Watching spiders," Conniff writes, "means narrowing the scope of your world and moving in millimeters" (2000:34). Web watchers, it seems, create a sense of travel that involves penetrating observation to locate and watch entire creations with very little movement. Conniff (2001:34) described his experience of accompanying a scientist into a spider's world over the course of a morning: "After a couple of hours, having journeyed through an entire universe in miniature, we turned back. We had covered all of 50 yards."

The Disciplines of Finding Place

I found in the description of the spider watchers an intriguing set of lessons for those interested in the application of social web watching. These lessons in many regards seem to entail both an attitude and a discipline. On one hand they could be called the disciplines of *scientific empiricism,* for they seem to involve the methods of observation about a phenomenon under study and the care with which one approaches the study. On another, they may constitute what practitioners call the *skills of social and conflict analysis*, for they also take up the need to understand a situation by breaking it down into manageable pieces in reference to what is going on and how exactly things are working in a given setting in order to develop a response. Those are both accurate descriptions of the lessons that could be derived from web watchers.

I was struck however with how the disciplines of web watching connected to an aspect of my work on a different plane, one that I have not often found attended to in the professional field of conflict resolution and for which I struggle to find adequate words to describe. I speak of matters of the soul. Picking up a phrase of Yeats, such matters engage the professional in a return to the deeper "heart's core." In short, I understand these matters as spiritual disciplines. They entail how we choose to be in the world. This involves the choice of how we enter into relationship with what exists and the degree to which we keep our senses attentive to the ever-present but rarely heard appeal for authentic dialogue bubbling in our surroundings, physical and social. Such attentiveness requires what I would call "soul-based disciplines." These I have come to appreciate as constituting a deeper plane that underpins the pursuit of authentic social change. In the geographies of violence, noise and busy-ness dominate our immediate senses. The moral imagination, if it is to penetrate and transcend, must find the soul of place. Finding soul requires that we go to the core, that we make our way to the voices behind the noise, that we see the patterns hidden beneath the presenting symptoms, that we feel the rhythms marking steady pace in spite of the cacophony.

The art of the moral imagination emerges from the soul of place, what Daniel Berrigan once called the "geography of faith" (Berrigan and Coles, 1971). It asks two questions that beg dialogue but not permanent answers: Who am I? Where am I? Those who invite and keep these questions throughout their journey in any geography will envision the soul disciplines as the spiritual underpinning of their work. They will struggle with the disciplines, and at times rare and fleeting as they may be, they will feel the soul of change. They will walk a pathway that invites the moral imagination. Those who do not invite or engage these questions see the disciplines of our field as scientific method or practitioner skill. They will develop eyes and ears that function mostly at the level of applied technique.

What are these soul disciplines? Three come to mind: stillness, humility, and sensuous perception.

Stillness

Web watching requires great patience, intense attention, careful movement, and observation. The zen of going nowhere requires the discipline of stillness.

Herein, by my experience, is one of the hardest lessons to learn for those impelled by social activism and a desire to understand how change can be sustained: Stillness is the prerequisite to observation and the development of a capacity to see what exists. Seeing what exists is the prerequisite of transcendent imagination.

The fundamental nature of stillness flies in the face of common notions of getting something to change. Change, we believe, is about promoting, nudging, and even pushing. Activism argues with the world: "Don't just stand there, do something!" Stillness says in response: "Don't just do something, stand there!" The paradox is this: Stillness is not inactivity. It is the presence of disciplined activity without movement. Stillness is activism with a twist. It is the platform that generates authenticity of engagement, for it is the stage that makes true listening and seeing possible.

What makes stillness possible? Stillness requires a commitment of patience and watchfulness. Its guideposts are these: Slow down. Stop. Watch what moves around you. Feel what moves in you.

Think for a moment about the nature of movement, be it in a car or on foot. You cannot see or listen to what is closest to you when you are moving. You see what is off in the distance but you cannot see what is at your feet. This is something I have learned from rock hounding, particularly for Pacific agates or aquamarines at the top of Mt. Antero in Colorado. The easy tendency is for your eyes to move quickly around, looking always just beyond where you are. The hardest discipline is to watch carefully right where you are. Most often the greatest find is sitting right in front of your face, invisible in its obviousness because the movement of your feet and eyes are traveling beyond what is immediately there.

As part of a recent doctoral study, Patricia Burdette made similar observations about the efforts in Lakota Country to develop a cultural-response resource for dealing with children who display severe emotional needs and deep trauma. Through participant observation of many years and extensive interviewing, she endeavored to understand how Lakota people understood *nagi kicopi*, a traditional ceremony through which "an ailing person's spirit is called back to begin the healing process" (Burdette, 2003:273). In her review of the literature and of the values underpinning the ceremony she remarks that one of the Lakota core values that accompanies the healing process is patience. As she puts it, commenting specifically about the Lakota people, "[P]atience as a value affects the understanding of time and it is the source of such personal attributes as humility and respect" (273).

This understanding of patience is prevalent among many indigenous peoples. It is the sine qua non of deep observation and is related to their seemingly innate capacity to imagine themselves in relationship not only with the human community but also with everything that surrounds them in the animate and inanimate world. The earth, the rocks, the trees, the sky, the air, the fish, the bear, the deer—all speak to them. I remember when Cheyenne peace chief Lawrence Hart arrived at a conference held in Harrisonburg, Virginia. He had just driven from Washington, D. C., across the mountains and then down the Shenandoah Valley. "I was glad to see," he laughed when he made his early introduction to the group, "that the people of the Valley have arrived at our conclusion. I passed just a few miles back a large sign on the road that said, 'Visit Luray Caverns: Hear the Rocks Sing.' " The marvel for indigenous people is not that rocks speak. It is that they, as a human community, retained a capacity to hear the rocks sing.

I recall an experience in the Philippines at the end of a seminar on conflict transformation with grassroots leaders from the indigenous areas of northern Luzon. As part of our seminar we held a midweek evening celebration. Several of the tribal members offered to do their native dances, titled the mosquito and the frog. We were mesmerized by their capacity to imitate the animals. It was as if in the dance they had become the insect or the amphibian, so accurate and detailed were their body movements and postures. In subsequent days, instead of talking about "conflict analysis" in the ways that it would typically be presented, we asked a different question: What does it take to be as observant about conflict as it took to be observant about the mosquito and frog, to the degree that the dancer could capture the whole picture? The answers boiled down to a simple idea: You have to be patient and watch a long time.

Stillness proposes that we pay attention to what is around us, at our feet. The greatest missed potentials of change are not those far-off things we missed because we could not envision them but those things we missed because our movement bypassed and made them invisible. A Chinese proverb says, "It is not the size of the mountain that obstructs our way. It is the pebble in our shoe." When we focus on the really big things, we often miss the greatest potential of resource, insight, and change that is present right in the location where our feet are planted.

What I found intriguing about web watchers was the care they took with every step. The universe they watch requires a slowness of movement, a stillness of observation precisely because a misstep could destroy the very thing they most wish to see and preserve. They understand that their every step affects the context they study. As such, stillness is a safeguard and protection.

Stillness engages the question "Where am I?" as a twofold inquiry in quest of meaning. The journey is inward, for in stillness I seek to understand my location within the broad geography of time and space, especially this place where I am now. The journey is outward, for in stillness I wish to truly see the place where my feet are set.

I have come to believe that the two greatest tragedies that negatively affect peacebuilding in settings of protracted conflict arise principally from the lack of the discipline of stillness by those who come from outside with good intentions. These are (1) the inability to recognize and see what exists in a place that could have potential or is already building the web infrastructure of constructive change; and (2) stepping quickly toward action to provide short-term answers to predetermined problems driven by a sense of urgency. In both cases the in situ web of change—people, processes, and relational spaces—are overlooked, ignored, and diminished, or, worse, replaced or destroyed.

In a fundamental way, stillness practices the imagination of authentic observation, the continuous nurturing of a platform that makes listening, watching, and learning possible. In the case of web watchers, this is about a way of approaching and being in a universe made up of intricate connections that must be seen before steps are taken. It applies equally to the case of web watchers in the context of building constructive social change.

Humility

In reflecting on those who study spiders and their webs, I found a quality that I can only describe as humility. At a first glance these scientists displayed a quality of methodical pursuit and meticulousness in their inquiry of empirical evidence. But looking deeper, something else jumped out. There was an art and a soul that can be summed up in two words: respect and connectedness. Their way of being in the context they were studying contained a near-spellbound awe around this micro-universe of arachnids. They spend a lifetime traveling into the universe by going virtually nowhere and finding new surprises at every turn and visit. They seemed gifted with a particular type of imagination: the capacity to see themselves in relationship with the context in which they traveled and studied. They knew, in deep, intuitive, and—I assumed by the way they talked about it—experiential ways that their every movement affected the context in which they were in moved. They saw themselves as connected. I see these qualities—respect and connectedness—as the core of humility. Humility is a journey toward understanding and locating the soul of place.

The *soul of place* is an odd turn of phrase. We are perhaps more accustomed to talking about the place of soul, that is, the place that our spirit, our faith, or the deep search for meaning should occupy in life. The soul of place seeks a different understanding. It represents a kind of inner voice that speaks to each of us personally, calling out to understand the nature of the place where we find ourselves and the nature of our place in that location. In professional jargon, we might speak in a much more sterile manner of this as the "definition of conflict roles," "the historical analysis of the conflict," or the "initial assessment of the needs and interests in the target setting." This jargon leaves the question and answer on the plane of technical inquiry, that is, they contribute to work, activity, and the engineering of process. To find the soul of place, we must go a step deeper where we wrestle with "Who am I?" and "Where am I?" as people. This is akin to the vision quests of the native peoples, the dream-songs of the aboriginals in Australia, or Jacob, who wrestled all night with an unknown being and then marked the place where he survived. This is the deeper search for meaning in identity, relationship, and geography. It is the birthplace of humility. For here is the place of encounter, where we come to recognize our sense of self and our sense of living in a much greater web.

The above discussion suggests two essences of humility. The first is acknowledgment that I am a small part of something really big. In that simple phrase, the word *acknowledgment* is the key. There is a world of difference between knowing and acknowledging. *Acknowledging* requires transparent recognition and intentional choice. Humility puts us in touch with the precarious life of meaning that we live. On the one hand, we must have a sense that we are, that we count, and that we make a difference. Without that sense, life itself is meaningless. At the same time we must understand and live in a way that recognizes what a small piece of a bigger whole our life and work is, including all of our projects and activities. Without that recognition, we fall prey to jealousy; become arrogant, territorial, and controlling; and in our presumed importance and bigness we become small. The challenge of humility is to combine a sense of meaningful contribution and place with intentional recognition that we are part of a larger whole.

The second essence of humility is to understand that learning and truth seeking are lifelong adventures. Humility ends when seeking truth is no longer needed and learning is over. Peacebuilding requires a type of humility that recognizes that no matter how much I know or have learned, there is always more. The essence of humility is found in the constancy of learning and adaptation. If I have the full truth, I have no need for further inquiry, question, or search. Without humility, processes of change themselves cease to exist, for they become final, rigid, and complete. The great lesson of the natural world, the lesson of spiders and their webs, the lesson of those who watch the webs is this: Without humility, there is no learning or adaptation. Without humility, extinction not transcendence is the outcome. The challenge of peacebuilding is how to develop processes of change to the best of our knowledge and continuously be able to learn and adapt what we have created as greater understanding is gained.

Finding the soul of place represents a journey to locate *who* I am in the particular place and *what* is the nature of this place *where* I am located. For peacebuilders, there is a pragmatic side to the essences of humility and the soul of place. Approach the context with care and respect. Walk carefully. Watch and listen to those who know the setting. Do not presume to know solutions or to provide preconceived recipes. Understand yourself as part of a larger whole. Recognize that no one person, no one process or project is capable of delivering and sustaining peace on its own. Adopt an attitude of constant learning in order to create adaptive processes capable of continuous response.

Those who have struggled and continue to wrestle with "Who am I?" and "Where am I?" nurture a sense of awe and connection. They build the soul of place. They come to see themselves as part of something, not as in control of something. Approaching social change with awe and humility opens the way for the moral imagination. Social change without awe, struggle, and humility quickly becomes an exercise in engineering.

Sensuous Perception

I have on many occasions in this text referred to the idea of *sense*. Common sense, to make sense of, sense of place, sense of self, are just a few typical points of reference. I want to talk about this word *sense*, and I want to connect it to the challenging concept that how and what we perceive, what we let ourselves take in, and what we are attentive to in the world are integrally tied to peacebuilding and social change. I call this the *discipline of sensuous perception*, which I am sure on first reading may well raise an eyebrow or two. I have been emboldened by the work of David Abram, who redeemed the word *sensuous* from a world of narcissistic pleasure and placed it back in its origins of how we are in and aware of the world we inhabit.

Sense is how we perceive. Most commonly we have five senses: touching, tasting, smelling, hearing, and seeing. The *Oxford English Dictionary* explains *sensuous* as that which is "derived from, pertains to, affects the senses, or is concerned with sense-perception," then adds in a second explanation: "keenly alive to the pleasure of sensation," as in poets or artists who are "moved by or are appealing to sensuous imagination" (Compact, 2000:1710). When the two words *sensuous* and *perception* are linked, the phrase points toward a way to be in the world. *Sensuous perception* is a capacity to use and keep open a full awareness of that which surrounds us by use of our complete faculties. As such, the two-word phrase represents an ontological affirmation, for it inquires into the nature of being. Sensuous perception intersects with the world via all of the means we are humanly capable of experiencing. It requires that we bring our full faculties of interaction to bear on the experience of being in the world.

The professional fields of conflict resolution and peacebuilding have not always taken a sensuous perception approach to interaction. We rely on, and therefore value, analytical capacities that draw on a narrow range of the available senses. Specifically, we more intentionally value and therefore develop perception and understanding of the universe we occupy, namely, the geographies of human conflict and in particular the terrains of violence in settings of protracted conflict, through the partial use of two senses: hearing and seeing. This is of course a reductionism justified on the basis of what constitutes useful knowledge according to those who have managed the field, the political and social scientists. We believe that social change and peacebuilding are essentially processes that evolve and are shaped in the world of language. Words carry the day. We are spellbound by words. However, if we are to awaken and engage the moral imagination, we necessarily must engage the fuller range of senses, which includes but goes beyond the world of words.

Web watchers captivated me in this regard. With every step they felt the ground upon which they were walking as if the ground spoke to them. Their eyesight was fixed and sharp, attuned to that which was visible and not so visible, looking for signs of what might be there but was not readily seen. Their skin seemed hypersensitive. At the slightest feel of a strand, all movements were stopped and multiple perceptions brought to bear in order to follow the strand to the web and the space. They whistled and sang. It seems that certain sounds, imitating insects desired by the spider, could bring the hidden master out and toward the realm of more direct visibility. Their manner suggested a holistic interaction with the setting by using every sense available. Their way of being suggested sensuous perception.

How might this be understood in the context of social change and peace-building? I have learned the lessons of sensuous perception more from people who live and survive in the geographies of violence than I have from professionals who practice or teach conflict resolution. I believe this is the case precisely because survival in these geographies, like survival in high-altitude treks, in the precariousness of rainforest life, or in the crossing of a desert creates, by necessity, resilience based on broad sensuous perception. People survive because they develop multiple sources of input, ways of sensing the environment and then choosing the appropriate response. I learned early in my first adventures to rock-hounding sites above 14,000 feet to watch and listen attentively to the people who had been there for years. At the first sign of weather change—the way the breeze shifts or the barometric pressure is felt by the skin, the distant sound of thunder, or the distant sight of lightning—they move, take action, descend. As an old-timer once put it, on the "bare mountaintop, move at the first sign of trouble." There is a respect for the power of the environment, storms, shifting weather, and the capacity to feel that calls on every available sense. This kind of sensuous perception is exactly what I learned from people who live in and survive settings of great violence.

A team of colleagues and I once had a lengthy conversation with a person who for years had been a key leader in the Basque underground about a proposal for a dialogue process. We described our proposal, the ideas we had for the process, and the conveners. We wanted his opinion as to how people he knew intimately would react to our idea. I remember quite clearly that his response was not initially in words. He lifted his face and sniffed the air. I recall it perhaps because of the prominence of his extraordinary Basque nose. "They will," he commented, lowering his nose following the olfactory exploration, "smell something wrong that has nothing to do with the words but with who is proposing it, who is financing it, who is included. It won't have much to do with the idea. It will have to do with what sense their nose gives them."

I have noticed ever since how often people whose lives depend on what happens assess proposals and processes through olfactory intuition. Phrases are not uncommon that suggest something in this "stinks," "smells of a trap," or in the words of Marcellus, a guard in Shakespeare's *Hamlet*, has the odor of "something rotten in the state of Denmark." We probably do not often think of change processes having an odor, but people who live in settings of violence have learned to smell change.

Or take another example. Why does significant change in peace processes often take place in off-the-record conversations around tea, supper, or a late-night drink? Why do we call it the peace or negotiation table? Why is a table connected to dialogue and change? I believe it has to do with eating and the sensuous perceptions of breaking bread, dipping stew, and sipping tea. Tables and eating, dating way back in human history, are often used to signify the place where enmity dissolves. The psalmist writes, "[T]hou preparest a table before me in the presence of mine enemies" (Psalm 23:5). Eating equalizes, humanizes, and creates a different space. Eating creates a space that includes sight, smell, taste, and conversation to be heard. I often find that negotiators, when eating together, bounce ideas that they would reluctantly externalize in formal negotiations. Around moments of eating, a feeling of transcendence emerges. By way of food and drink around a table, the old world is suspended momentarily. A new world is entered. At the very least, the formal process is transcended; at best, people move beyond the blockage of exchanged demands. Something new, something unexpected emerges. It is as if, when a space is created that incites the broader use of sensuous faculties, people become more human. It is also why, in many instances, some negotiators refuse and even fear the space of eating, preferring the formality of a process that protects interests in the negotiating agreements, processes that are reduced almost exclusively to the senses that interact with the written or spoken word.

Sensuous perception suggests that attentiveness to process, the construction of meaning, and the understanding of place require the full engagement of all of our senses. Remember the warning from the gift of pessimism: Words are cheap. While language and words are and will remain a mainstay of how social change is understood, shaped, and conveyed, unilateral dependence on one faculty of perception creates narrowness and weakness. Those who survive in settings of violence do so by using all of their senses. They not only see, they smell, taste, and feel our processes. We must learn to smell, feel, and hear what surrounds their reality and processes. They have learned to speak the many languages of the environment, which rarely relies on words. We, too, must learn to speak these languages of the environment. For the moral imagination to emerge and transcend, it depends on and must incite the fullest of all possible sensuous imaginations.

Conclusion

Peacebuilders talk a lot about the need for networking. However, we are overly simplistic and superficial and lack a deeper understanding of what this endeavor actually requires. Networking is not just about instrumental connections among organizations that help us to achieve our goals or that minimize friction and competition. That is a narrow view of networking. Web watching as a discipline requires us to locate change processes in the web of how organic relationships occupy social space, how the connecting points create the flow and function of constructive, life-giving energy, and how pieces and strands of change are located within a larger system.

The web approach has a suggestion to make about constructive social change in protracted conflict: The way out of the pattern of repeated violence goes through the web of relational spaces in the context. Find the relational spaces, and you will find the location for sustaining social change in the context.

But the approach of web watching also suggests that the process of locating webs demands careful attention to how we are in and how we relate to the setting. What has not always been easy for us to imagine in the universe of conflict transformation and peacebuilding is the simple notion that the womb and home of conflict are relationships, in situ, and that we are part of that womb. We are features of a common landscape embedded in a social geography. The disciplines of web watching are aimed at how we enter, move in, and relate to this social geography. This is particularly true of protracted conflicts. Web watching suggests that locating and understanding the fabric, the relationships that comprise a setting, represent the single most important feature that should be taken into account if change in the patterns and relationships is to occur. Spider watchers have rules of thumb that are worthy of close attention and social application.

Be still. Take time to really observe before you step. Vigilantly seek to see and uncover the universe of relationships that is in place before you step.

Recognize that you are in relationship with the setting and the web you study. Imagine your connection even when you don't see it.

Develop a full range of capacities that help you sense what is around you. Be attentive with eyes, ears, nose, mouth, and skin. Never narrow to a single way to sense the soul of place.

Web watching requires deep observation. It can only be done with patience and time. You must imagine the whole even when it is not visibly present, and you must follow the strands that you touch. Web watching leaves us with perhaps two of the most important questions peacebuilders must keep present early and often: What exists? And how are we in relationship to it? Web watchers propose a simple idea: Relational spaces create and hold the center of social change. Finding, understanding, and relating to the webs that exist require stillness, humility, and our full senses. Web watching, the zen of going nowhere, attends to whole universes with gentle movement. It touches the soul of place.

II

On Serendipity

The Gift of Accidental Sagacity

You don't reach Serendip by plotting a course for it. You have to set out in good faith for elsewhere and lose your bearings serendipitously.

—John Barth, *The Last Voyage of Somebody the Sailor*

While writing this book I gave a university lecture on the challenges of modern-day peacebuilding. I decided I would explore with the audience the challenge of understanding the moral imagination. I shared the four guiding stories found in chapter 2 and at the end of the storytelling I asked the rhetorical question: What made these shifts possible? And I answered: the serendipitous appearance of the moral imagination in human affairs. After the lecture a conversation was struck up with several of the professors. Their concern, as expressed that evening, pushed at intriguing questions. As I remember their concerns, they were "Of what use is the moral imagination if it is not something that can be harnessed and applied? You spoke of the spark of change as a serendipitous element. How would we possibly convince politicians, much less hardcore realists, that such an attitude is reasonable or even responsible in the conducting of human affairs?"

They were and remain legitimate and most puzzling questions. They don't have nor deserve easy answers. These questions beckon a series of thoughts, wanderings, and probings, perhaps exaggerated, but a direct inquiry nonetheless, for these questions take us to the art of several matters. Serendipity pushes us to think about attitude and humility, the nature of developing theories of social change, and the building of adaptive processes that can sustain change. If taken seriously, serendipity increases our capacity to be responsive in the real world. And it all starts with a fairy tale.

There are lots of words with interesting etymologies and original uses, but there are only a few with stories so compelling that their very birth has created books and, in the electronic age, Websites. Such is the case with serendipity.

Horace Walpole, novelist, the fourth earl of Orford, the son of Prime Minister Robert Walpole, and a prolific producer of correspondence, did not set out to invent a word. That, in fact, was the serendipitous nature of his eventual fame. On the morning of January 28, 1754, he simply sat down to write a letter to Horace Mann to acknowledge that the portrait of Bianco Capello had been received in London from Italy. Walpole's letter contained the first written usage of *serendipity*. To quote the letter directly, while discussing an aspect of the portrait Walpole wrote:

> [T]his discovery indeed is almost of that kind which I call serendipity, a very expressive word, which as I have nothing better to tell you, I shall endeavour to explain to you: you will understand it better by the derivation than by the definition. I once read a silly fairy tale called *The Three Princes of Serendip*: as their highnesses traveled, they were always making discoveries, by accident and sagacity, of things which they were not in quest of (Walpole: 1754)

By most accounts *The Three Princes* dates back to stories of Persian origin. While different versions exist, the core of the story remains the same. The king of Serendip sends his three sons on a voyage, to be trained by the best scholars of the day and to gain experience such that they may become wise and worthy of the throne. They travel the roads of common people, encountering their problems and dilemmas. As fate would have it, the princes make their mark by way of their great capacity for astute observation and an equal proclivity toward trouble, their future and good character redeemed time and again through an unexpected turn of events.

The fable is filled with ironies. The princes travel toward ascendance to royalty in Serendip by leaving it. They move among commoners, finding their way unexpectedly into the hearts of these people through mishaps, unforeseen events, and a growing wisdom based on common sense, which brings them eventually into the great favor of other kings. These adventures, as Walpole put it, constituted the journey of discovery emergent from "accidental sagacity." He used the travels of Serendip to describe these types of processes and phenomena. Many years later Theodore Remer (1964:14) suggested that Walpole's expressive term, serendipity, must be understood as "a gift for discovery by accident and sagacity while in pursuit of something else." This is the definition that stuck.

Serendipity, it seems, is the wisdom of recognizing and then moving with the energetic flow of the unexpected. It has a crablike quality, an ability to accumulate understanding and create progress by moving sideways rather than in a direct linear fashion. Serendipity requires peripheral vision, not just forward-looking eyesight. It is the single greatest antidote to static politics and tunnel vision. Serendipity describes the fascination and frustration of sideways progress that constitutes the human endeavor of building peace in settings of violence, for constructive social change is often what accompanies and surrounds the journey more than what was originally and intentionally pursued and produced.

For many years I struggled with this nagging paradox of my work in peacebuilding: The more I wanted to intentionally produce a particular result, the more elusive it seemed to be; the more I let go and discovered the unexpected openings along the way, at the side of the journey, the more progress was made. I found myself reflecting on the notion that my greatest contributions to peacebuilding did not seem to be those that emerged from my "accumulated skill" or "intentional purpose." They were those that happened unexpectedly. At a certain point, I came to call this "divine naiveté," which originally I defined as the practitioner's dilemma of learning more from mistakes than successes. The reality was that these were not mistakes in the proper sense of the word; they were important things that happened along the way that were not planned. Hence I needed the combination of divine and naiveté. *Divine* pointed to something transcendent, unexpected, but that led toward insight and better understanding. To see that which is not readily planned for nor apparent, however, requires a peripheral type of vision, the willingness to move sideways—and even backward—in order to move forward. The ability to make that movement requires *naiveté*, an innocence of expectation that watches carefully for the potential of building change in good and difficult times. Divine naiveté and serendipity share this in common: They both foster the art of the possible. In a recent chapter (Lederach, 2003b:36–37) I wrote:

> Naiveté does not take what is presented on the surface and generally accepted as final truth as the primary measuring stick of how things work, are held together or fall apart. Naiveté is unafraid of being perceived as stupid and has the courage to raise basic questions, both of optimism when all seems impossible and of common sense realism when everybody expects peace to happen because a paper was signed. In both instances, the art is in seeking a way to reach toward a deeper source of what is possible and needed to keep a constructive change process alive and healthy.

One of my earliest and most formative experiences with serendipity came during the Sandinista East Coast negotiations as part of the Nicaraguan peace process. Looking back, the most significant components of the conciliation process happened not through direct planning but through serendipitous openings that led to relationships, breakthroughs, and ultimately direct negotiations.

I started the journey via an invitation from the Mennonite Central Committee (MCC) to conduct training sessions on conflict resolution with a variety of grassroots leaders in Central America. Gerald and Joetta Schlabach, then country representatives of MCC in Nicaragua, decided that the first pilot workshop would take place with Miskito and Creole Moravian church leaders. These leaders were at the time displaced in Managua due to the war on the East Coast. As events would unfold, some of them later became the primary conciliators between the warring sides. When our family moved to Central America we went through several rounds of finding an appropriate rental property. On a second round of searching in San Jose, Costa Rica, we rented a house that—at the time unknown to us—sat within blocks of the person who would become the chief negotiator for Yatama, the East Coast opposition movement that was at war with the Sandinista government.

Little events like these, not particularly noticed at the time, created the basis of what became my primary work for a number of years: to help support a conciliation effort to end a war. When I look back at those years some of the most important things I did as a conciliator were not what I had been trained to do in the classes that I had received on the structure and skills of facilitating direct negotiations. In fact, I did not do much "direct facilitation." And the things I did do were most probably things against which knowledgeable process advisors and experts would have cautioned.

My wife, Wendy, tells a good story in this regard. There was a time early in the conciliation process when, due to an unexpected turn of events, I was involved in hosting meetings of the leadership of the Southern Front of Yatama. On one occasion I was joined in San Jose by the head of the Moravian church, Andy Shogreen, who was the principal liaison between the East Coast fighters and the Sandinista government for almost two years prior to the start of direct negotiations. It was not easy to find places for East Coast leaders and *comandantes*, half of whom were undocumented, to meet in Costa Rica. Our newly rented house was somewhat off the beaten path and became a convenient rendezvous point. With unpredictable schedules, meetings would often happen at the spur of the moment.

One morning, such a meeting took place. Around fifteen leaders of various factions of the East Coast came to our house. Halfway into the meeting the leaders looked over at Andy and me and said in typically clear fashion, "We do not wish to insult you or abuse your hospitality but we need to sort some things out here, alone." So while the leaders took up their internal deliberations in our house, Andy and I headed to a downtown auto shop to buy some Toyota car parts he needed back in Nicaragua.

At about noon Wendy came home from her teaching job with our three-year-old daughter, Angie, in tow. On arrival she was startled at the door by someone whom she had never met. *Comandante* Coyote, a baseball cap perched on top of his head, ponytail to his waist, stood in the doorway and asked her, "Who are you?"

"I'm Wendy," she somehow mustered the gumption to respond. "I live here."

"Oh, well, come in, we are having a meeting."

She walked into a living room full of Indian leaders she had never met and no sight of Andy or her husband. "Well," she said as she surveyed her house, "can I make you guys some lunch?"

What took place that morning, through the lunch that Wendy made, which Andy and I, the great conciliators, eventually ate in the kitchen while the Indian leaders talked by themselves in the living room through the afternoon, was the meeting that created the consensus decision that overcame a key internal obstacle in whether to pursue negotiations with the Sandinistas. Serendipitously, we had a house, a set of useful connections, lunch, a willingness to risk what we had, and sufficient insight to stand aside when we were not needed. Trust sprouted and grew. We also had a computer, a telephone, an American Express card, organizations to help pay bills, and the know-how to put a phrase on paper that helped shaped certain concerns, along with the people who could walk that paper into the offices of the minister of the interior back in Managua. But when I look back, the most critical shifting points of change that made a process possible were never coerced, forced, or intentionally planned. They happened, more often than not, through the little serendipitous things nobody ever told me about in school.

In conflict resolution studies, from university to professional training courses, my preparation had focused on a set of skills to analyze substantive problems, solve them, or conduct communication processes to facilitate face-to-face dialogue by which those who have the problems solve them. These skills are important. They have formed an important base that constitutes a now almost unnoticed part of who I am and what I do as a peacebuilder. Without them I am sure I would be far less effective in my work. However, these same skills and training can easily contribute to a form of tunnel vision.

A tunnel essentially creates an avenue for cutting through a huge, immovable obstacle situated in the pathway. While there are tunnels with some curves, most move through the obstacle by cutting the pathway of least resistance that connects two points: where we are now and where we want to be. Tunnels are linear. Seeking the light at the end of the tunnel is the metaphor of the goal: to reach the way out. The metaphor describes well how conflict resolution is conceptualized as a process to create a pathway that cuts through the problems and permits people to reach the light at the end of their tunnel.

Working with conciliation processes, however, I have been surprised time and again with how un-tunnel-like the experience of peacebuilding really is.

Tunnel vision provides the important element of visualizing a guiding light at the far side. But the focus of tunnel vision neglects two important components that are not easily reduced to conflict analysis or communication skills, for they really are about attitude, art, and creativity.

First, tunnel vision assumes a far too static environment. By this assumption it suggests social change is like a process of seeing a mountain and devising a pathway through it that links point A on one side with point B on the other side. Our difficulty in peacebuilding is this: The mountain through which we have to devise a path is more akin to a sea than a rock. It occupies a great space that links the past with the future, and we live in a constantly moving, ebbing and flowing present. The mountain—if you will—is dynamic. To continue the mountain parallel, we should ask: How would you carve a tunnel through an active volcano? What we were not always taught in conflict resolution school was this: We are introducing a change process into a historically patterned and permanently changing environment. The challenge of peacebuilding is how to introduce constructive change that affects the patterns while living in and adapting to a dynamic environment.

This leads to the second difficulty with tunnel vision: It never develops peripheral vision. It looks unidirectionally toward a preconceived process and goal. If you have ever watched a crab work the sands of sea tides, you will have a concrete image of a creature that has peripheral vision and a sense of purpose at the same time. Peripheral vision, or what I have come to call the *art of serendipity in social change*, is the capacity to situate oneself in a changing environment with a sense of direction and purpose and at the same time develop an ability to see and move with the unexpected. People with tunnel vision can only see in a forward direction. Peripheral, or serendipitous, vision watches and sees forward, backward, and sideways. It can move in any of those directions, adapting to the changing environment while maintaining a purpose in mind but without a singularly defined process or pathway. Without peripheral vision, change processes are fragile because they are rigid. With peripheral vision, change processes have a flexible strength, never find dead ends that stop their movement, and relish complexity precisely because complexity never stops offering up new things that may create ways forward, around, or behind whatever jumps in the way. In peacebuilding you rarely reach Serendip by heading straight at it. You reach Serendip through the art of close observation and creative adaptation.

Before proceeding further, let us return for just a moment to the question of being reasonable and responsible in the conducting of human affairs in the world of politics and change. I should like to posit for the reader that the real world is one of constantly shifting environments and constant adaptation to these shifts. This is particularly true of settings of deep-rooted conflict and violence. The most realistic, as in the most *realpolitik*, thing we could do in peacebuilding would be to create processes with peripheral vision, capable of maintaining purpose while constantly adapting to the difficult and shifting sands and tides they must face and survive. The least realistic thing we could do would be to devise rigid processes of politics and social change that are incapable of adaptation.

We have for some time lived under the myth that somehow we increase our ability to control the outcome of processes through an equation that links power and military capacity. At a political level, our assumption is that since violence and violent patterns are the result of the capacity to produce violence we ultimately believe that we can control and overcome these processes by introducing more of the same. Those with the greatest capacity to introduce coercion or violence control the process and outcome. What we fail to recognize is that deep-seated patterns of violence are not controlled and overcome by that which creates them. They are brought asunder by changing the environment within which the pattern is given life. Authentic change and hardcore realism do not aim at the symptomatic, most visible expression of violence but rather adapt to the environment that generates the symptom and change the nature of the environment from within. Realism requires peripheral vision.

This has been, in fact, the hardest lesson, the lesson mostly left unlearned, from September 11, 2001. The attacks on the United States changed the game. Terrorism, at its horrific worst, is the negative side of peripheral vision. It never attacks the mountain directly. It understands that the mountain is more like a sea, offering up enormous power but many options. It uses the power of the sea against itself. In the case of September 11, civilian planes, easily available pilot training programs, tickets by Travelocity, and a box cutter—not a single gun, missile, or weapon of mass destruction—wreaked the greatest havoc on a superpower in its history. The most expensive and greatest logistical response to this event under the rubric of a "war on terrorism" fell prey to the trap of tunnel vision, to a rigid unidirectional understanding of war, which resulted in the waging of traditional battles of landed warfare against an enemy that is not land-based. The greatest weakness of tunnel vision is its inability to see peripherally, to feel, understand, and move in response to dynamically changing environments without losing a sense of purpose and direction.

In answer to the question: But what does serendipity have to do with real politics? I respond, "Everything." In the real world, the element that historically assures extinction is unidirectionality and tunnel vision, a single-mindedness of process and response in pursuit of a purpose. Survival requires adaptation to constantly changing environments, finding ways to move sideways while maintaining clarity of purpose. The key, as suggested by Walpole, is how to build from the unexpected, how to connect accident with sagacity. What we can expect in peacebuilding is the permanence of the unexpected. The strength of our processes of change, however, will depend on our capacity to innovate, imagine alternatives, and adapt to shifting sands while sustaining our goal in mind.

What then are the capacities that create the serendipitous moment, the capacity to give birth to discovery and through discovery to give birth to constructive change? Involving fewer skills than a shift in world view, finding the serendipitous moment suggests three guideposts: acquire and build a capacity for peripheral vision, develop creative learning disciplines, and sustain platforms that are smart flexible.

Guidepost 1: Peripheral Vision

In the original story, the three princes had a single capacity that provided the foundation of sagacity: astute, continuous, and rigorous observation. This cannot be overstated for understanding the nature of serendipity. Serendipity was not an act of random chance that somehow resulted in a good outcome. Serendipity involved engaged observation of what was found along the way. This notion of having eyes attentive to the along-the-way is the core of peripheral vision. Peripheral vision pays attention primarily to the purpose of the process rather than to the rote delivery of the process designed to provide a desired outcome. It is attentive to the surroundings, that which can be seen around, under, and behind presenting problems. Peacebuilders must be crablike in their approach to obstacles. As an astute observer from the Fiji islands, Paolo Baleinakorodawa, once suggested in a training workshop, crabs, when surrounded on all sides, will bury themselves in the sand and then rise again at a later point. A crab has the instinctual capacity of multidirectionality.

In peacebuilding, peripheral vision is attentive—we might even say hypersensitive—to certain kinds of phenomena that are directly connected to the foundation of the moral imagination. For example, obstacles in the pathway of constructive change present themselves more often than not in the form of procedural impasses and substantive issues accompanied by deep disagreements over solutions to the same. For the most part, peripheral vision ignores what appears as the symptomatic expression of the conflict and looks through the content of the problem to the broader pattern of how things are related (Lederach, 2003a). Peripheral vision has a lens that brings into focus the historical patterns of these relationships. Patterns of relationship, like complexity, offer up a sense of the larger picture and myriads of small openings and opportunities. Relational spaces and the patterns of how things are connected create continuous opportunities for addressing obstacles in new ways when finding solutions directly to those same problems appear as dead ends. The great gift of relational spaces is their ongoing dynamic nature. They continue to offer up accidents, unexpected twists, and opportunities. Peripheral vision watches the relational spaces of the process more than what appears as the content of the looming obstacle.

With peripheral vision, multiple avenues are held simultaneously within the panorama of the possible. This is the essence of nonpolarity. Peripheral vision does not frame the process or the decisions exclusively in terms of either-or choices. It holds connections and choices within a wider frame. When one avenue offers resistance, peripheral vision does not counterpush against the resistance. It sidesteps, locates other avenues, and watches for openings and indirect channels.

If sports metaphors are useful, the style of observation of peripheral vision, as I once heard from Kenyan peacebuilder Bethuel Kiplagat, is much more like soccer (what most of the world calls "football") than the sport of American football. In soccer, the field is wide. The motion is constant. In order to create a goal, the ball moves back, across, forward, and back again. Multiple sets of players coordinate and create a complex pattern of relationships and relational spaces from which openings are derived for pursuing the goal, more often than not in totally unexpected ways that require imagination and skill. Unlike American football, progress is not measured by each play and whether forward movement was created. As a metaphor, soccer, like peacebuilding, is serendipity built on peripheral vision.

Peripheral vision attends to several things often ignored or seen as unimportant. It watches all accidents along the way, be they events that take place that seem to derail a process or something as simple as a slip of a word from a key negotiator that creates a new twist on the situation, gives insight into a hope or a fear. Peripheral vision attends to and explores the metaphors that people in the conflict create to describe their situation. I recall that in some particularly tense off-the-record meetings with people from different political affiliations in the Basque conflict two metaphors popped out and became useful to understanding much better the perspectives and options that were under debate between the participants. One was found in the question: What does the final picture of this conflict look like? As a metaphor, it raised the visual picture of where the process was headed, who would be in that painting when the conflict ended, and how would the surrounding political environment be painted. The second was a short phrase that one of the participants pulled from a Hollywood-style script in response to statements others had made in reference to their group. "You keep acting as if this is a 'Surrender! You are surrounded!' scene. That is not," he said, "an accurate depiction of how we see the situation." In both cases, going directly at the problems separating the sides was less helpful than moving sideways with the metaphors, exploring the experience, probing for options and ideas that emerged from those discussions.

A final form of peripheral vision comes from a most unexpected source: common sense. Perhaps the most productive form of observation for the three princes was not their formal training under the great scholars of the day. It was their interactions with common folk, listening carefully to what they said and watching the environment surrounding these people's problems. This led them down the pathway to serendipity and can provide a moral of the story for peacebuilding: Never talk only to politicians and militia leaders. Talk to taxi drivers. Talk to construction workers and housewives. Talk to elders, shamans, and for goodness' sake, talk to children. Art Linkletter developed an entire television show based exclusively on the serendipitous wisdom of children: "Kids Say the Darnedest Things." The darnedest things often capture the wisdom of serendipity in commonsense phrases. A simple, straightforward statement of how things are, what they look like, can offer greater clarity than a complexified but misleading analysis. Common sense, like haiku, offers images that synthesize more than analyze. Serendipity sees a picture and cuts to the core in ways that often bypass what appear as insurmountable obstacles and difficulties.

Conversations with everyday people create connections to the environment and context. They provide insight and a capacity to cut through a confused morass. A long coffee break, a construction site, sitting in a teahouse, chewing the fat on a street corner—all constitute the spaces of peripheral vision. Ideas pop out, new ways of looking at old problems and old ways of looking at new problems can spark insight and new options. The stream of new possibilities often traces to the endlessly available well of common sense.

Guidepost 2: Creative Learning

Some things in life cannot be taught. They are qualities of being that distinguish one category of people from another. This is the case with creative learning. This kind of learning distinguishes rote technical application from creative artistic endeavor.

The technician has learned a response to a stimulus and works only to perfect the recipe offered for every problem. A hammer has been provided. Nails are expected and found. For the most part the technician has come to content herself with repeating and perfecting what someone else has discovered.

The artist on the other hand has never bumped into the same problem twice. Artists live an everyday ontology built on three pillars: an insatiable curiosity, constant invention, and attentive critique. They learn from everything and everyone, but they never stop creating.

At one point we were all artists. Pablo Picasso is reported to have said, "Every child is an artist. The problem is how to remain an artist once you grow up" (Cameron, 2002:85). For the technician, education took the life out of learning and replaced it with predetermined management. This may be useful for some functions of production but it loses its luster when the challenge is how to respond to the ambiguous beauty of our conflicted world. The artist has retained the capacity of innovation. Artists are on a journey to find and reflect the beauty that surrounds them. Curiously, you can find artists washing dishes at a restaurant, planting corn, or devising housing policy for an inner city. And you can find technicians managing universities, directing a church choir, or purchasing eighteenth-century art for a national museum. The difference is not in what they do or where they are located. The difference is in how they are attentive to and interact with the world that surrounds them.

Creative learning is the road to Serendip, the discovery of things by accident and sagacity. An insatiable curiosity does not translate into some form of disrespect for what others know or have learned. In fact the opposite is true. Curiosity wants to know more, not just about the idea, solution, or process proposed by someone else's journey. It wants to know how those things were generated. And most of all, curiosity just wants to know how things are and how they work. When applied to social change, insatiable curiosity has a single question: How exactly do things change?

I once taught a university course and decided I would ask that question early and often. I proposed a single paper that the students would have to write by the end of the semester. Every paper would have the same title: "How I Believe Social Change Happens." I was asking them to struggle with something that happens when artists become note technicians: They lose curiosity about their own theories of change.

We have often had an odd gap in our field of social change between practitioners and theoreticians. On the one hand we have theoreticians who, from a variety of disciplines, have provided major frameworks for our consideration. They often seek empirical evidence by watching what others do, but they rarely enter the swirling river of social change itself, particularly in settings of protracted conflict or deep violence. On the other hand, we have practitioners who live in that river, but only on rare occasions venture out to a place of reflection that translates their experience into proposed theory. We have few who do both.

I come more from the practitioner-who-occasionally-reflects school. That has been my challenge over the years. For many years I was reluctant to call any of my musings "theory." Theory, it seemed to me, was something more formal, more definitive and precise. However, one of the gifts of serendipity and creative learning is that they permit us to demystify theory.

I spend a lot of time with practitioners in settings of protracted conflict and—much like I did in earlier phases—I find that they have a certain distance from and fear of theory. For many of them, theory is connected to images of doctoral studies, books they can barely read, and ivory towers they have never visited. It is the world of the "really intellectual" folk. Practitioners, on the other hand are "just" hands-on people. In many workshops I endeavor to disabuse them of this image. I tell practitioners that beyond a shadow of a doubt each and every one of them is a theoretician, even if they have no formal education. I start with a little example and a question: "When you head from your home village or town into the big city, into Nairobi, Bogotá, or Manila, where do you put your money?" A few chuckles later the hiding places are described: in socks, tucked in blouses, under a belt line. "You see. You are theoreticians! You have a sense about the way things work in your everyday environment, and you adjust your action according to your theory." And I end with the well-known adage: "And there is nothing more practical than a good theory."

In the field of conflict resolution we have for far too long taken the art out of education and learning. With art removed, the former becomes training and the latter becomes evaluation. For those not familiar with the field or for those who have not noticed in such detail, training and evaluation have become defining epistemological pillars nearly overshadowing direct resolution practices. *Epistemology* refers to knowledge, how it is constituted and what kind of knowledge is valid. Thus, *training* determines what is useful and needed for practice. *Evaluation* determines whether the practice worked and is worthy of further funding. What would the lenses of serendipity and creative learning suggest to these two pillars?

On the purpose of training, I believe we have fallen prey to a model of education that produces technicians more than artists. The justification for this, which does indeed carry a certain weight, is the need for a skill base to conduct the management of processes. Missed in the pedagogical endeavor is the artistic side of our work. We do not expend an equal amount of time supporting people in trusting and developing their capacity to invent and create adaptive processes responsive to real-world situations and shifts. This requires something beyond rote skill training. It requires that we open a space for the development of the moral imagination, the capacity to recognize patterns and relational contexts yet think beyond the repetition of what already exists.

This kind of imagination is close to what Paolo Freire called "conscientization" (1970). He described this as the ability to pose the problems existing in a setting and let people interact, discover what they know, and innovate responses, seeing themselves as actors, part of the context of change. What they invent, he argued, will emerge from a growing belief in and understanding of the strengths and weaknesses of their own insights and understandings. Key to this process is the naming of the realities and the inventions, which he called the first and greatest of all human powers. Transforming training back toward education must create space for the art of imagination and provide space for naming the knowledge and the process. When this happens we assure a greater probability that rising generations will rediscover time and again the art that invents but always lies under and goes beyond the technique.

On the purpose of evaluation, we have been held hostage to two defining metaphors that, while well intended, have weakened rather than strengthened our capacity to build and sustain constructive change. I speak of the "project" and the "results." The two are linked. We have accepted and primarily oriented our work around the concept of projects. Projects are the way we propose, define, and fund peacebuilding. In essence, projects are activities conducted under a broad, often vague purpose aimed at producing amazingly concrete results in a discrete time frame, most typically one to three years. Reductionism par excellence, most projects quickly render even the most insightful artist a technician in short order. It is important to recognize that the project mentality assumes two important but rarely accurate truisms: (1) Social change is linear; and (2) social change is best measured by visible and verifiable results.

Serendipity proposes that attentive observation and learning are the keys to transformative evaluation. This suggests that theory building, learning, and the practice of peacebuilding are linked. Serendipity requires practitioners to be more explicit and intentional about their theories of change rather than relying on rhetoric that sounds good or promising and thereby focuses mostly on short-term results. In other words, good practice requires the capacity of theory building.

Serendipity pushes us to demystify theory. Theory is not writing perfectly defined but intangible explanations of social realities. It is about the common sense of how things are connected, how they influence each other, and how they may relate to desired change. Theory is our best speculation about how complex things work.

Serendipity requires that evaluation focus on creative learning. Results are one lens for learning but, serendipity argues, in the journey of social change, it is rarely the most important for it draws our attention exclusively toward the destination, and we lose sight of what is to be discovered, by accident and sagacity, along the way. An important shift in the development of evaluation methodology is the capacity to test and learn about our theories of change as much or more than the results that any one project produces.

Serendipity suggests that peacebuilding practitioners should not complain that funders and evaluators do not understand the unpredictable nature of their context and work. They should become as adept at articulating their theories of change, and engage funders with how those theories can be tested, as they have become at articulating the results they believe they can produce and the rhetoric of why their work is important and worthy of attention.

Serendipity suggests that those who fund and evaluate peacebuilding should concentrate less on results as the primary standard of success and failure. Those results, mostly forms of counting—how many agreements were produced, how many guns were turned in, how many people participated in workshops, or how many cases were removed from litigation—produce data that look impressive on paper but lend little to the deeper learning process. Practitioners, funders, and evaluators should participate together in the far more complex process of exploration: How did change happen or not happen? What has been learned about your theory of why things work from the experience of this setting? What unexpected insight was gained along the way that had little or nothing to do with the original proposal?

Serendipity nudges us toward the *art* of social change. It asks us to be attentive to how things are connected. It opens our eyes to the great learnings along the way that were not originally expected or intended. It builds an insatiable curiosity and love for learning.

Guidepost 3: Smart Flexible Platforms

The lenses of serendipity and spiders have much in common. They both are attentive to the surrounding environment. Their lives, so to say, are woven with the winds. They intuit, observe, and learn. And they both survive with a capacity to innovate and adapt. The best definition of *accidental sagacity* perhaps is found in the simple idea of being smart flexible. But how does that translate into a strategy for social change? It is found, I believe, in the idea of building platforms for change.

In the early writing of *Building Peace* I talked about strategic change requiring four broad categories of attention and innovation (Lederach, 1997). Not to be understood as a linear inquiry but rather as a process of multitasking, the titles of the four spheres of attention placed on the matrix were crisis, people, institutions, and visions. The third category represented an effort to move beyond the courageous efforts of a few individuals toward a capacity to sustain desired changes in social settings over time. This requires developing not just initial ideas but processes that sustain themselves beyond the individuals who initiated them. At the time, for lack of a better term, I called this *institutional inquiry*.

In subsequent years I questioned my choice of terms. I found time and again, particularly in settings of protracted conflict where peace agreements had been signed, that the negotiators of the peace with all good intentions placed the infant change processes into an institutional home. "Departments" and "ministries of" housed them and were responsible for their implementation. It makes perfect political sense. Responsibility and accountability need a formalized space. Nonetheless, in the process, something seemed to be lost. Sociologist Max Weber (1947) perhaps had the key insight: Social institutions, as they solidify and formalize, also codify and rigidify. In a word, they bureaucratize and in the process focus on self-perpetuating behaviors, independent of their original purpose. The form they take becomes more important than their originating function. Herein was the disease I felt. The environment, the context in which social change needed to grow and stick, was dynamic and constantly changing. The process of bureaucratization, however, seemed increasingly rigid, caught up in the form, in its social legitimacy, and the perpetuity of its institutional base. In turn, the institutions became increasingly less responsive to the realities of change they needed to support. Institution building in this sense of the word was not what I had in mind. A different kind of concept was needed and I landed one day by serendipity, in the midst of a lecture, on the idea of *platforms* for constructive change. The challenge remained the same: How do we sustain the social capacity to support constructive change while constantly innovating and adapting to a dynamic and demanding environment?

A platform provides a base for response. However, the focus is on the purpose of the platform rather than on the platform itself. A platform has permanency of purpose and flexibility to generate new responses to emerging challenges. It is in this sense smart flexible. Institutions are notorious for creating structures but are not typically known for their capacity to shift and change according to shifts and changes in environmental demands. They are permanent in purpose but not flexible in how they might pursue that purpose. Since the 1990s, much has emerged in systems theory and organizational development that argues that this is precisely why corporations and organizations live or die in fast-changing environments (Wheatley, 1994). Institutions that become like platforms understand the interdependency of purpose and flexibility of form for survival.

In this sense, smart flexible platforms for change have a capacity to move with the shifts that are presented along the way and from that place generate responsive processes and solutions to rising and constantly shifting demands. In the arena of social change this requires a capacity to continuously think in strategic ways about the context, the who, the overall purpose, and the innovation of process. The great irony is this: Innovation of process and the form of the platform are constantly adaptive; while the purpose of the social change provides meaning and orientation. Strategic peacebuilders do not confuse the more permanent nature of purpose with the far more fluid nature of responsive innovation and the forms it must take. In other words, platforms are social constructions of what the "new sciences" has termed *process-structures* found in the natural world (Wheatley, 1994).

Let me give two examples of process-structures. The first is as close as the back of your hand. I often tell the story of my childhood experience of visiting great-grandma Miller. I was about six. She was just over a hundred. She would sit in her rocking chair and we would go, usually one at a time, to hold her hand. I will never forget how century-old skin felt in my young hand. It was so soft, almost silklike. It was fragile yet unbelievably stretchy. She used to laugh when we would pull on the skin of the back of her hand. Sometimes she would lift it up and it would stretch for inches off her hand. "Look," she would say, "you can see through it." At six years old my skin was tight on my hand. But grandma's stretched and was translucent in the light, exposing the veins and even bones below it. "It's been with me a long time," she would joke.

Now, in my late forties, I suddenly notice things about my skin. Sometimes when I look down I have a flashback: My skin looks like what I remember of my dad's when he was in his mid-forties and I was in my teens. Today I can stretch my skin off the back of my hand a good bit more than I care to think about. I imagine, should I live to be a hundred, it will lift for inches and my great-grandchildren will laugh at the amazing translucent sight.

Skin, like all of our body parts, is a process-structure. Skin renews itself every few weeks. It is dynamic, adaptive to things that happen. Over time, it changes in significant ways, but the big change is not noticeable day to day. At the same time, skin has a purpose, a place, and a form. There is a permanency and tenacity of purpose. Simultaneously, skin is adaptive, constantly renewing itself, and it has a structure that permits it to fulfill its mission in life.

A river is another process-structure. When you step into a river, you enter a dynamic environment. Water moves. It is fluidity defined. You can never step into the same river twice. It is impossible, given the intrinsic nature of its dynamic quality. Yet you step back from the river and walk to the top of the mountain, or watch from the heights of an airplane window, and suddenly you can visualize the form and the structure the river has carved. You gain a sense of its purpose, direction, and flow. Herein is the paradox: From a great distance, you cannot see the dynamic movement of the river. You see its form and structure. From the middle of the river, you cannot see the bigger picture of its purpose and ultimate shape. You feel and understand its dynamic movement and power. Simultaneously, a river is a dynamic, responsive process *and* a structure with purpose.

Process-structures, like skin and rivers, more than anything I can think of describe the nature of peacebuilding and the quality of building platforms that support social change. It is not that structures are bad. Structures provide a sense of direction, meaning, and a base of support for the ultimate purpose of social change. However, structures alone are not sufficient. Pursuing change in a constantly shifting environment requires a constancy of innovation in both process and response. Social change needs dynamic adaptive platforms that respond to the nature of the environments where they must live. But processes that are adaptive without purpose create chaos without direction or ultimate shape. The challenge of social change is precisely this: How do we create smart flexible platforms, process-structures with purpose and the constant capacity for adaptation?

Conclusion

Serendipity nudges us in the direction of discovery and innovation. Accidental sagacity links the unexpected in the social environment with a capacity to observe it, see what it means, and innovate appropriate responses. Wisdom and survival are most clearly found in this capacity to recognize and adapt.

Serendipity is the gift of life. It keeps us alive to constant growth and unending potential, if we develop a capacity to see what is found along the way and adapt creatively while keeping a keen sense of purpose. Spiders, crabs, skin, rivers, and peacebuilders are artisans of social change.

12

On Time

The Past That Lies before Us

When the last person who knew the departed also dies, then the former passes out of the horizon of the Sasa (the Present) period; and in effect he now becomes completely dead as far as the family ties are concerned. He has sunk into the Zamani (The Past) period. But while the departed person is remembered by name, he is not really dead: he is alive, and such a person I would call the living-dead. The living-dead is a person who is physically dead but alive in the memory of those who knew him in his life as well as being alive in the world of spirits. So long as the living-dead is thus remembered, he is in the state of personal immortality. . . . Paradoxically, death lies "in front" of the individual, it is still a "future" event; but when one dies, one enters the state of personal immortality which lies not in the future but in the Zamani.

— John Mbiti, *African Religions and Philosophy*

In the mid-1980s during the conciliation process between the indigenous groups of the East Coast of Nicaragua and the Sandinista government I had my first lessons about living in coexistent but quite different understandings of time.[1] It took me more than a decade to recognize them as lessons. My teachers were the indigenous peoples, the Miskito, Sumo, and Rama Indians, and the Afro-Caribbean Creoles, including the day-to-day interactions with several of my close colleagues, notably Andy Shogreen, son of a Miskito-Creole marriage, who at the time was the superintendent of the Moravian church.

I was a young aspiring professional who wanted to help this

process of conciliation between two warring sides. I was anxious because there was much to be accomplished. Proper descriptions of my inner feelings—and most probably on more than one occasion my outer expression—would probably include intense, busy, and operating with a deep sense of urgency. Andy, though keenly aware of the task and completely given to the challenge of ending the war, rarely displayed my sense of urgency. We were different in this regard: I wanted to control time. Andy let time come to him. I was pushed and was pushing to get things done on time. Andy read time, as in paying attention to the *coyuntura*, the meaning of the moment. He commented as much to me. "You know the difference between you guys up north and us guys down south," he once said with his big chuckle and East Coast English accent. "You have the watches, but we have the time."

It was not just that I saw time as a commodity. I saw the flow of time as moving forward, toward a future goal that I could somehow control if enough skill and planning could be brought to bear. The present was an urgent fleeting moment that somehow must be taken advantage of and shaped. Andy saw himself in an expansive present in which he moved toward much that was unknown, little of which could be controlled directly. What he knew were the patterns of the past and the potentialities of the expansive moment.

In 1989 I made my first trip to the Philippines. It was an exchange of experiences. With some members of the Nicaraguan Conciliation Team we traveled and shared stories with indigenous peoples of northern Luzon, who were embroiled in their own set of internal conflicts. We observed and listened to the intriguing intertribal and indigenous dominant-culture processes in that setting. Some of the tribal elders were *budong*, peace-pact holders. They held the peace between groups that had a history of fighting. The holder held the peace not for his own tribe, but was responsible for assuring the well-being of the other tribe.

Time and again, discussions emerged around a term that I have heard in other settings but which most prominently sticks in my mind from the Philippines: ancestral domain. I remember one of the first times (in the 1980s) it was explained to me by an indigenous elder in Luzon. "Some believe that ancestral domain is essentially a term that refers to land fights, you know, where indigenous people claim historical rights to a piece of land when outside groups want the land, or the minerals, forests, or water. I suppose that is true," he commented. "But for us, ancestral domain is not about the land as if it were a legal question of title. For us, this place is where the ancestors live. Where they live is where we are people. That is why we say *ancestral domain*. It is the domain of our ancestors, the place where we as a people go to join them." He paused and then finished: "You take away our place, you take away our past. You take our past, and we cease to be. That is what people do not understand."

In the summer of 1990 I found myself in a longhouse community meeting in Kahnawake, one of the few remaining land bases of the Mohawk Nation. It was a gathering of elders, clan mothers, and chiefs. The context was again urgent and anxious. A land dispute near the city of Oka had sprouted armed barricades on the outskirts of Montreal. Each passing hour and day felt as if an imminent and violent disaster would explode.

In the meetings, different viewpoints were expressed about whether and how to negotiate the standoff. At one point in the conversation, when someone highlighted the dire urgency of the situation, the simple words of an elder reminded everyone of Mohawk time. "Decisions made seven generations ago affect us yet today," he said, "and decisions we make today will affect the next seven generations." It was the first time I had heard this used in a context of urgent crisis negotiation. "Fourteen generations," I thought to myself. "How do people think, much less negotiate, in a context of fourteen generations?"

A month later, direct, face-to-face negotiations opened for a few short days in Montreal between the Mohawk Nation and the Quebec and Canadian government officials, lawyers to be more accurate. The government officials noted early and often that the only question on the negotiation table at the time was when and how the barricades of the Mohawk would be dismantled in the next days. The Mohawk spokespersons framed their concerns and proposals with the phrase "from time immemorial . . ." Their negotiations on the crisis began at a place before memory.

The face-to-face negotiations collapsed within a week. I have come to believe, all else aside, that it is possible to explain the failure of those negotiations purely from the standpoint of time. For the Mohawk, the past was alive. It accompanied every step of their journey. The very nature of who they were in that crisis and how they were in relationship with other peoples and nations arose from a historical context that was alive in their physical and social geography. Most important, the past was alive in the responsibility they felt for the well-being of the lands and the lives of their great-grandchildren. For the Mohawk, it was as if the negotiation table were an expansive space of time that connected the voices of a distant but very much alive past with a distant but very much present future. The active present was fourteen generations.

For the governments' representatives, the relationships at the negotiation table were defined by the nature of the immediate issues. If history were relevant for negotiations, it was the history of recent events and their potential impact on political futures. Political futures are, at best, the immediate polls of popularity and the upcoming timeframe of elections. The past was irrelevant as a useful frame of reference for responding to a crisis. The entire time span of the present was, for all practical purposes, several years at most.

For one group, the past lay before them. For the other, pragmatic politics forced a short view of recent events, demanding immediate decisions in order to secure political stability in an equally short-term future. One could argue that negotiations failed in the Oka crisis when no common or mutually meaningful conjugation of relationship and time could be found. From the eyes of officialdom, it was pragmatic politics and the control of time that carried the day, described as dismantling the barricades without loss of life. For the Mohawk, ancestral domain is alive and well in relationships between indigenous people and the dominant culture, evident in the post-Oka Canadian context where land transfers from the federal government to aboriginal peoples have gained a new prominence and saliency. The past, it would appear, still lies before us.

I recall quite well my first visit to Belfast in the early 1990s. Accompanied at various times by Joe Campbell and Brendan McAllister, I toured the different neighborhoods of the city between our meetings. Murals stood out, supporting heroes and denigrating enemies, which from one street to the next would switch perspective. One mural stuck in my mind. It contained a quote from Irish Nationalist Padraig Pearse: "The fools the fools, they have left our Fenian dead. While Ireland holds these graves, Ireland unfree shall never be at peace." From that day forward I kept noticing how the "graves" of one group or another were not a bygone static entity. The past was alive, in fact, literally circulating in the streets each year in the parading season when violence would erupt around who had the right to remember what date in history, in which way, and on whose geography. I was surprised to discover that ancestral domain was walking and talking in the streets of Belfast.

When the ceasefires were first declared in Northern Ireland, we had a series of visits inside the Maze prison. The Maze was the prison for politically motivated prisoners who had committed violence during the thirty-year Troubles. Moving around the H-blocks in the course of a day we would meet with representatives of the various paramilitary groups who controlled the corridors they now inhabited. Thinking that the ceasefires were signs of movement forward, we were struck time and again with the deep concern expressed that this "peace" could not, in fact, represent significant or trustworthy change. It was as if the seasoned voices of the past were leading the discussion. Following a conversation with a commander in one of the cells, I jotted a few lines in my journal that over the years became this poem:

> Inside the Maze
> "My fear of peace?" he responds.
>
> We sit hunched under bunks.
> Men with tattoos bring us tea,
> Roll cigarettes,
> And watch even our breathing.
>
> "That at the end of the day,"
> he says to us twice,
> "I'll be back in this prison visit'n'
> me children's children."

So powerful and alive was the past that it occupied his grandchildren's future.

Then Came Naivasha

Naivasha is located partway up the Rift Valley, several hours' drive from Nairobi. For a few days in March 2001, a small group of people met from the National Council of Churches of Kenya (NCCK) and the Nairobi Peace Initiative, Africa (NPI-Africa). It was the culmination of several years of effort that had looked at how organizations working in peacebuilding in places like the ethnic clash regions of the Rift Valley can monitor and evaluate their peace work. Our process had started two years earlier, dating back to a period of earlier external evaluation, when the NCCK and NPI-Africa had taken up the challenge of more proactively developing a framework for evaluation for the purposes of learning and planning (Nairobi Peace Initiative, Africa, 2002).

The meeting was filled with interesting reports of activities, the evolution of evaluation models and experiments, a range of visual doodles, and an ongoing struggle to come to grips with the topic. Suffice it to say, it was never boring nor were we ever far from that creative space that connects lived frustration with new insight. Harold Miller, a steering committee member of NPI-Africa, long-time Africanist, and vocational philosopher, began our morning mediation with the famous words of Apostle John: "In the beginning was the Word." Harold then launched us deep into reflection about African perceptions of time based on the work of philosopher John Mbiti (1969). Harold lifted out the intriguing view of Mbiti that in Africa time moves from the present toward the past and that collective memory is accessible through the wisdom of the elders (Nairobi Peace Initiative, Africa, 2002). Such a view contrasts with much of how Western planning and evaluation of any social endeavor are conducted. This was the subject with which we were struggling with regarding peacebuilding in Africa. Planning and evaluation take for granted that time is forward-moving: We conduct a particular set of activities now in order to create a certain set of outcomes in the future.

Following a rather animated discussion of these multiple time realities, one participant, Jebuwot Sumbeiywo, shared a linguistic insight accompanied by a graphic body movement. She noted that for years she had wondered about the language used by her parents and grandparents when it came to talking about time. JB reported that in her native Kalenjin:

> [People say,] the past that lies before me and the future that lies be-
> hind me. They point ahead of them when they talk about the past.
> They point back when they refer to the future. I always thought
> there was something wrong with the language because once I

started in school and studied in English I learned that the future lies before us and the past is behind us.

JB then stood up to explain a new insight. "This morning I understand that what we know, what we have seen, is the past. So it lies before us. What we cannot see, what we cannot know is the future." Then she began to walk backward. "So the past we see before us. But we walk backward into the future. Maybe my grandparents' way of saying it is more accurate."

Accurate indeed! What JB had described, linguistically and with her walking motion, was very close to Mbiti's argument. When John Mbiti first released his book *African Religions and Philosophy*, in 1969, he was hailed for his originality though he was critiqued for some provocative statements. It was among the first African-based explanations of world view, religion, and philosophy that directly took on much of what had been up to that point Western-based anthropology, which was filled with subtle ethnocentrism if not overt racism.

In reference to time, Mbiti proposed that African languages and ceremonies reflected a movement that was paradoxical by its very conception. People saw their lives in a series of simultaneous dimensions. The living was the world of everyday life. When people physically died, they entered the world of the "living-dead." Ceremonies and conversation kept memory of those people alive. Mbiti commented that as long as they are remembered they stay in the sphere of the living-dead and can shape and influence the events of everyday life. This is the presence of ancestors, who are remembered, appealed to, conversed with on a range of matters. The past is not dead. It is alive and present. Wisdom and a sense of deep identity are carried as the accumulated understanding held by the elders of the group, who function nearly as a walking and talking library and who have the longest capacity of memory, putting them in touch with the widest range of ancestors. The term used in our Naivasha discussion was *wazee hukumbuka*, Swahili for "old people remember." Memory is a collective act by which people and the past are kept alive, present among us. When memory stops, when the last person who remembers the departed physically dies, the departed then passes from the living-dead to the sphere of the dead.

Herein lies the paradox: The journey of life moves toward physical death, which is a future event. Yet when people die and pass into the sphere of the living-dead, they join the ancestors in the past. As such, the journey is toward a past that lies before us, just as Jebuwot had indicated from her maternal language in our seminar. The past and future are not seen as dualistic, polar opposites. They are connected, like ends of a circle that meet and become seamless.

The critique of Mbiti seemed to emerge around the metaphors of time, which may be interpreted to suggest that Africans have, at best, a vague concept of the future and an orientation toward the past. Some, both from within and outside Africa, seemed to take Mbiti's time description as suggesting that such an orientation would make Africans backward, unenlightened, and doomed to not make "progress." A careful reading of Mbiti, however, suggests this could hardly be further from his intent or actual description. "Backward" conjures up a pejorative metaphor if "forward" notions of time are only those of Eurocentric enlightenment, rational thought, or capital-based industrialization indicating "progress." Mbiti's concern was, in fact, to debunk the notion that Africa as determined by others' standards of progress was "backward." He was describing an understanding of space and time as multidimensional spheres, polychronistic in quality rather than exclusively linear, and based on a deep understanding of human place within creation, which—ironically—by the latter half of the twentieth century became the cutting edge of scientific developments in physics, biology, ecology, and the social sciences. At the time of his writing Mbiti was receiving inquiries from scientists intrigued by "your description of the African concept of time which seems to accord much more with the modern physicist's views of 'spacetime' than does our usual notion" (Mbiti, 1969:27).

Mbiti proposed that ancestors and the living-dead were not just the artifacts of traditionalism or the backwardness of native peoples, nor were they a kind of unenlightened mystical worship requiring cleansing by modern religious insight and orthodoxy. On the contrary, ancestors were embedded in a world view of time whose only apparent difficulty was that it flew in the face of the dominant Western cultural world view of the proper interpretation of reality. Contrary to the practice and beliefs of the postindustrial West, with its emphasis on progress and the scientific and technical management of human affairs, in the African view, time does not flow forward. Time moves backward toward those who have come before us. But that does not mean Africans are backward. Just the inverse is true: They more properly see their place in the worlds they inhabit, and they have retained a keen sense of their journey toward the past that lies before them.

Such discussions of traditional, indigenous, and African views may strike the reader coming from dominant modern faith perspectives as odd or even antithetical to the common Western religious understandings. Surprisingly, I found the opposite to be true for my own faith journey. With the lens of the past that lies before us, the reading of New Testament writers takes on a whole new perspective. Less congruent with the sacred text are the modern notions of time, control, and future destiny. Far more congruent are the simple understandings of multidimensionality, a past that is alive and guides, and a future of hope that journeys toward those who have gone before us, ancestors who give us light. Consider under these lenses the Letter to the Hebrews in which the author writes, "Faith is the assurance of things hoped for, the conviction of things not seen. Indeed, by faith our ancestors received approval. By faith we understand the worlds were prepared by the Word of God, so that what is seen was made from things that are not visible" (Hebrews 11:1–3). The author then goes on to list the ancestors, who by all accounts, given the active memory of them, are among the living-dead, who form "a great cloud of witnesses that surround us," and to whom we turn for guidance and example.

In Naivasha, a brief and dynamic conversation suddenly linked up a series of insights I had heard, mostly from indigenous people, about the nature of time. The Miskito conciliator, the Mohawk elder, the Budong peace-pact holder describing ancestral domain—all came together. My peacebuilding framework and much of what is conceptualized as professional process management in the conflict resolution field at large had a gap: We have not developed a deep capacity to imagine the past that lies before us. And it made sense. The past was alive and kept showing up on the doorsteps of constructive social change. A new kind of imagination was required, one that was, so to say, as old as the hills.

Time and Peacebuilding

The stories and experiences with time, like little windows into the complexity of multiple worlds, have floated around my work and occasionally into my writing over the past twenty years. But they never made their way directly into the conceptual framework proposed in *Building Peace*. The thrust of that book was defined by a forward-looking understanding of time found principally in an "integrated framework for peacebuilding" (Lederach, 1997:80).

Briefly, the integrated framework created a matrix that combined a horizontal time axis with a vertical axis of levels of conflict based on the excellent work of Maire Dugan (1996). In my earlier book, I proposed that within the broader peace studies and conflict resolution fields, separate communities of analysis and action had emerged that could be found on this matrix. My ultimate purpose was to suggest that a transformative approach to constructive change would require a much greater integration of these efforts rather than the current state of competitiveness and isolation of schools of thought and practice that seemed to dominate the field. The central question raised seemed logical and simple enough: How do we move from the current patterns of crises to desired and more constructive relationships in the future? The answer, I proposed, would require attention not just to proposed substantive solutions, but to the need for the strategic design of change processes at different levels with different sets of people. The framework therefore required a capacity to understand the patterns of the present, imagine a desired future, and design change processes. I would often draw this as a circle that linked the present (where we are now), the longer-term future (where we hope to go), and the emerging future (the range of change processes needed to make that journey). The framework proposed a capacity to imagine the future. It did not explore

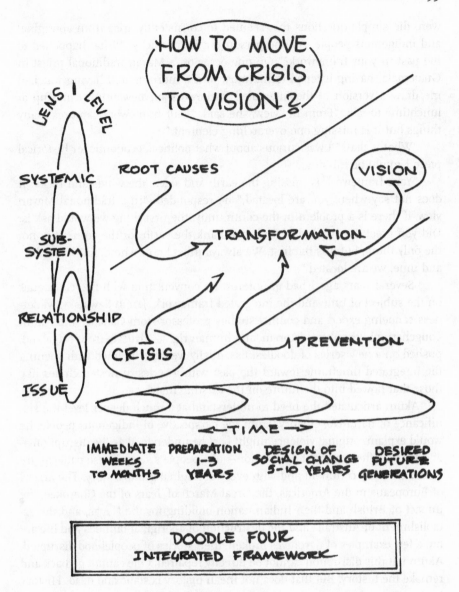

HOW TO MOVE FROM CRISIS TO VISION?

LENS / LEVEL

SYSTEMIC

SUB-SYSTEM

RELATIONSHIP

ISSUE

ROOT CAUSES

TRANSFORMATION

CRISIS

PREVENTION

VISION

← TIME →

| IMMEDIATE WEEKS TO MONTHS | PREPARATION 1-3 YEARS | DESIGN OF SOCIAL CHANGE 5-10 YEARS | DESIRED FUTURE GENERATIONS |

DOODLE FOUR
INTEGRATED FRAMEWORK

what capacity might be needed to imagine a past that was alive and accompanying us at every step of the way.

There is much that is useful and holds great promise in the integrated framework for building constructive change that I suggested in 1997. But there is always much to be discovered, which happened for me through classroom and training sessions. Over the years, as I would present the integrated framework, I received feedback from participants. The most daunting and insightful were the simple questions that seemed to consistently arise from aboriginal and indigenous people. As one person put it succinctly: "What happened to the past in your framework?" On one occasion a Mayan traditional priest in Guatemala, having listened to me most of the morning and having watched me draw a version of the integrated framework on newsprint, came up at lunchtime to talk. "From my view," he said, "your framework captures many things but it is missing one overarching element."

"What is that?" I was curious about what political, economic, or historical piece I might be missing.

"Your framework is missing the earth and skies, the winds and rocks. It does not say where you are located," he responded. "In a traditional Mayan view, if there is a problem in the community, the first thing we would ask is: Did you greet the sun today? Did you thank the earth for the corn? It is not the only thing, but it is the first. We always must know where, [in] what place and time, we are located."

Several years ago I had an interesting conversation with two colleagues on the subject of time and the integrated framework. Jarem Sawatsky, wilderness canoeing expert and conflict studies professor from Canada, and Aküm Longchari, philosopher, historian, and human rights advocate from Nagaland, pushed on a new series of doodles. Essentially we experimented with opening the integrated timeframe toward the past with a series of nested circles like those that flowed into the future on the existing matrix.

Aküm articulated the need to understand at a much deeper level the significance of narrative, of story. From the perspective of indigenous people, he would explain, original violence might best be understood as the disruption—and far too often, outright destruction—of a people's story. These patterns are found on every continent and with every aboriginal group's story. The arrival of Europeans in the Americas, the Great March of Tears of the Cherokee, the impact of British and then Indian nation-building for the Nagas, and the establishment of Australia and the destruction of aboriginal families and life are but a few examples of narratives broken, their stories of peoplehood disrupted. Aküm felt this disruption cannot be directly repaired. One cannot go back and remake the history. But that does not mean history is static and dead. History is alive. It needs recognition and attention. The challenge, Aküm would often express, lies in how, in the present, interdependent peoples "restory," that is, begin the process of providing space for the story to take its place and begin the weaving of a legitimate and community-determined place among others' stories. Aküm essentially was pushing for a long view of a living history. Narrative has the capacity to create, even heal, but it has had its voice taken. A return to giving narrative a place and a voice was needed.

Jarem's notion was that one could identify specific ways to understand past-oriented lenses by exploring several other fields, including narrative theology and indigenous world views. He began to experiment with how the field itself has endeavored to take this up, though we had not located this within an expansive understanding of time connected to social change (Sawatsky, 2003). Our ideas converged and an initial matrix expanded toward the past settled on four nested circles, drawing rough symmetry with those that run toward an imagined future.

The diagram suggests a set of embedded circles that flow toward the past as a way of exploring a more holistic understanding of the settings of cycles of violent conflict. This starts with a circle that includes recent volatile events, to which people from the setting often refer as they explain why the current situation is so explosive. This circle of recent events lifts out the most visible expressions of the political, military, social, or economic conflicts. It is rarely a timeframe that goes beyond months or a year or two.

The recent events circle then phases into a wider sphere, which we are calling "lived history." The idea of lived history tries to capture a more expansive view of time, which will vary from younger to older people. My lived history is what I have experienced directly in my lifetime, which is more expansive than my children's but much less so than my grandparents'. The key here is that these are not experiences that were conveyed to me by others, but a history I have seen, touched, and tasted. Intriguingly, a local or national community has within it multiple ranges of lived history. The older people have experienced events that go back across decades, the youngest less than a decade. Thus, a circle of lived history for a community can run from one to about eight, maybe nine, decades.

Critical for settings of protracted conflict is the understanding that people's

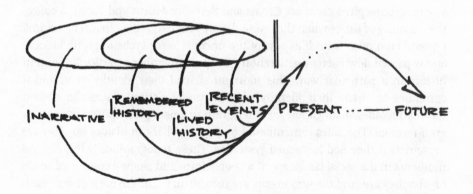

DOODLE FIVE
THE PAST THAT LIES BEFORE US

stories in this lived history timeframe are experiences that have flesh and blood attached to them, and more often than not, they are experiences that have repeated themselves into the next generation. It is not just that my grandmother told me about those people from the next village over who have harmed us. I have experienced it myself. Lived experiences create, recreate, and reinforce the story of our collective life, which is embedded in the patterns that accompany our community.

A third, wider circle of time pushes us to enter what we might call the context of memory, or "remembered history." This is history kept alive and present by what is remembered from a group's topographic map of time. In mapmaking, topography shows the contours, heights, and depths of landscapes. In a similar way, applied to protracted conflict, there exists a kind of landscape of social memory that is kept alive. In the group's view of its history, certain events stand out, that is, they rise to a level of heightened recognition. These events shape and form the collective identity. These points in history are often the moments, exactly as Aküm suggested, when the story of who people are, their self-understanding, was transformed in unexpected ways, disrupted, or even destroyed. Recently this understanding has been explored in the conflict literature, particularly from the discipline of psychology, as remembered events that create a "chosen trauma."

While the term *chosen trauma* has bounced around counseling and therapy circles, theorists and practitioners Joseph Montville and Vamik Volkan have applied the concept to international relations and in particular to settings of deep-rooted conflict (Volkan and Montville, 1991; Volkan, 1999). Simply put, a group's identity is linked in large part to what its members remember and keep alive. In settings of protracted conflict the mixed history of violence among groups gives each, say Croats and Serbs, or Hutus and Tutsis, a collective memory of times when they were deeply violated by the other. The trauma remembered renews itself as part of the unconscious psyche of group identity and is passed down across generations. People remember a particular point in history in a particular way. This moment shaped their identity then, and it continues to shape their identity now. In many circumstances the chosen trauma provides justification for intergroup defense, preemptive violence, or even revenge. The dates remembered may go way back in history but they are present as if they had happened yesterday. These topographically highlighted moments in the social landscape of a people form and shape a continued sense of who they are, and the very events are reconstructed in the present with each new encounter, or as the case too often may be, with each cycle of renewed violence at the hands of the other. The chosen trauma forms the context of memory.

Finally, the deepest history, all the way to time immemorial, is the "narrative." Narrative creates the formative story of who we are as a people and a place. These are, according to many of the authors who have written from the perspective of narrative, the understandings of how people come to see their place on this earth, in a figurative sense and their place as tied to a specific geography, in a literal sense. Narrative, the deep, formative telling of one's story, has increasingly found its way across academic disciplines and their respective practices. There are approaches and even schools of narrative psychology and therapy (Freedman and Combs, 1996; Monk et al., 1997; Crossley, 2000), narrative theology (Hauerwas and Jones, 1997; Stroup, 1997; Goldberg, 2001), narrative analysis of political science (Roe, 1994; Almond, 2002), and narrative methodologies in the social sciences (Polkinghorne, 1988; Riessman, 1993; Lieblick. Tuval-Mashiach, and Zilber 1998), to mention but a few. More recently, these approaches have been explored in application to specific professions within the field of conflict resolution, most notably by Winslade and Monk (2001), who applied the narrative lens to the mediation of social conflict.

For our purposes, this circle titled "narrative" suggests lenses that explore the interpretation and understanding of meaning in an expanded view of time and the development of group identity over generations tracing to the stories of origin, which are the approaches that are closest to this deeper reach into history. In other words, beyond a particular methodology of scientific inquiry or the practice of personal therapy, the use of narrative that we wish to explore is one which involves the formative stories of genesis and place (Hauerwas and Jones, 1997). If we take such a long view of identity and group formation seriously, we shall come to recognize that the formation of group identity arising from the past, the construction of its future, and its very survival are about finding place, voice, and story.

When we connect these nested spheres that explore the past into the integrated framework, we can begin to explore the challenges posed by a range of activities that are increasingly practiced in the field of peacebuilding. Doodle 6 suggests that we can locate these activities by connecting our spheres of memory to the levels of conflict.

The rise and evolution of truth commissions and war crime tribunals, for example, are efforts to create a public and systemwide accountability for crimes and atrocities committed within the period of recent violence. These are social, political, and legal initiatives that attempt to bring into the public sphere a collective acknowledgment of what happened, who suffered, who was responsible, and how they are accountable. As those who have studied these phenomena indicate, we are still in what might be called exploratory and experimental efforts to create adequate public truth and accountability, but we are increasingly aware at social and political levels that such efforts must be pursued (Hayner, 2001). Public acknowledgment, we could argue, is the sine qua non of finding place, voice, and story for the communities affected.

In the bottom quadrant of the doodle, we locate initiatives of restorative justice, which are alternatives to the formality of Western notions of jurisprudence and include approaches like victim-offender reconciliation programs or

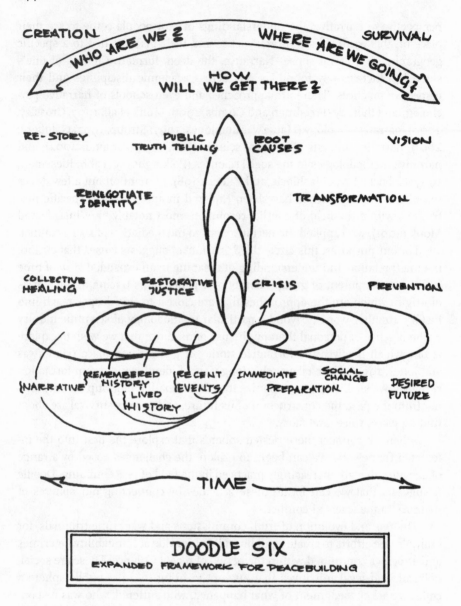

CREATION   WHO ARE WE?   WHERE ARE WE GOING?   SURVIVAL

HOW
WILL WE GET THERE?

RE-STORY   PUBLIC
TRUTH TELLING   ROOT
CAUSES   VISION

RENEGOTIATE
IDENTITY   TRANSFORMATION

COLLECTIVE
HEALING   RESTORATIVE
JUSTICE   CRISIS   PREVENTION

NARRATIVE   REMEMBERED
HISTORY   RECENT
EVENTS   IMMEDIATE   SOCIAL
CHANGE   DESIRED
FUTURE
LIVED
HISTORY   PREPARATION

TIME

DOODLE SIX
EXPANDED FRAMEWORK FOR PEACEBUILDING

community circles (Zehr, 2002). These are efforts to explore the impact of broken relationships in the context of specific interpersonal and community relationships. For many, these models may appear to be micro-oriented in application, but therein lies their genius. The impetus that drives restorative approaches is not one that awaits the policy and decision from the highest level, nor does it assume that its particular action provides a comprehensive response to systemwide problems. Rather these efforts paint a different canvas of social change, which depends on the practices of accessibility, reconnecting people in actual relationships, and local responsibility. These practices assume that the capacity of people to heal and "restory" their identities and relationships requires more than the rule of law expressed as a remote bureaucratic concern. Healing requires proximity that touches the web of community life, which includes both the recent events and the lived histories of a community. The locus of the initiative is therefore placed in the context of actual relationships and community (Zehr, 2002).

The center block, which in the wider integrated framework connects a subsystem level of analysis with the historical timeframe we call "remembered history," requires exploration of how chosen traumas involving whole communities and ethnic and religious identities emerge and are sustained. Jarem Sawatsky (2003) suggested that such an exploration requires more than personal healing. As he put it, addressing generational trauma must "renegotiate history and identity." Deeper collective group trauma goes beyond counseling or dealing with a form of post-traumatic stress syndrome. While involving individuals, this arena of trauma healing must be understood and developed in collective and communal forms. Recent efforts of Strategies of Trauma Awareness and Recovery (STAR), jointly sponsored with the World Council of Churches U.S. and the Conflict Transformation Program at Eastern Mennonite University, provide a useful illustration. The programmatic initiative began as a response to the trauma felt by caregivers of all faith traditions living in close proximity to the events of September 11, 2001. Rather than focus on the provision of direct trauma healing, efforts were made to support caregivers in their context, connecting the trauma produced by that particular event and timeframe to the larger context of a framework for justice and peacebuilding. The program has linked people in local settings in the United States with counterparts struggling to work with systemic trauma in other parts of the world, including Colombia, Northern Ireland, the Balkans, and East and West Africa. Their effort explores not only the implications and challenges of healing at the level of individuals affected, but also how responses to trauma and healing can be conceptualized as wider social processes. This is exactly what is meant by "renegotiating history and identity," for it attends to the ways that historic trauma connected with specific violent events forms and shapes the identity of individuals and of whole communities, and how those events can be channeled toward constructive engagement that responds to individual needs but seeks to shape the wider public and even national ethos.

At the far edges of the integrated framework as it explores the past, we find memory captured in the more expanded notion of narrative. In the event-driven field of international mediation this is not an easy sphere of activity to conceptualize. For many, it feels too remote and distant. The key that opens greater understanding may well be found with careful attention to the world views of indigenous peoples. The Budong peace-pact holder in northern Luzon commented that losing a geographic place meant losing the past, and if the past is lost, "we cease to be." The world view of indigenous peoples suggests that story, place, and identity are linked. They understand that collective narrative and survival are connected. In other words, "time" is not a commodity found in a linear sequence where the remote past and remote future are separated at the extreme ends. Time is best understood, as was written by the physicist to Mbiti, as spacetime. And spacetime is a circle. As the indigenous world view suggests, social meaning, identity, and story are linked through narrative, which connects the remote past of *who* we are with the remote future of *how* we will survive in the context of an expansive present *where* we share space and relationship. The space of narrative, the act linking the past with the future to create meaning in the present, is a continuous process of restorying. In Mbiti's notion of spacetime this was the place and role of accumulated wisdom, the *wazee hukumbuka*, memory of the old ones.

One way to understand cycles of violence and protracted conflict is to visualize them as a narrative broken. A people's story is marginalized or, worse, destroyed by the dominant culture, and by this act, meaning, identity, and a place in history are lost. This is the deeper challenge of peacebuilding: How to reconstitute, or restory, the narrative and thereby restore the people's place in history. For many of us who come from outside the settings of protracted violence or are from cultures that have not had their stories destroyed, we have perhaps a hard time understanding this notion of peacebuilding as narrative restored. In the United States, one of the most poignant examples of this kind of imaginative narrative is found in the work of Randall Robinson (2000) and the exploration of accountability for the centuries of slavery and systemic racism suffered by the African-American community. Strong reactions are often expressed in response to his and others' calls for reparation. Common is a reaction that says, "What happened was wrong, but it took place centuries ago, with many different people who were responsible for the atrocity then. How can we today possibly be responsible for what happened so long ago?" What we can observe in this reaction is how "time" comes to be defined by individualistic understandings of responsibility embedded in an extraordinarily narrow world view of our place in both cosmos and chronos. Contemporary Western ethos has little or no imagination of location in a wider, polychronic spacetime. Yet, deep narratives in settings of protracted conflict beg for this to be repaired.

The professions of conflict resolution and peacebuilding are equally spacetime challenged. We have no real tradition of frameworks that address the deepest questions of collective story, identity, and place nor an expansive view of time. Our modus operandi drives us toward problem analysis and problem solving. Narrative is useful to our approach when it involves the establishing of what happened in order to gain a sense of the issues and the horizon that generates solutions. When deep narrative raises its head, we listen for a time, sympathize, and do a "reality check" defined by the parameters of what is possible according to the pragmatics of the existing dominant story. We have rarely engaged ourselves in the deeper search, which requires an imagination that explores narrative as long history, the location of whole peoples' place in local, national, and global history and as part and parcel of collective healing and the building of justice.

When deep narrative is broken, the journey toward the past that lies before us is marginalized, truncated. We lose more than just the thoughts of a few old people. We lose our bearings. We lose the capacity to find our place in this world. And we lose the capacity to find our way back to humanity.

This notion of spacetime, found most clearly among indigenous peoples, is in many regards the heart of the moral imagination for it requires that we recognize and build imaginative narrative that has the capacity to link the past and the future rather than force a false choice between them. The art and soul of such a linkage goes beyond the more instrumentalist view of "storytelling" as a stage of problem solving in mediation. By *instrumentalist* I mean the opening of a small space for people to recount what happened in the recent events of conflict from their view in order to establish the parameters of negotiation so that a solution can be found to the immediate problems. Restorying as imaginative narrative looks for the deeper social story and meaning, not just of what happened, but how stories are connected to a far more profound journey of discovering what these events mean for who we are as both local and global communities.

We have among us those who engage such journeys, though we don't often afford them their due place as peacebuilders: the storytellers, the traditional sages, the shamans, the healers. David Abram (1996:6) called them the magicians whose intelligence "is not encompassed *within* the society; its place is at the edge of community, mediating *between* the human community and the larger community of beings upon which the village depends for its nourishment and sustenance." Ten years later, the Mayan priest's observation about the gap in my framework makes much greater sense: Peacebuilding requires respect for the center and the edges of time and space, where the deep past and the horizon of our future are sewn together, creating a circle of time. The circle of time, constantly in motion, moves around our biggest inquiries: Who are we? Where do we belong? Where are we going? How will we journey together? The capacity to hear and then constructively engage this level of inquiry is the art and soul that makes up the moral imagination.

Conclusion

If the above discussion suggests anything for our professional fields, it proposes that the moral imagination requires us to develop the art of living in multiple time and space spheres. Even in the moments of greatest crisis, when the urgency of the situation seems to hinge on quick short-term decisions, multidimensionality is present. Thus we need the imagination of the past that lies before us. This kind of imagination does not see the past as something to be laid aside, overcome, or forgotten in order to move into a better future. It does not engage the past by relentlessly revisiting bygone events so as to purge and release them, as if the past were a beast that needed taming or defeat. Nor does it see the past as a magical formula that somehow miraculously solves the problems of today. The imagination of which I speak is the capacity, to use Aküm's word, to restory, to find the narrative that gives meaning to life and ongoing relationships.

In her monumental writing, Hannah Arendt chose much of this pathway as she reflected on the nature of the human condition and healing in the aftermath of World War II (Arendt, 1998). Paraphrased broadly, her insight was this: We live in a certain paradox as human beings precisely because we are beings that live by the meaning things have for us. Our God-given place is this. We have the capacity to remember the past, but we have no capacity to change it. Not even God can change the past. We have the capacity to imagine a different future, but we have no capacity to fully predict much less control it. Try as we might, nobody controls the future. The web of life is juxtaposed between these realities of time, between memory and potentiality. This is the place of narrative, the art of restorying.

In practical terms, if one can speak of "practical" when entering the realm of something so fundamentally nebulous as time and space, narrative expands the basis of how we envision the moral imagination as part of our work. It requires an imagination that must more fully be aware of and embrace the multidimensionality of time rather than reduce it to its narrowest configuration. What does this suggest for our inquiry?

First, the four disciplines are readily apparent in our discussion of the past that lies before us. A capacity to imagine relationship necessarily sees the past as alive, as part and parcel of how people, communities, and their futures evolve. It watches and listens for the deep questions of narrative often present but hidden from the eyes of pragmatic politics and quick solutions, which occupy so much space in the symptomatic discussions of immediate problems. The art of imagining the past will, without fear of entering unpredictable territory or fear of recrimination, develop a curiosity about the patterns, the cycles, and the story that repeats itself. Knowing that the past is a generative energy, it will seek to find and engage where the narrative has been broken. The moral imagination will see itself in relationship with this energy.

The refusal to frame process and change as dualistic choices is precisely the unique characteristic of finding the seamless connection between the past and the future. If we take seriously the insight of traditional wisdom, and I believe we should, it suggests that collective memory and survival are linked.

The repetitive, too often destructive, and violent energy that explodes around immediate crises in settings of protracted conflicts attests to the idea that much is at stake for those involved. It is not a matter of talking them into rationality, bringing them to pragmatic solutions, or finding a way to let go of the past that they hold dear. Our challenge is to engage the source that generates the energy while creating processes that move it toward constructive expression and interaction. This requires that we hold together the past and the future, not as separate entities or as separate phases on a linear chart of change.

This is the challenge of restorying: It continuously requires a creative act. To restory is not to repeat the past, attempt to recreate it exactly as it was, nor act as if it did not exist. It does not ignore the generational future nor does it position itself to control it. Embracing the paradox of relationship in the present, the capacity to restory imagines both the past and the future and provides space for the narrative voice to create. As such, the art of imaging the past that lies before us holds close the deep belief that the creative act is possible.

To live between memory and potentiality is to live permanently in a creative space, pregnant with the unexpected. But it is also to live in the permanency of risk, for the journey between what lies behind and what lies ahead is never fully comprehended nor ever controlled. Such a space, however, is the womb of constructive change, the continuous birthplace of the past that lies before us.

13

On Pied Pipers

Imagination and Creativity

Everywhere I go I find a poet has been there before me.
                                        —Sigmund Freud

"Bring me a musician," the Prophet Elisha called. And while the
musician played, the power of the Lord came on him.
                                        —2 Kings 3:15

As a young child I remember hearing the fairy tale of the Pied
Piper.[1] A town was beset with a great rat infestation and had no
hope on the horizon that it would change soon. Experts and advisors
came and went but nobody could move the rats. Then a stranger
showed up and promised, for a considerable sum of money, to clean
the town of this life-destroying problem. The mayor agreed. The following day the stranger turned out to be a piper, a flutist of sorts,
and lifting the pipe to his lips, he played a melody that floated out
across the streets. The rats began to move, drawn to the music.
More and more rats gathered, following the sounds of the music.
He led them out of town and straight into a river where the rats
drowned. Back in town, celebrations were breaking out everywhere.
The piper, pleased with his work, approached the mayor for his due
compensation. With the problem now gone the mayor hemmed,
hawed, feigned financial difficulties, and finally turned the piper
away without a single coin. Disgruntled, the piper returned the next
day to the streets and lifted his flute in melody again. This time, the
children came and then followed the piper out of town, leaving the
community without the joys of young voices or life for the future.

The moral of the story seemed clear: When you give a promise, you had best keep your word.

Four decades later, when I read the story again, this was not the moral that caught my attention. What I saw was the power of a flutist to move a town, address an evil, and bring the powerful to accountability. Without any visible power or even prestige, much less a violent weapon, a flutist transformed a whole community. I was struck with the nonviolent power of music and the creative act. The moral of the story now seemed to be: Watch out for the flutist and his creative music for, like the invisible wind, they touch and move all that they encounter in their path.

Artful Change

In 1996 I found myself sitting in the Killyhevlin Hotel in Fermanagh, Northern Ireland. I was a keynote speaker at a conference titled "Remember and Change," a phrase that had been pulled from a talk I had given in Belfast a year earlier (Lederach, 1995). In 1994, at the time of the ceasefire declarations by both republican and loyalist paramilitary groups, people engaged in conflict transformation and peacebuilding work had requested some reflections on what might beset them as they entered a post-accord phase of violent conflict. In that talk I suggested that reconciliation was not "forgive and forget." It was "remember and change." A year later I was in Enniskillen to address a conference. Delegates attended from peace and reconciliation partnerships across Northern Ireland, representing all sides of the conflict and a wide range of community, economic, and political interests, now trying to move toward a new horizon.

The Killyhevlin Hotel was the chosen site. It is located on the shore of Lough Erne, near Enniskillen. The venue was not without symbol and purpose. On a number of occasions, bombs had all but destroyed it. The conference was for the most part a series of talking heads like myself giving speeches and exchanging insights and ideas that were to translate into programs. The one exception was just following the lunch. The planners had decided to take a risk on what was considered a delicate addition. They had commissioned a troupe of dancers made up of young local Catholic and Protestant women to choreograph an expressive dance to music. The song chosen was Irish folk artist Paul Brady's "The Island." Behind the stage, there was a large screen. While the young women performed their dance, slides—pictures everyone knew and that captured the scenes of the thirty-two-year-old Troubles—would appear without comment.

The artistic process was not without its risks. Brady's song had first emerged a decade earlier, during the heat of the worst cycles of violence in the Irish conflict. "The Island" raised a question about the reasons for and logic of the violence and those who justified it on one side or another. Performed by a solo voice accompanied by a piano, the lyrics are profound, suggesting that violence is trying to "carve tomorrow from a tombstone" and is wasting our children's future "for the worn-out dreams of yesterday" (Brady, 1992).

When first played publicly, the song generated immediate controversy. Perceived as written by a well-known artist from one community criticizing people engaged in the violence, threats went out from the paramilitaries against the artist, radio stations that would play the music, and stores that would sell it. For years "The Island" was not played or circulated publicly.

In the early afternoon of the conference, I found myself seated between one of the highest standing officials of the police force in Northern Ireland and the mayor of the town, both fine and dedicated men, from different sides of the conflict, and both pleasant but also rather formal in demeanor, toughened, you might say, by the years of their experience and the nature of their positions. The song began and the dance troupe's graceful first steps brought hundreds in the audience to complete silence. The color slides of Belfast's troubled murals, children running from fire bombs, funeral processions, and parades riveted the eyes and captured the haunting feel of the music and lyrics juxtaposed against the ballet-like movements of these young women dancing together though from different sides of the violent divide. The whole of the Irish conflict was held in a public space, captured in a moment that lasted fewer than five minutes.

Near the end of the performance I suddenly noticed that the two men on either side of me were discreetly pulling handkerchiefs from pockets and wiping tears. Behind me I could hear and feel the same thing happening. One of the men leaned over and apologized to me, as if somehow it were a lack of professional etiquette to have displayed such emotion in public. The seminar proceeded. Speeches were given. Program initiatives were proposed and evaluated. It was a day in the process of a long, slow transformation. Looking back now, nearly a decade later, it would be interesting to know what people remember of that day. Without locating the specific documents I know that I cannot remember a single speech, proposal, or formal panel response. I do however remember, vividly, the image and feeling of those five minutes of combined music, lyrics, choreography, and photos. It created an echo in my head that has not gone away. It moved me.

In the larger picture of politics and social change many would say, "And so what? What difference does something like this artistic five minutes actually make?" I am not sure I can answer that question. On the other side of the coin I would ask a different but parallel question: How, when, and why did politics and developing responses to needed social change come to be seen as something separate from the whole of human experience? The artistic five minutes, I have found rather consistently, when it is given space and acknowledged as something far beyond entertainment, accomplishes what most of politics has

been unable to attain: It helps us return to our humanity, a transcendent journey that, like the moral imagination, can build a sense that we *are*, after all, a
human community.

In the Old Testament there was a time when the prophet Elisha was sum-
moned by two kings, Jehoram and Jehoshaphat. The two were surrounded by
enemy forces, were facing a drought, and were nearing the end of all their
resources. The prophet was to advise kings, which of course put him in a rather
tough position. Needing to sort through what response should be given, Elisha
cried, "Bring me a musician." A musician? This is the rough equivalent of
President Bush and Prime Minister Blair contemplating a world war and calling on the great religious leaders of our day for guidance, and their response
would be, "Bring us a musician." What does music have to do with the *real*
world? The biblical text records that while the musician played, the power of
the Lord came on the prophet. It also records that a great deal of bloodshed
took place the following day. Music, it seems, has the power to push things
either in the direction of greater violence or toward reconciliation. Is this yet
another isolated incident? Perhaps. I have anecdotal, not scientific evidence.[2]
But consider the anecdotes for a moment, from history remote and close.

Exhibit A. Through the research of Patricia Burdette (2003) I came across
a text written by Chief Leon Shenandoah in 1946. He describes how the process of creating the Great League of Nations—sometimes called the Iroquois
Confederacy—overcame one obstacle. The various chiefs of the nations had
agreed to the peace with one important exception: Onondaga chief Tadodaho
would not be persuaded. Led by an extraordinary woman, Jikonhsaseh, a del-
egation was formed to go and meet the resistant chief. Shenandoah (1946:12–
13) writes:

> They discovered him in a swamp—rough, dirty place. His ap-
> pearance, they said, was very frightening. Snakes were woven in his
> hair, and his body appeared crooked and misshapen, and everything
> about him was unpleasant to behold. The expression on his face let
> the people know he was unbearably cruel. They were singing a
> song, which was provided especially for this meeting. When he
> heard that song, Tadodaho at first felt threatened. But it was that
> song that turned him; and he melted when [he] heard that song. He
> agreed to listen to them. He had long been the worst human being
> in the world, so terrible that people had said, "The mind in that
> body is not the mind of a human being." And he was the last to
> reform, but they were able to comb the snakes from his hair and to
> transform his mind using songs and words to bring him health and
> peace. Jikonhsaseh had told them to use songs and words to trans-
> form his mind, and that he would be the leader—like the facilitator—
> of the Grand Council. That is the story of the remarkable leader of

the Haudenosaunee—the Six Nations. His title has been handed down from generation to generation, like the title of the Dalai Lama or Pope. I am Tadodaho today.

This can of course be taken as a quaint folk story passed down through the generations. Or it could be taken for what it is: the capacity of the oral tradition to remember and keep alive the identity of peoplehood and how it came to be. A brief reminder is in order not to lose our sense of historical context. The crafting of the Great Peace, the formation of the six-nation confederacy led by Chief Tadodaho, was a forerunner to and inspired the writing of the U.S. Constitution (Brown Childs, 2003). At a given moment in time the Indian people of the six nations called on the Pied Pipers of their day, who had the moral imagination to transcend the challenge of their patterns while addressing the concrete challenges of their enemy through "song and words" to become "sane human beings." One could argue that a song changed a person and transformed our globe.

Exhibit B. In the 1980s, 200 years later, the countries of Burkina Faso and Mali exploded into war over border issues. International mediation efforts failed on numerous occasions to stop the fighting. Then the president of neighboring Guinea, Ahmed Sekou Toure, persuaded his fellow presidents Thomas Sankara of Burkina Faso and Moussa Traore of Mali to attend a meeting at his palace. Samuel Doe and Emmanuel Bombande recount the unexpected events that followed:

> In front of the Presidential Palace in Conakry, one of West Africa's celebrated griots (praise singers), Kanja Kouyate, put on a spectacular performance before the host and visiting presidents.
>
> The performance took on the form of entertainment, but Kanja Kouyate was calling on the two presidents at war to make peace. He did this by evoking their ancestors and appealing to their inherent human goodness as leaders to lead their people out of conflict. Through poetry, song, and dance he brought out qualities that were a hallmark of a true African leader and challenged the two presidents to look to their ancestors and bring back dignity instead of shame and suffering to their peoples. So emotional was the performance that the two presidents not only shed tears and embraced publicly, but took a solemn oath before the public and witnessed by their ancestors not to return to war. (Doe and Bombande, 2002:164)

The story does not end there. In the next months, pushed by the presidents, a peace agreement was signed. It has not been violated since. It would seem that the peoples of Burkina Faso and Mali serendipitously received a visit from the Pied Piper.

Exhibit C. On May 27, 1992, in the center of Sarajevo, a bread shop opened for a few short hours. A long queue snaked from the door out into the streets as people waited, anxious though patient, for the staple that had become a scarce resource during the horrific siege of the city. On a hill miles away, snipers locked their sights down on the bread line. A shell exploded at the feet of the people waiting. As people scrambled to help the injured, the snipers began to shoot emergency workers and anyone who ventured near the explosion. Twenty-two people died. The bread store was in the neighborhood of Vedran Smailovic, an internationally renowned cellist who had refused to leave Sarajevo during the war. He rushed to the square that afternoon and passed a frightful night of anguish watching more of his neighbors die senselessly. He recounted:

> Filled with sorrow, I eventually fell asleep at dawn, and was awakened by new explosions and [the] shouts of my neighbors, who were carrying children and blankets to shelters. I went to the shelter myself and returned home after the shelling was over. I washed my face and hands, shaved, and without thinking, put on my white shirt, black evening suit and white bow tie, took my cello and left home.
>
> Looking at the new ruins, I arrived at the place of the massacre. It was adorned with flowers, wreaths and peace messages; there were posters on local shops saying who had been killed. On a nearby table was a solemn book of condolences, which people were signing. I opened my cello case and sat down, not knowing what I would play. Full of sadness and grief, I lifted my bow and spontaneously made music. (Smailovic, 1998)

When his spontaneous playing was done, Smailovic discovered that people had gathered to listen near the square. Around coffee late that evening close friends told him how meaningful it was and begged him to play again, that they felt better when he played. "I understood then," he wrote, "that Albinoni's Adagio is healing music, that music heals, and that this was no longer a purely personal issue." He decided to return to the Bread Massacre Square and play every day for twenty-two days in a row, one day for each person killed in the massacre. Shelling never ceased during those days, but neither did his music. He became a symbol of civilian resistance against the tyranny of hatred and violence.

On one occasion, during a lull in the shelling, a TV news reporter approached the cellist seated in the square and asked, "Aren't you crazy for playing music while they are shelling Sarajevo?" Smailovic responded, "Playing music is not crazy. Why don't you go ask those people if they are not crazy, shelling Sarajevo while I sit here playing my cello." The moral imagination that gave hope and the strength to resist, a creative act that transcended the madness of violence, was found in the hands of a cellist who sat fast in the midst of the geography of hate. Sarajevo, it seems, found the gift of the Pied Piper.

Exhibit D. The last major bomb that destroyed buildings and lives during the Troubles of Northern Ireland came several years after the ceasefire had been declared. On August 15, 1998, in the town of Omagh, the warnings about the bomb were misleading. As a result, instead of people being directed away from the threat, they were evacuated into the path of the bomb. The hidden device exploded. Twenty-nine people and two unborn children died. More than 400 were injured. The events in the community of Omagh sent waves of shock across the world. Many feared the Irish peace process would collapse. Return to the cycles of violence seemed imminent.

The public—local and well beyond—responded much as they had to the death of Princess Diana the previous year. Flowers and wreaths arrived by the hundreds, filling the bomb site, the surrounding streets, and the grounds of the local hospital. It was an extraordinary outpouring of grief and solidarity. Some weeks later, still reeling with the devastation, town officials felt a certain quandary that was expressed openly by the mayor in a radio interview. "What are we going to do with all the flowers?" The flowers were now wilting, yet they were like a sacred shrine that could not be removed. Traveling in her car, artist Carole Kane listened to that interview and had an immediate idea: Make paper. She called Frank Sweeney, head of the Department of Arts and Tourism of the Omagh district. Thus began the healing journey that came to be known as the Petals of Hope (Kane, 1999).

Men, women, and children from all walks of life and both sides of the identity divide in Omagh participated in a series of workshops that saved the flower petals and processed the raw material of the wreaths and arrangements. Over time, the organic mush became textured paper of different hues. Common everyday people seeking for a way to respond became the artists that crafted small and large pieces from the paper, incorporating the preserved petals. Carole Kane developed a number of pieces alongside them. As people worked with their hands, they talked about where they had been when the bomb went off, what they remembered about what they had experienced. Touching and making something while talking began the healing.

On March 10, 1999, a private viewing of the paper pieces produced was opened for the families who had lost members in the bombing. Those who had worked and created the art chose one piece to give to each family who had lost someone in the bombing. In a book of condolences sent to Omagh, Nobel poet Seamus Heaney had written three stanzas from "The Cure of Troy." He gave permission for these lines to be used as titles of three pieces.

> So hope for a great sea-change
> On the far side of revenge.

> Believe that a farther shore
> Is reachable from here.
>
> Believe in miracles
> And cures and healing wells.

The exhibit was then opened to the public and has since traveled around Ireland and Europe. Kane (1999:32) recounts her experience watching the families see the pieces for the first time:

> On the night of the private viewing there was a quietness about the exhibition space. It felt like a sanctuary. . . . families spoke quietly to each other. . . . This wasn't like an ordinary opening, where I'd be concerned about people liking the images and buying the work. None of the normal things mattered. . . . I spoke to Stanley McCombe about his picture as the lady who had made this piece had requested it would be given in memory of Stanley's wife. This was the picture of the dove, which was given from a Roman Catholic person to a Protestant person. This summed up what all my work was about and Stanley was touched by this gesture.

Belief in the creative act, as Heaney puts it, is belief in "cures and healing wells." How do we transcend the patterns that create such great pain and still attend to the difficult bogs where our feet seem mired? I have come to believe that it has something to do with the artistic endeavor more than the feat of engineering. It is a process that must breathe life, put wings on the pepper pod, and paint the canvas of what could be while not forgetting what has been. Omagh, too, found its Pied Piper.

Artful Application

What does all this mean for the world of conflict transformation and peacebuilding? There are two arenas I believe merit exploration. The first relates to our notion of process, change, and healing, particularly around the challenge of reconciliation. The second I will share through a personal journey, a look into what it might mean if we saw ourselves as artists.

The quality of my reflections on and interactions with art and peacebuilding was pushed forward through another of those serendipitous adventures—for the last place you really would expect to discover things about art and social change is by serving as a member of a Ph.D. dissertation committee. But such was the process of accident and sagacity with my close friend and professional colleague Herm Weaver, though both of us are still struggling to locate the sagacity.

Herm calls himself a husband, father, songwriter, roofer, and psychology professor, roughly in that order. He usually leaves off his informal resume that he was once a reverend. Some years back he decided to pursue his doctoral degree. He wanted to look into the psychological processes that underpin reconciliation and healing. As part of his research he began an inquiry into the nature of music and healing. Herm had peripheral vision so it was not long until the side interest came front and forward. He embarked on a journey to take his music as seriously as he took his intellectual studies and to focus more directly on music in the process of healing and reconciliation. In essence, he wrote songs and paid attention to how the creative process might be related to the process of healing.

There were of course many fascinating outcomes of this process, including the production of a musical CD, *Travellin' Home and Back*, and a full-blown thesis explaining it (Weaver, 1999a, 1999b). For me, however, one of the best elements of the entire process was the formation of a single question, which I would now frame as: What if reconciliation were more like a creative artistic process than a linear formula of cumulative activities aimed at producing a result? Sometimes, it takes a whole dissertation to formulate one good question.

Herm arrived at an intriguing summary of what came from the creative endeavor and empirical research. He concluded with the elements that he found guided the artistic process and then how these elements might explore pathways toward answering the question of the connection between art and reconciliation. The list was as follows, in his case, framed around the creation of music:

1. The music was to be guided by an *internal standard* rather than external.
2. The music was to be *honest*.
3. We valued *simplicity*.
4. We tried to make *space for the listener to participate*.
5. We aimed at creating music that *arose from the heart as much as from the head*.
6. We were committed to *having fun*. (Weaver, 1999b:105–106).

In relationship to reconciliation, this points us in a challenging direction. The artistic process is not linear; it moves around and pops out in all kinds of unexpected ways. Taking the relationship of art and reconciliation seriously would then suggest that reconciliation should not try to obligate people to think or act linearly, as in "if you do A and then B, you will get C."

The artistic process has its own sense of time and it is not chronological. When the creative process is forced or obligated, less than desirable and artificial outcomes emerge. People working with reconciliation need to rethink healing as a process paced by its own inner timing, which cannot be programmed or pushed to fit a project. People and communities have their own clocks.

The artistic process rises to its highest level when it finds expression that is simple and honest. Elegance and beauty are often captured when complexity is reflected in the simplest of lines, curves, textures, melodies, or rhythms. Reconciliation that is framed as an intellectually complex process will too often create so much noise and distraction that the essence is missed. The key is to find the essence. Honesty of experience, ahead of correctness of perception, Weaver argued, is the key to reconciliation. Art and reconciliation may share this guideline: Be honest early. Be honest often. In healing, there is no replacement for straight honesty, even when it hurts.

The artistic process cannot be understood as something that mostly deals with the head. Intellectual rationality is but one element of the human experience but it is the element that most wishes to control the others. The artistic process initially breaks beyond what can be rationally understood and then returns to a place of understanding that may analyze, think it through, and attach meaning to it. This is much like the process of reconciliation. Brokenness wanders all over our souls. Healing requires a similar journey of wandering. It is not possible to cognitively plan and control the healing. "Healing," W. H. Auden quoted his papa's advice, "is not a science, but the intuitive art of wooing nature" (quoted in Cameron, 2002:247).

The artistic process is fun. The greatest artists of all time had a knack for playfulness, for seeing the life inside of things. Too much seriousness creates art with a message but rarely creates great art. There is no scientific evidence that seriousness leads to greater growth, maturity, or insight into the human condition than playfulness. This is even truer of healing—an understanding I first gained from Edwin Friedman (1990). Reconciliation is dealing with the worst of the human condition, the effort to repair the brokenness of relationships and life itself. It appears as a very serious business. Ironically, the pathway to healing may not lie with becoming more serious. This may explain one reason that people of so many geographies of violence have developed such extraordinary senses of humor and playfulness.

A few years after writing his thesis and reflecting back on his list, Weaver added this thought to his initial work:

> Reconciliation gets complicated and compounded when we try
> to address it purely on the intellectual level. Somewhere along the
> way we came to think of hurt as lodged in the cognitive memory.
> Hurt and brokenness are primarily found in the emotional memory.
> The reason I like the arts—music, drama, dance, whatever the form—
> is precisely because it has the capacity to build a bridge between the
> heart and the mind. (Weaver, 2003)

Without a doubt, there is something of a transcendent nature that takes place in both the artistic endeavor and authentic reconciliation. This transcendent nature is the challenge of the moral imagination: the art and soul of making room for and building the creative act, the birthing of the unexpected.

A second artful application comes in another simple question: What would it mean if peacebuilders saw themselves as artists? It would be an error if we thought only those who are artistically gifted in a particular discipline could pull this off. In her book *Walking in the World*, Julia Cameron called this the "scenario of leaving those we love and going somewhere lonely and perhaps exotic, where we will be Artists with a capital A" (Cameron, 2002:17). The goal of bridging art and peacebuilding is not that we endeavor to become something we are not. Nor is it the pursuit of the "Arts" in order to find a way to somehow become miraculously gifted in one of the forms, like music, poetry, or painting. Experimenting and working at those can create tremendous insight, inner strength, and sustenance. But I am not appealing for nor advocating that peacebuilders must be artists in the professional sense of the word in order to connect art and social change. The key is simpler than that: We must find a way to touch the sense of art that lies within us all. As an example, let me clarify the context from which my own sense of artful connection to the world emerges.

I am a Mennonite by family affiliation and adult choice. I grew up in rural communities in the West and I was lucky enough to know all of my grandparents and two of my great-grandmothers. My heritage was never far from the farm, so to say, from people who lived a relatively simple country life. In my living room corner sits a ceiling-high writing desk and cabinet that was made as a wedding present for my great-grandparents in 1888 by a Mennonite carpenter. In our kitchen is a cherry table my grandmother had commissioned from a local Amish man in eastern Pennsylvania. On our bed is a quilt my aunt bought as a gift for our wedding, sewn by Mennonite women and sold to raise money for humanitarian relief efforts overseas. On my wall a small fraktur hangs, hand printed by a Mennonite woman capturing the statement of one of our founders. Each of these pieces has a simple elegant beauty. Yet if you asked any one of the people who created them, "Are you an artist?" I doubt that any of them would say yes. Knowing my people, I would guess they might say, "No, I just enjoy working with my hands and taking care to do it well." Art is a form of love. It is finding beauty and connection in what we do.

I remember as a little child watching my grandmother Nona and great-aunt Leona making apple pies on the Miller farm in northern Indiana. Two memories stick with me to this day: how good those pies tasted and how those women made crusts. There was a craft to rolling the dough flat then flopping it into the pie pan, but it did not stop there. I can still hear the knife blade hit the side of the pie pan rim as the excess dough was cut. Then the edge of the crust was pinched, thumb and fingers bouncing along the rim, but an awesome symmetry followed their fingers and stayed perched on the pan. Apple filling, probably with too much sugar, was poured to the edges. Then, the last movement, the top of the pie was covered with crisscrossed strips. To be honest, when the pie came out of the oven, anyone with any sense of aesthetics would have hesitated to eat it. That was never our problem. Mennonites are a pragmatic bunch. It may look good but the purpose is to eat!

That is my context. I grew up with a whole community of artistic pragmatics. They saw what was and generally said it. They saw work to be done and generally did it. But somewhere along the line they nurtured a sense of beauty. From housewife to farmer, barn builder to quilt maker, no matter how mundane the task, it could be filled with the respect of simple beauty. If you don't believe me, take a drive to your local Amish country in about the month of June, before the corn is too high. Stop and look for a minute or two at how a garden is laid out, cared for, and nurtured. There you will find love and art.

The challenge of the artful connection is how to respect what we create, nurture love for what we do, and bring beauty to what we build, even in the simplest tasks. We have come to see our work for social change and peacebuilding too much in the line of an intellectual journey, the cognitive processes of getting the analysis right and developing the technique that facilitates the management of the change process. We have failed to nurture the artist. To nurture the artist however does not require becoming whom we are not. The opposite is true. It requires that we pay attention to what already lies within us, within our capacity.

Conclusion

I am not sure that I can answer the questions raised in this chapter about the connection of art to the pragmatics of political change in the world. I do know this: Art and finding our way back to our humanity are connected. Politics as usual has not shown itself particularly capable of generating authentic change for the good of the human community. We have to recognize that constructive social change, like art, comes in fits and starts. The greatest movements forward, when you look really closely, often germinated from something that collapsed, fell to the ground, and then sprouted something that moved beyond what was then known. Those seeds, like the artistic process itself, touched the moral imagination. To believe in healing is to believe in the creative act.

14

On Vocation

The Mystery of Risk

Since I was cut from the reedbed,I have made this crying sound.
—Rumi, *The Reed Flute*

Along our way in the preceding pages, I have hinted at but not fully
explored the fourth discipline: risk. Commitment to relationship always entails risk. Sitting in the messy ambiguity of complexity while
refusing to frame it in dualistic terms requires risk. Belief that creativity can actually happen is an act of risk. Walking into the camp of
a warlord is taking a risk. Meeting with all of the armed groups in
Magdalena Medio was pure risk. But what exactly is risk?

Risk is mystery. It requires a journey. Risk means we take a step
toward and into the unknown. By definition, risk accepts vulnerability and lets go of the need to a priori control the process or the outcome of human affairs. It is the journey of the great explorers for it
chooses, like the images in the maps of old, to live at the edge of
known cartography. Risk means stepping into a place where you are
not sure what will come or what will happen.

The word *mystery* has been cropping up continuously in my
work. In a recent research initiative, I could find no word other than
mystery to explain certain kinds of attitudes, activities, and responses
of people who live in settings of great violence. The Maryknoll Center for Research had taken up an effort to study grassroots community responses to violence. When I was first contacted by Tom Bamat, the research director at Maryknoll, I thought he had made a
mistake. He wanted me to accompany the research process, listen to
the findings, and then make *theological* comments on what I heard

and saw. After several go-rounds of clarification about my likely shortcomings as a theologian, I accepted.

During the research I very much did what Tom described. I attended meetings and listened to the on-the-ground researchers who were interviewing local people and conducting ethnographic and survey research in communities affected directly by violence. The research was carried out in Mindanao, Sudan, Rwanda, Northern Ireland, Guatemala, Sri Lanka, and inner-city gang territories from Los Angeles to Philadelphia. The people to whom the researchers talked were not professionals of peacebuilding, nor did they use such a title at an informal level. They were common, everyday folk who were sorting through how they should respond to violence in order to survive. The researchers looked into how people thought about broad themes like peace, violence, and images of the Divine. The result is found in *Artisans of Peace*, which captures these studies and grassroots responses (Cejka and Bamat, 2003).

Toward the end of the first phase, preliminary case studies and findings were presented. My task at that meeting was to present my early impressions about the theology of what I had picked up as initial themes emerging in the voices and findings of the case studies. I shared some thoughts on the topics of time and space, which became subsections in that book and subsequently are being explored more fully in this book. The third section I suggested was the "Theology of Mystery."

In our meeting that afternoon, I described what I meant by the *theology of mystery*. It was my sense that the people being studied at the grassroots levels in the case examples had responded with their lives, in many cases undertaking extraordinary actions, but the researchers were somewhat perplexed that these same people did not have an explicit cognitive theology nor theory of peace. When asked about their view of peacemaking, since they were engaged in reconciling with their enemies, many of the respondents did not have a well-honed speech or practiced explanation. It was as if they had not fully thought it through. They had to stop and think what words to give to their actions. They had found ways to constructively engage and even reconcile with their enemies in the midst of violence. But they did not have words to describe what they had done. The results were initially reported by the researchers as apparently insignificant, simple phrases: "It was the right thing to do," "We believe in stopping violence" "Peace is God's way." This was, I suggested, not a reflection that these folks lacked theology or sophistication. It was a reflection that the action taken was mysterious. They had ventured on a journey toward a land totally unfamiliar. Exploration of that unknown land called peacebuilding, I thought, was akin to the mysterious journey toward the sacred. It is the same land, I have come to believe, that the moral imagination requires us to explore.

In response to what I was suggesting, our Northern Irish researcher, John Brewer, provided an extraordinary insight. Reflecting on Northern Ireland he commented:

In our context of thirty plus years of the Troubles, violence, fear
and division are known. Peace is the mystery! People are frightened
of peace. It is simultaneously exciting and fearful. This is mystery.
Peace asks a lot of you. Peace asks you to share memory. It asks you
to share space, territory, specific concrete places. It asks you to share
a future. And all this you are asked to do with and in the presence
of your enemy. Peace is Mystery. It is walking into the unknown
(Cejka and Bamat, 2003:265)

I found in the case studies, in people's explanations, and in the researchers' descriptions something I have often found in settings of protracted conflict. People find innovative responses to impossible situations not because they
are well-trained professionals or particularly gifted. Innovative responses arise
because this is their context, their place. The essence of the response is not
found so much in what they do but in who they are and how they see themselves in relationship with others. They speak with their lives.

When we approach the mystery of risk as part of peacebuilding in settings
of violence, I believe we are exploring life purpose more than professional
effectiveness. The two are not unrelated or antithetical but life purpose takes
us to a deeper soil not readily available if we stop only at the level of professional
ethics and conduct. Risk and the moral imagination dig into this special kind
of soil, one that is not commonly discussed in either the scientific or professional literature on conflict transformation and peacebuilding. It is the soil of
finding our voice, finding a way to speak with our lives. It is the potentially
rich but too seldom tapped or fed soil of vocation.

I first understood this from Parker Palmer's book *Let Your Life Speak* (Palmer, 2000). *Vocation*, he clarifies, is rooted in the Latin for "voice." As he put
it, "[V]ocation is not a goal that I pursue. It means a calling that I hear. Before
I can tell my life what I want to do with it, I must listen to my life telling me
who I am" (Palmer, 2000:4).

In conflict resolution and peacebuilding we expend a lot of energy teaching
people how to listen. The focus is on how to listen to others. I have often been
struck with how little energy we invest in listening to our own voices. Yet the
two are intimately connected. I am increasingly of the view that people who
listen the best and the deepest to others are those who have found a way to be
in touch with their own voices.

To deeply understand vocation as voice, we must go beyond what is initially
visible and audible, to that which has rhythm, movement, and feeling. Voice
is not the externalization of sound and words. Literally and metaphorically,
voice is not located in the mouth or on the tongue where words are formed.
Voice is deeper. Words are only a small expression of that depth.

Consider the ways we talk about and perceive voice. We speak with ad-
miration of a person who has a deep, resonant voice. Baritones or sopranos

whose voices ring in such captivating ways that you nearly forget to breathe never sing from their mouths. They sing from deep within, from a place that sustains the longest of vowels and notes. I once had voice lessons to improve my singing. Although it did not improve my stature as a singer, I do remember the instruction. The one thing upon which the voice teacher insisted was this: Push from deep, from the diaphragm up. The sound and sustenance of music must tap deep, or it is weak and incomplete. The least important element is the mouth. The most important is the foundation of the voice, the home where voice is found. That place is literally where heart and lungs meet.

Voice is located where breath dies and is born, where what is taken in gives life, where what has served its purpose is released anew. Voice is located at the source of rhythm, the internal drumming of life itself. When the poet Emerson said we walk to the "beat of a different drummer," he was talking about voice, the sense of internal rhythm. We cannot underestimate the enormity of the Genesis stories, and of parallel narratives in many traditions, of how life itself came to be: God breathed into clay. Life was created from the place where breath and earth met, and from that place voice arose. Voice is the essence of being a person.

Where you find that meeting place, the home where heart and lungs gather, where breath meets blood, there you will find voice. When you find your way to that home, there you will find yourself, the unique gift that God has placed on this earth. You will find the place from which your journey begins and to where it returns when the road is confused and hard. This is the deeper sense of vocation.

I have been reading Persian poets as part of my personal education for working in Central Asia, mostly in Tajikistan and the Ferghana Valley. I have had the great privilege of coming to know new friends in this part of the world. One of them is Faredun Hodizoda, the son of the most prominent living scholar on Persian literature in Tajikistan, Rasul Hodizoda. As we traveled recently through the most southern part of the Ferghana Valley, where Faredun works, I inquired about the poets I was reading. I have found that the poetry, written from within an Islamic context and tradition, has a feel much like the wisdom literature I find in Proverbs, the Song of Solomon, and the Psalms with which I am familiar from the Old Testament. Attar, Saadi, Saanai, Rumi, Hafez—the names are familiar to a few specialists in the West and nearly household words in the oral traditions in much of Central Asia. Within Islam, these poets are the mystics, the Sufis. They speak of love, life, and the nature of the Divine. They often write in teaching parables and stories. I began to notice that many of these poets used references to the reed flute. I asked Faredun on one of our trips about the meaning of the flute.

"Ah, the reed flute," he replied. "You see, the flute is made by cutting the cane, the reed. When the flute is played, lips are placed on the mouthpiece and breath is blown into [the] reed. The sound, you may have noticed, is mournful.

It calls out. It is said that the reed always wants to return home, to its place. Rumi once wrote the story told by the reed."

> Since I was cut from the reedbed,
> I have made this crying sound.
> Anyone apart from someone he loves
> understands what I say.
> Anyone pulled from a source
> longs to go back. (Barks: 1988:17)

"You see," Faredun continued:

the sound of the reed flute is a call to find a way home. The poets use the reed flute to say it is like God placing lips on humans and breathing life. The breath creates a sound, a voice in the body that searches for this source of life. So the reed wants [to] return home. It is a return to God. The poets say the voice of the flute is a longing for true home.

Longing for a true home, this is vocation. Finding a way to that home is a journey toward understanding who I am. At its essence, home provides a sense of place. Vocation is the same. Knowing who you are is finding where you are, as in "I have a sense of my place in this world." We often seek our sense of place by what we do professionally. This is where the confusion comes that links vocation with work, jobs, and titles. But vocation is not a profession. It is definitely not "work" and even less a "job." Vocation is knowing and staying true to the deep voice. Vocation stirs inside, calls out to be heard, to be followed. It beckons us home. When we live in a way that keeps vocation within eyesight and earshot, like the needle of a compass, vocation provides a sense of location, place, and direction. This is why we may say to friends as a deep compliment of appreciation for their genuine acceptance, "I feel comfortable here with you. I can just be myself. I feel at home."

People who are close to home no matter where they live or travel or what work they do are people who walk guided by their voice. They are voicewalkers: They can hear the reed flute. On a permanent journey, they always are within earshot of home.

Voicewalkers

I have known a lot of voicewalkers in my life. They rarely stand out immediately. You come to recognize them after a while more than from first impressions. Lives don't speak in one-time conversations. They speak over time.

You may notice them first for the things they don't confuse. They don't confuse their job or activities with who they are as people. They don't confuse getting credit with success, or recognition with self-worth. They don't confuse criticism for an enemy. They don't confuse truth with social or political power. They don't confuse their work with saving the world. They don't confuse guilt with motivation.

Then you may notice something that is not easy to put a finger on: It is not so much what they do as who they are that makes a difference. They listen in a way that their own agenda does not seem to be in the way. They respond more from love than fear. They laugh at themselves. They cry with others' pain, but never take over their journey. They know when to say no and have the courage to do it. They work hard but are rarely too busy. Their life speaks.

Rose Barmasai, to whom I dedicate this book, was a voicewalker with an extraordinary moral imagination. She gave her life to walking, literally, up and down the ethnic clash areas of the Rift Valley in her native Kenya. She helped initiate and then carry the Community Peace and Development Project of the National Council of Churches of Kenya. She was a magician in the best sense of David Abram's definition for she was at the edge of her own community, moving and mediating between the worlds of tribal wars while being a part of the fabric where they happened. She was, in the words of the Van Morrison song, a "dweller on the threshold."

I had the privilege of many meetings and conversations with her and was able to watch her be among her people. She never feared talking to the highest-level political or religious leader about what was happening on the ground, the impact of their words and actions on real people's lives, or what new ideas needed to be pursued. And she never lost their attention or respect. Rose was known for walking, seemingly without fear, into enemy tribal areas when things were about to explode. This middle-aged woman called on every intuition she could muster, from motherhood to ancestors, when on more than one occasion she waded into open and violently explosive *baraza* meetings (open town square meetings) that could avert or lead to war. She moved with equal courage toward those from her own tribe, never forcing a false choice between love and truth.

I saw her laugh, contagiously. I sat with her when she wept from deep inside. I saw her give birth to hope in others. With a life portfolio of experiences and accomplishments in on-the-ground peacebuilding few of us could possibly imagine, I watched her insatiable desire to learn in seminars and classrooms. But mostly I saw a person who walked in touch with her voice, and from that place she gave voice to others. Rose lived the mystery of vocation, the mystery of risk.

In October 1999, Rose died in a tragic car accident returning from meetings in the Rift Valley. Two years later, Kenya, through a process of national elections, passed to a new era of leadership. For perhaps the first time in contemporary Kenyan history, the electoral period took place unmarred by extensive violence. A decade of Rift Valley voicewalkers with their seminars, workshops, *barazas*, elders meetings, conversations with parliamentarians—but mostly with their presence—had given birth to a nearly imperceptible gift: a space for change to happen without violence. I am sure the ancestors watched. And I am sure Rose laughed contagiously.

Conclusion

There is a sense in which the whole of peacebuilding could be summed up as finding and building voice. It happened between the warlord and the philosopher, between the young man and the chief. This was the case when the peasants engaged the range of violent actors around them in Magdalena Medio. Starting with a few women in the market, a whole community found a voice that stopped a war.

These are the kind of things we usually visualize as our work: how to help people find that voice that sustains and makes change possible. The journey toward change that those people make requires more than a strategy of good ideas or technique. Fundamentally, it requires a willingness to risk and great vulnerability. They are stepping into the unknown, into the mystery of risk. The journey of voice finds its source at the level of life and vocation.

In the important process of the professionalization of our fields, we have not adequately attended to the need that we touch and listen to the voice of vocation. We cannot expect others to enter the mystery of risk that takes the step beyond violence and into the uncharted geography of relationship with the enemy unless we ourselves understand and engage the mystery of risk and vocation. We cannot listen and provide support to others as they find their voices if we ourselves see this only as a technique or the management of a process. The capacity to incite the moral imagination connects at this level for it taps the source of what makes transcendent change possible: the capacity to risk.

15

On Conclusions

The Imperative of the Moral Imagination

Logic will get you from A to B.
Imagination will take you everywhere.

—Albert Einstein

Conclusions are never easy to write. They walk a narrow pathway
that winds between redundancy and useful synthesis. For the reader
entering our conversation from the back of the book, welcome! This
may be as good a place to start as any. Our inquiry was not a linear
one. The preceding chapters wove a tapestry of spiders' webs, yeast
and siphons, haikus and ancestors, Pied Pipers and the princes of
Serendip—all in search of something imminently available and yet
extraordinarily elusive: how to invoke the moral imagination in the
midst of human conflict and violence. As Einstein is widely pur-
ported to have remarked, "Imagination will take you everywhere."

Books are not exactly a timely enterprise. Somewhat attentive to
but not driven by day-to-day events, ideas follow an anachronistic
pace and evolution as they make their way to the finality of the written page. This book was produced during the three years that followed the events of September 11, 2001. From the perspective of international relations, little can be found at the level of official politics
in those intervening years that provide examples of the moral imagination. In fact, the major events and patterns have demonstrated the
antithesis of what we have explored in this book.

In the first years of this new century, many of the places of conflict where I have worked for decades with dedicated colleagues or
encouraged and supported students as they promoted peacebuilding

initiatives have seen significant deterioration. The Middle East spiraled into relentless cycles of violence and counterviolence. Deadly conflict inside Colombia worsened and expanded. Mindanao collapsed into renewed fighting. Liberia broke into another round of devastation. The war on terrorism was declared. In fewer than three years, the leaders of the United States took the single remaining superpower into two full-fledged land-based wars in pursuit of elusive enemies.

News about these deadly cycles dominates our daily papers and televisions. The rhetoric justifying involvement on one side or another of these violent conflicts promises a horizon of increased security, well-being for the human community, and freedom. Yet the actions and reactions that sustain protracted violence replicate a guiding narrative antithetical to the birthplace of the moral imagination. Isolation and fear paralyze the capacity to imagine the web of interdependent relationships. Harsh lines of enmity and narrow ideological lenses force people and political decisions into false either-or frames of reference that belie the complexity of the challenges facing our local and global community this century. Economic and military power become the bulwarks that seek to control outcomes and assure the security of the more powerful, and in so doing narrow or destroy the capacity for creative alternatives to our deepest-rooted global conflicts. The risks taken by leadership in response to perceived imminent threat in any of the above-mentioned settings of violence have in each and every case placed defenseless civilian populations at greater vulnerability and given over the global treasure of our younger generations to the implacable destruction of violence. Daily rhetoric has floated over airwaves during these past three years appealing to our loyalty and justifying violence on the basis of seeking a higher moral ground. Songwriter Paul Brady's words (1992), written more than a decade ago in Northern Ireland, seem prescient on a global level. "Up here," he sang, "we sacrifice our children for the worn-out dreams of yesterday." In cycles of violence, "up here" does not refer to a higher moral ground and has not led us toward the promised horizon of security. The inverse is true. The past few years have spawned a veritable industry of fear and insecurity driven by the logic of violence and incapable of transcending and transforming it.

The conclusion from the preceding tapestry of chapters is that if we are to survive as a global community, we must understand the imperative nature of giving birth and space to the moral imagination in human affairs. We must face the fact that much of our current system for responding to deadly local and international conflict is incapable of overcoming cycles of violent patterns precisely because our imagination has been corraled and shackled by the very parameters and sources that create and perpetrate violence. Our challenge is how to invoke, set free, and sustain innovative responses to the roots of violence while rising above it. The stories in this book recount ways that people in the worst of conditions spawned precisely that kind of imagination and suggest four pathways to assist its birth:

- We must move from isolation and attitudes of "dominate or be dominated" toward a capacity to envision and act on the basis that we live in and form part of a web of interdependent relationships, which includes our enemy. Our grandchildren's destinies are one.
- We must not fall prey to the trap of narrowly defined dualisms, which severely limit the framing of our challenges and choices. We must find ways to nurture an inquisitive capacity that explores and interacts constructively with the complexity of the relationships and realities that face our communities.
- Below and above, outside and beyond the narrow walls with which violence wishes to enclose our human community, we must live with trust that creativity, divinely embedded in the human spirit, is always within reach. Like a seed in the ground, creative capacity lies dormant, filled with potential that can give rise to unexpected blossoms that create turning points and sustain constructive change. We must expose and break the false promise that places trust in violence as *the* defender and deliverer of security.
- Accepting vulnerability, we must risk the step into unknown and unpredictable lands and seek constructive engagement with those people and things we least understand and most fear. We must take up the inevitably perilous but absolutely necessary journey that makes its way back to humanity and the building of genuine community.

A Few Implications

These pathways have significant implications for peacebuilding and for the conducting of human affairs in general. They show the need to expand how we—as conflict, justice, and peace professionals—envision our theories and our practice. In broad terms, the imperative of the moral imagination requires us to reflect deeply on our work as embedded in the wider purpose of initiating and promoting constructive social change processes, and it poses challenges and questions to the development of our professions. Several broad inquiries arising from the preceding chapters, illustrate the nature of these challenges:

- What happens to peacebuilding practice if we shift from a guiding metaphor that we are providing professional services to one that we are engaged in a vocation to nurture constructive social change? The web approach, for example, suggests that we develop lenses that sharpen our capacity to envision the relational context as the space within which

change happens and our services are offered. As such, our ability to
initiate, design, and support specific services is embedded in and
builds from the capacity to understand and develop strategic approaches to social space—the know-who of the immediate and wider
relational context within which we operate. Rather than narrow and
specialize, we expand how we view "services" in the context of the
wider society and social change processes. Our designs and interven-
tions are not defined so much by the parameters of particular process
management skills but rather our technical skills are defined and fit
into the horizons of wider change and the potential for building transformative relational spaces. The web requires us to think strategically
about change processes in the context of immediate relationships, ultimate purpose, and social space.

• What happens to process design if we think of ourselves as *artists and
professional specialists* with technical expertise? Among the most basic
ideas put forward in this book was the simple notion that transcending
violence requires imagination, which translates into creative acts. Over
years of working with people in a wide variety of applied peacebuilding
initiatives, I have come to firmly believe that there clearly exists a constant element of creativity in our practice. However, I am struck rather
consistently with how this aspect of our work is pushed into categories
that we seem to understand and to which we refer as the building of
skills and technical expertise. The case I wish to make is that we must
give room to the artistic side of this work. What would happen to process and intervention designs if we intentionally created spaces that
made room for categories we would name "artistic moments and attitudes" in the design of professional responses to social change? This
could, for example, suggest that we encourage in far more intentional
ways the disciplines and joys of journaling, storytelling, poetry, painting, drawing, music, and dance as part of the design process itself.
The particular results of any one of these creative activities should not
be seen as a "product." Rather, we now understand that to build artistic space requires that we open the design process itself to different
and critically important ways of knowing what has, is, or could happen
in the complex reality under consideration. Two consequences could
emerge. First, we would at various times find significant ah-hah, haiku-
like moments that penetrate complexity in the form of breakthrough
insights. Second, we would nurture a far more constructive attentiveness to both individual and group intuition. Over time, I believe, we
would keep our professions alive with a sense of wonder and awe, and
we would replenish our work-as-craft with art and soul.

• What happens if we envision an understanding of serendipity as an integral part of our professional education and practice? This rings like

an oxymoron. But let us remember that serendipity is the discovery by accident and sagacity of things we were not in quest of. The primary discipline of serendipity is attentiveness to those things present along the way that were not initially seen as the defined goal but that in the end created significant new insight that built creatively toward an ultimate purpose. Serendipity creates a shift from tunnel to peripheral vision. The most significant implications of this shift may well have to do with how we as professionals truly become reflective practitioners rather than rote technicians. Reflective practitioners sustain a curiosity about their work, purpose, and learning. This attitude and way of being is the space that links experience with theory and theory back to practice. Serendipity is not just openness to the unexpected. It requires us to hone the disciplines that build both knowledge and wisdom.

• What happens if building intuition and art are included in conflict resolution, mediation, and peacebuilding training? Training is typically thought of in these fields as the development of skills for analysis and process management. If the moral imagination lies within us as a dormant seed of potential, and this seed holds the key to breaking cycles of destructive conflict, then our challenge is how to invoke the growth of this kind of imagination as an integral part of developing innovative professionals. Much of what currently takes place in "skill training" orients itself toward understanding and managing cognitive and behavioral responses in human interactions. Tapping the creative side, touching intuition, knowing things kinetically, visually, metaphorically, and artistically requires avenues of exploration in the educational process that tap whole other parts of human "being" and "knowing." It suggests that training programs build in spaces for listening to the inner voice, recognizing and exploring a variety of ways of knowing and touching reality. For example, I have for some time incorporated music, poetry, and visuals (paintings, photography, and sculpture) into my teaching and training. In my more experimental modes, I take whole mornings of five-day training events in peacebuilding to teach the rudimentary elements of haiku or invite a musician to write music with the class. There is not an exact formula or an immediacy of results that emerges from these endeavors, but there is a growing sense that if we are to invoke the moral imagination, we must incite and excite the artist within us.

• What happens if we envision training and education as supporting not only professional expertise but also vocation? The moral imagination proposes that engagement of the kind that sparks turning points and transcendence in settings of violence arises not primarily from the technical skills side of our peacebuilding professions. The guiding stories of this book (chapter 2) suggest that this kind of imagination bursts forth as part of a life journey that cares about the nature and quality of our relationships and communities and about how we move from relationships defined by division and fear toward those character- ized by respect and love. One of the things I have discovered over the years is how often people who have worked professionally in settings of violent conflict struggle not so much with the specifics of their skills and specialties but with the deeper questions posed by the setting itself: Who are we? What are we doing? Where are we going? What is our purpose? These are the questions that keep cropping up but as things stand have precious little space to be explored within the professions themselves. The moral imagination suggests that education and train- ing are incomplete in any of the fields related to social change if they do not build early and continually the space to explore the meaning of things, the horizons toward which to journey, and the nature of the journey itself. This quest is one that must take seriously the process of listening to the deeper inner voice, a spiritual and deeply human ex- ploration that should not be relegated to occasional conversations among friends or, worse, to the couches of therapy when professional life crises emerge. This is the heart, the art and soul of who we are in the world, and it cannot be disconnected from what we do in the world.

- What would happen if leaders of national and global politics invoked the artist, particularly at times when violence is present or its use is about to be justified? Our thesis suggests that the common ways that politicians and leaders invoke artists rarely incite the moral imagina- tion. Too often artists are called at celebrations, inaugurations, and vic- tories, or when leaders' decisions need to be blessed, or when group and national ethos need to be solidified and sentiments of loyalty and allegiance affirmed, or when national grief needs to be expressed. Rarely, if ever, when faced with large-scale life-and-death issues do leaders invite artists—from musicians and poets to painters, filmmak- ers, and playwrights—to respond imaginatively from within their disci- plines to the challenges they face as leaders. Yet in the aftermath of the events that follow, it is often the artist who penetrates the deeper es- sence of humanity's plight. Why not in the foremath? Why must poli- tics be a field of human activity that relies almost exclusively on cogni- tive understandings of complex realities and by virtue of its self-definition limits its capacity to imagine whole new possibilities and insights?
- What would happen if local and national elected officials and signifi- cant civic, religious, and educational leaders who direct the course of public and human affairs were required to attend continuing educa- tion in a School for the Moral Imagination? Granted, it may be hard to

imagine, though perhaps a few guidelines would be helpful. It could start with one week a year. That is not too much to ask. The classroom would be made up of people who rarely interact with each other, including political and ideological enemies and a creative mix of the people they purport to serve. There would be lots of tea and coffee time and few lectures. Participants would be asked to do one simple thing: talk openly and honestly with each other about their hopes and fears, about their lives and families. Teachers would only be storytellers, mostly common folk chosen for their life stories of how they overcame what seemed insurmountable odds to break out of injustice and threat without resorting to violence. They could be children or refugees, wise old farmers or wartorn community survivors. At least part of each day, the participants would listen to music, write poetry, or make paper together with their hands. Near the end of each week, they would spend a day planting a garden, four or five people to a plot. Above the door that exits the school there would be a small plaque that each leader would be asked to read before leaving and to comment on the following year. It would read:

Reach out to those you fear.
Touch the heart of complexity.
Imagine beyond what is seen.
Risk vulnerability one step at a time.

Epilogue

A Conversation

Epilogue: A speech or short poem addressed to the spectators by one of the actors at the conclusion of the play.
—*Compact Oxford English Dictionary*

No epilogue, I pray you, for your play needs no excuse.
—Shakespeare, *A Midsummer Night's Dream*

"How do I make the moral imagination appear?" a reader asked.

"I don't have a magic formula. No recipe exists," the playwright answered. "But if you pay attention, advice may accompany your search. Watch and listen!"

"When you feel denigrated," said the young Konkomba man, "offer respect."

"In the face of fear," Abdul advised, "offer your vulnerability."

"When division and hate is all around you," the women of Wajir responded, "build solidarity with those close at hand and then reach for others as far as you can touch."

"In the face of violence and threat," Josué and the *campesinos* of Magdalena Medio said, "offer truth, transparency, and dialogue."

"When overwhelmed by complexity," the haiku master laughed, "seek the elegant essence that holds it together."

"Think of the space that lies before you," suggested the orb spider. "Think how much silk you have. Be smart flexible."

"Step carefully," said the web watchers. "You are part of something greater than you even if it is not visible."

"Don't let the goal of your journey blind you," advised the princes of Serendip, "from learning about your purpose along the way."

"Let the music in," sang the Pied Piper.

"Follow your voice toward home," said the reed flute. "Keep walking. The ancestors await you."

Glossary

Constructive change: The pursuit of shifting relationships from those defined by fear, mutual recrimination, and violence toward those characterized by love, mutual respect, and proactive engagement. Constructive social change seeks to move the flow of interaction in human conflict from cycles of destructive relational patterns toward cycles of relational dignity and respectful engagement.

Critical yeast: Rather than *critical mass*, commonly believed to be the moment of shift when large enough numbers of people get behind an idea or movement, critical yeast does not focus on producing large numbers of people. Critical yeast asks the question in reference to social change: Who within a given setting, if brought together, would have the capacity to make things grow toward the desired end? The focus is not on the number but on the quality of people brought together, who represent unique linkages across a wide variety of sectors and locations within the conflicted setting.

Haiku attitude: The discipline of preparation, a predisposition for touching and being touched by the aesthetic, in other words, to perceive and be touched by beauty. Haiku poets talk of humility and sincerity as the two guiding values that underpin their work as they face life and seek to see the true nature of things.

Haiku moment: Penetrating insight; the appearance of deep resonance, which connects deeper truth with the immediacy of experience. Haiku poets call this the ah-ness, which some may consider as the ah-hah moment, the moment when people say, "I see exactly what you mean." In the midst of complexity, the haiku moment penetrates and results in insight that is held in a simple, elegant, and organic whole.

Horizontal capacity: The ability to build and sustain relational spaces of constructive interaction across the lines of division in systems and societies divided by historic patterns of identity conflicts.

Justpeace: An orientation toward conflict transformation characterized by approaches that reduce violence and destructive cycles of social interaction *and at the same time* increase justice in any human relationship.

Moral imagination: To imagine responses and initiatives that, while rooted in the challenges of the real world, are by their nature capable of rising above destructive patterns and giving birth to that which does not yet exist. In reference to peacebuilding, this is the capacity to imagine and generate constructive responses and initiatives that, while rooted in the day-to-day challenges of violent settings, transcend and ultimately break the grips of those destructive patterns and cycles.

Platforms: Ongoing social and relational spaces, in other words, people in relationship who generate creative processes, initiatives, and solutions to the deeper-ingrained destructive patterns and the day-to-day ebb and flow of social conflict. As such, a platform has a continuous generative capacity that is responsive to longer-term relational patterns and is adaptive to changing environments. The focus of a platform is to create and sustain a foundation capable of generating responsive change processes that address both the immediate expression of the conflict and the deeper epicenter of the conflictive relational context. A platform is like a moving sidewalk in an airport combined with a trampoline. The sidewalk continuously moves across time and the trampoline has the capacity to spring forward new ideas in response to unexpected and emerging problems while sustaining the long-term vision of constructive change.

Process structures: In the physical world, these are phenomena that are simultaneously dynamic processes and take shape and form in identifiable structures. Some examples are skin, rivers, and glaciers. They are changing and adapting, yet have a form and shape that from a distance appear static. Applied to social change, building justpeace is a process that must be both responsively adaptive to the context and the evolution of events, yet must have a vision, direction, purpose, infrastructure of support, and a shape that helps sustain its movement toward the desired changes.

Serendipity: The discovery, by accident and sagacity, of things for which you were not in quest which creates an emphasis on learning about process, substance, and purpose along the way, as initiatives for change develop. To nurture serendipity, one must pay special attention to the development of peripheral vision, the capacity to be observant and learn along the way while sustaining a clear sense of direction and purpose.

Siphon strategy: A siphon seeks to move liquid from one container to another using only the natural energy available. A tube is inserted in one container. At the other end of the tube, a person inhales, creating a vacuum that lifts an initial portion of the liquid against gravity until it begins its descent into the other container, pulling with it the remainder of the liquid in the original container. The physics of a siphon does not concern itself with moving all of the liquid. It is only concerned with getting the initial portion to move against gravity, knowing that momentum will pull the rest. Applied to social processes, the siphon strategy raises this question: Who, if they are linked together and make the journey against social gravity, would have the capacity to pull the rest of the system/society along toward a desired change?

Social spaces: The locations and places where relationships are built and interaction takes place. In reference to constructive social change, these spaces refer to the locations of interaction among people who are not like-minded about the conflict and not like-situated across the social divisions and levels of leadership within the setting.

Strategic what: Analysis of the wide range of issues and problems that focuses on the challenge of which of the many options holds the greatest potential for creating a wider impact on the setting. Primary in this regard is the choice of investment in a particular issue because it has an inherent convening capacity (these are issues around which people who are not like-minded and not like-situated in the conflictive setting can be convened). The *strategic what* avoids, at all costs, crisis-hopping and fire-fighting approaches to conflict resolution.

Strategic where: Provides lenses that focus on the place and geography that have strategic significance in addressing social processes and conflicts. Rather than looking at conflict exclusively in terms of issue content or process, the *strategic where* inquires into the interdependence of people and the locus of their conflict. It looks for geographies of unique social interaction and intersection, then explores the design in reference to those locations. Examples are riverways, markets, schools, hospitals, or highways as strategic places, geographies for the emergence of potentially constructive transformations of conflict by virtue of the unique relational interdependencies and intersections created in the confluence of those places.

Strategic who: Analysis of conflicted social systems aimed at identifying key agents of change, particularly those with the capacity for building vertical and horizontal integration.

Vertical capacity: Relationship building across levels of leadership, authority, and responsibility within a society or system, from grassroots to the highest, most visible leaders. This approach requires awareness that each level has different needs and unique contributions to make, but ultimately they are interdependent, requiring the explicit fostering of constructive interactions across the levels.

Vertical and horizontal integration: Strategy for seeking change within a divided system or society that explicitly engenders and supports processes that link individuals, networks, organizations, and social spaces that demonstrate a capacity for both vertical and horizontal relationship building.

Vocation: The deeper listening to an inner voice that relates to the purpose and unique place of people and their life callings.

Web approach: The pursuit of social change initiated through spatial strategies and networking. This strategy identifies, reinforces, and builds social spaces and intersections that link individuals, groups, networks, and organizations, formal and informal, across the social divides, sectors, levels, and geographies that make up the settings of protracted conflict.

Notes

CHAPTER 2

1. The following story was received during multiple conversations with
Emmanuel Bombande, who works with the West Africa Network for Peacebuilding in Ghana. I also want to acknowledge personal conversation on
this story with Hizkias Assefa and Father Clement Aapenguayo.

2. This story is based on personal conversations with women and men
from the Wajir Peace and Development Committee. I am especially indebted to Dekha Ibrahim for her advice and input on the development of
this particular short version. For more information, see *The Wajir Story*, a
documentary video produced by Responding to Conflict. For further reading, see Dekha Ibrahim and Janice Jenner, "Breaking the Cycle of Violence
in Wajir," in *Overcoming Violence: Linking Local and Global Peacemaking*, ed-
ited by Robert Herr and Judy Zimmerman Herr.

3. This account is taken from Garcia, *Hijos de la Violencia*. I had the
privilege of meeting and working with some of these *campesinos* in the early
1990s. The translation of the text from Spanish into English is mine.

CHAPTER 3

1. *Justpeace* as a term was proposed to fill a gap in the English language
and refers to conflict resolution approaches aimed at reducing violence and
increasing justice in human relationships (see Lederach, 1999).

2. I have included in the bibliography a range of books that used *the
moral imagination* in their titles or subtitles. The list includes: Price, 1983;
Clausen, 1986; Kirk, 1988; Coles, 1989; McCollough, 1991; Allison, 1999;
Beidelman, 1993; Johnson, 1993; Tivnan, 1995; Babbit, 1996; Bruce, 1998;
Guroian, 1998; Stevens, 1998; Williams, 1998; Brown, 1999; Werhane,

1999; Fernandez and Huber, 2001; Fesmire, 2003; McFaul, 2003; and Newsom, 2003.

CHAPTER 5

1. Portions of the next two chapters were first presented at the RIREC conference sponsored by the Joan B. Kroc Institute for International Peace Studies, University of Notre Dame, under the working title of "The Horizon of Peacebuilding," September 26, 2002.

2. All of the figures in this book will be presented as "doodles," drawings that look similar to the way I would present them in off-the-record meetings with people involved in conflicts or with students in class. I am indebted to the gifted hand of my father, John Lederach, in the elegant production of these graphics. For more of an explanation, see chapter 7.

CHAPTER 7

1. Jack Kerouac wrote this sentence in exactly this form.

2. An example of this can be found in chapter 12. *Inside the Maze* is a poem I wrote, which emerged from a conversation inside the Maze prison in Northern Ireland.

CHAPTER 9

1. Portions of this chapter were first published in "Building Mediative Capacity in Deep-Rooted Conflict," *Fletcher Forum of World Affairs* 26(1) (Winter–Spring 2002): 91–101.

2. While these emerged over a number of conversations, I am indebted to a small handwritten note from Deborah Overholt after one of these lectures, which was very helpful in identifying several factors specific to yeast.

CHAPTER 12

1. This chapter owes significant debt to conversations with Aküm Longchari and Jarem Sawatsky.

CHAPTER 13

1. I want to acknowledge the guiding hands and help of Dr. David Bolton and Dr. Herm Weaver in the development of this chapter.

2. It is important to add that there are a range of scientific inquiries and essays exploring this topic of arts and peacebuilding. A sampling could include the following listed in the bibliography: *Peacemaking Creatively Through the Arts* (Wezeman, 1990) "Arts" Chapter 7 in *People Building Peace* (European Center for Conflict Prevention, 1999); *Art Toward Reconciliation* (Gernika Gogoratuz, 2000); "Constructive Storytelling: A Peace Process (Senehi, 2002); "Symposium: Artists of Resistance" (Varea and Novak, 2003).

Bibliography

Abram, David. 1996. *The Spell of the Sensuous*. New York: Random House.

Allison, Dale. 1999. *The Sermon on the Mount: Inspiring the Moral Imagination*. New York: Herder and Herder.

Almond, Gabriel Abraham. 2002. *Political Science Narrative and Reflection*. Boulder, Colo.: Rienner.

Arendt, Hannah. 1998. *The Human Condition*. Chicago: University of Chicago Press.

Babbit, Susan E. 1996. *Impossible Dreams: Rationality, Integrity, and Moral Imagination*. Boulder, Colo.: Westview.

Barks, Coleman. 1988. *The Soul of Rumi*. Atlanta: Maypop Books.

Barnes, Catherine. 2002. *Owning the Process: Public Participation in Peacemaking, Accord 13*.

Beidelman, T. O. 1993. *Moral Imagination in Kaguru Modes of Thought*. Washington, D.C.: Smithsonian Institution Press.

Berrigan, Daniel, and Robert Coles. 1971. *Geography of Faith*. Boston, Mass.: Beacon.

Boulding, Elise. 1990. *Building a Global Civic Culture: Education for an Interdependent World*. Syracuse, N.Y.: Syracuse University Press.

Boulding, Kenneth. 1984. *The Image*. Ann Arbor: University of Michigan Press.

———. 1985. *Human Betterment*. London: Sage.

———. 1989. *Three Faces of Power*. London: Sage.

Brady, Paul. 1992. "The Island," *Songs and Crazy Dreams*. Compact disc. London: Fontana.

Brown, William P. 1999. *The Ethos of the Cosmos: The Genesis of Moral Imagination in the Bible*. Grand Rapids, Mich.: Eerdmans.

Brown Childs, John. 2003. *Transcommunality: From Politics of Conversion to the Ethics of Respect*. Philadelphia, Pa.: Temple University Press.

Bruce, Cicero. 1998. *W. H. Auden's Moral Imagination*. Lewiston, N.Y.: Mellen.

Brueggemann, Walter. 2001. *The Prophetic Imagination*, 2d ed. Minneapolis, Minn.: Fortress.

Burdette, Patricia Wells. 2003. "The Power of the Spirit: American Indian Worldview and Successful Community Development Aamong the Oglala Lakota." Ph.D. diss., Union Institute and University.

Burke, Edmund. 1864. "Reflections on the Revolution in France, in *The Works of the Right Honorable Edmund Burke*, vol. 2, 515–516 London: Henry G. Bohn.

Call, Charles T., and William Stanley. 2003. "Military and Police Reform Aafter Civil Wars," in *Contemporary Peacemaking*, ed. John Darby and Roger MacGinty, 212–223. New York: Palgrave.

Cameron, Julia. 2002. *Walking in the World*. New York: Penguin Putnam.

Cejka, Mary Ann, and Thomas Bainat. 2003. *Artisans of Peace: Grassroots Peacemaking Aamong Christian Communities*. Maryknoll, N.Y.: Orbis.

Charters, Ann, ed. 1995. *The Portable Jack Kerouac*. New York: Penguin.

Clausen, Christopher. 1986. *The Moral Imagination: Essays on Literature and Ethics*. Iowa City: University of Iowa Press.

Coles, Robert. 1989. *The Call of Stories: Teaching and the Moral Imagination*. Boston, Mass.: Houghton Mifflin.

Compact Oxford English Dictionary. 2000. Oxford: Oxford University Press.

Conniff, Richard. 2001. "Deadly Silk," *National Geographic*. (Aug.): 30–45.

Crompton, John. 1951. *The Life of the Spider*. Cambridge: Riverside.

Crossley, Michele. 2000. *Introducing Narrative Psychology: Self, Trauma and the Construction of Meaning*. Philadelphia, Pa.: Open University Press.

Darby, John, and Roger MacGinty. 2003. *Contemporary Peacemaking*. New York: Palgrave.

De Gruchy, John. 2002. *Reconciliation: Restoring Justice*. London: SCM Press.

Doe, Samuel Gbaydee, and Emmanuel Habuka Bombande. 2002. "A View from West Africa," in *Into the Eye of the Storm*, ed. John Paul Lederach and Janice Moomaw Jenner, pp. 159–172. San Francisco, Calif.: Jossey Bass.

Dugan, Maire. 1996. "A Nested Theory of Conflict," *Women in Leadership* 1 (Summer): 9–20.

Elmi, Asha Hagi, Dekha Ibrahim, and Janice Jenner. 2001. "Peace Is Milk, Peace Is Development, Peace Is Life: Women's Roles in Peacemaking in Somali Society," in *Rethinking Pastoralism: Gender, Culture and Myth of the Patriarchal Pastoralist*, ed. Dorothy Hodgson, 121–141. London: Curry.

European Platform for Conflict Prevention. 1999. "Arts Chapter 7" in *People Building Peace*. Utrecht, Netherlands: European Platform for Conflict Prevention.

Farah, Ahmed Yusef. 1993. *The Roots of Reconciliation*. London: Action Aid.

Fernandez, James W., and Mary Taylor Huber, eds. 2001. *Irony in Action: Anthropology, Practice, and the Moral Imagination*. Chicago: University of Chicago Press.

Fesmire, Steven. 2003. *John Dewey and Moral Imagination: Pragmatism in Ethics*. Bloomington: Indiana University Press.

Fisas, Vicençe. 2002. *La Paz Es Posible*. Barcelona, Spain: Intermon Oxfam.

Fox, Matthew. 2002. *Creativity: Where the Divine and the Human Meet*. New York: Penguin Putnam.

Freedman, Jill, and Gene Combs. 1996. *Narrative Therapy: The Social Construction of Preferred Realities*. New York: Norton.

Freire, Paulo. 1970. *Pedagogy of the Oppressed*. New York: Seabury.

Friedman, Edwin H. 1990. *Friedman's Fables*. New York: Guilford.

Garcia, Alejandro. 1996. *Hijos de la Violencia*. Barcelona, Spain: La Catarata.

Gernika Gogoratuz. 2000. *Art Towards Reconciliation*. Bilbao, Spain: Gernika Gogoratuz.

Gladwell, Malcolm. 2002. *The Tipping Point*. New York: Little, Brown.

Goldberg, Michael. 2001. *Theology and Narrative: A Critical Introduction*. Eugene, Oreg.: Wipf and Stock.

Gopin, Marc. 2001. "The Use of the Word and Its Limits: A Critical Evaluation of Religious Dialogue as Peacemaking," in *Building Peace through Interfaith Dialogue*, ed. David Smock, pp. 42–56. Washington, D.C.: U.S. Institute of Peace Press.

Guroian, Vigen. 1998. *Tending the Heart of Virtue: How Classic Stories Awaken a Child's Moral Imagination*. New York: Oxford University Press.

Hauerwas, Stanley, and Gregory Jones, eds. 1997. *Why Narrative: Readings in Narrative Theology*. Eugene, Oreg.: Wipf and Stock.

Hayner, Priscilla B. 2002. *Unspeakable Truths: Confronting State Terror and Atrocities*. New York: Routledge.

Heinrich, Wolfgang. 1997. *Report on the Life and Peace Institute's Somali Initiative*. Uppsala, Sweden: Life and Peace Institute.

Helmick, Raymond, and Rodney L. Petersen. 2001. *Forgiveness and Reconciliation: Religion, Public Policy and Conflict Transformation*. Philadelphia, Pa.: Templeton Foundation Press.

Herr, Robert, and Judy Zimmerman Herr. 1998. *Transforming Violence*. Scottdale, Pa.: Herald Press.

Hofer, Eric. 1951. *The True Believer*. New York: Harper and Row.

Honeyman, Chris. 1990. "The Common Core of Mediation," *Mediation Quarterly*. 8: 73–82.

Johnson, Mark. 1993. *Moral Imagination: Implications of Cognitive Science for Ethics*. Chicago: University of Chicago Press.

Kane, Carole. 1999. *Petals of Hope*. Omagh, Northern Ireland: Omagh District Council.

Kirk, Russel. 1988. *Eliot and His Age: T. S. Elliot's Moral Imagination in the Twentieth Century*. Peru, Ill.: Sugden.

Lakoff, George, and Mark Johnson. 2003. *Metaphors We Live By*, 3d ed. Chicago: University of Chicago Press.

Leatherman, Janie. 2003. *From Cold War to Democratic Peace*. Syracuse, N.Y.: Syracuse University Press.

Lederach, John Paul. 1988. "Of Nets, Nails and Problemas: A Folk Vision of Conflict in Central America." Ph.D. diss. University of Colorado.

———. 1986. *La Regulación del Conflicto Social*. Akron, Pa.: Mennonite Central Committee.

———. 1992. *Enredos, Pleitos y Problemas: Una Guia Practica para Resolver Problemas*. Guatemala City, Guatemala: Semilla.

———. 1995. "Beyond Violence: Building Sustainable Peace," in *Beyond Violence*, ed. Arthur Williamson, 3–8. Belfast: Community Relations Council.

———. 1997. *Building Peace: Sustainable Reconciliation in Divided Societies*. Washington, D.C.: U.S. Institute of Peace Press.

———. 1999. "Justpeace: The Challenge of the 21st Century," in *People Building Peace*, ed. Paul Van Tongeren, 27–38. Utrecht: European Centre for Conflict Prevention.

———. 2001. "The Challenge of Terror: A Traveling Essay." Posted on the Website of the Joan B. Kroc Institute for International Peace Studies, University of Notre Dame.

———. 2002. "Building Mediative Capacity in Deep-Rooted Conflict." *Fletcher Forum of World Affairs*. 26(1) (Winter–Spring): 91–101.

———. 2003a. *The Little Book of Conflict Transformation*. Intercourse, PA.: Good Books.

———. 2003b. "Cultivating Peace: A Practitioner's View of Deadly Conflict and Negotiation," in *Contemporary Peacemaking*, eds. John Darby and Roger MacGinty, 30–37. New York: Palgrave.

Lieblick, Amia, Rivka Tuval-Mashiach, and Tamar Zilber. 1998. *Narrative Research: Reading, Analysis and Interpretation*. Thousand Oaks, Calif.: Sage.

Mayer, Bernard. 2000. *The Dynamics of Conflict Resolution*. San Francisco, Calif.: Jossey Bass.

———. 2004. *Beyond Neutrality*. San Francisco, Calif.: Jossey Bass.

Mbiti, John. 1969. *African Religions and Philosophy*. Portsmouth, N.H.: Heinemann.

McCollough, Thomas E. 1991. *The Moral Imagination and Public Life*. Chatham, N.J.: Chatham House Publishers.

McFaul, Thomas R. 2003. *Transformation Ethics: Developing the Christian Moral Imagination*. Lanham, Md.: University Press of America.

Mills, C. Wright. 1959. *The Sociological Imagination*. New York: Oxford University Press.

Mitchell, Christopher. 2003. "Mediation and the Ending of Conflicts," in *Contemporary Peacemaking*, ed. John Darby and Roger MacGinty, 77–86. New York: Palgrave.

Monk, Gerald, John Winslade, Kathie Crocket, and David Epston, eds. 1997. *Narrative Therapy in Practice: The Archeology of Hope*. San Francisco, Calif.: Jossey Bass.

Nairobi Peace Initiative, Africa. 2002. *Strategic and Responsive Evaluation of Peacebuilding*. Nairobi: Nairobi Peace Initiative and the National Council of Churches of Kenya.

Newsom, Carol A. 2003. *The Book of Job: A Contest of Moral Imaginations*. New York: Oxford University Press.

Paffenholz, Thania. 2003. *Community-based Bottom-up Peacebuilding*. Uppsala, Sweden: Life and Peace Institute.

Palmer, Parker J. 2000. *Let Your Life Speak*. San Francisco, Calif.: Jossey Bass.

Polkinghorne, Donald E. 1988. *Narrative Knowing and the Human Sciences*. Albany, N.Y.: State University of New York Press.

Pound, Ezra. 1913. "A Few Don'ts by an Imagist," *Poetry: A Magazine of Verse*, 1 (March).

Price, Martin. 1983. *Forms of Life: Character and Moral Imagination in the Novel*. New Haven, Conn.: Yale University Press.

Rashid, Ahmed. 2002. *Jihad: The Rise of Militant Islam in Central Asia*. New Haven, Conn.: Yale University Press.

Remer, Theodore. 1964. *Serendipity and the Three Princes*. Norman: Oklahoma University Press.

Riessman, Catherine Kohler. 1993. *Narrative Analysis*. Newbury Park, Calif.: Sage.

Robinson, Randall. 2000. *The Debt: What America Owes the Blacks*. New York: Penguin Putnam.

Roe, Emery. 1994. *Narrative Policy Analysis: Theory and Practice*. Durham, N.C.: Duke University Press.

Sawatsky, Jarem. 2003. Personal correspondence.

Senehi, Jessica. 2002. "Constructive Storytelling: A Peace Process," *Peace and Conflict Studies* 9, no 2: 41–63.

Shenandoah, Leon. Forward. 1946. *The Iroquois Book of Life: White Roots of Peace*. By Paul A. W. Wallace. Philadelphia: University of Philadelphia. Reprint, 1994. Sante Fe, N.M.: Clear Light.

Smailovic, Vedran. 1998. "Memento Mori Albinoni Adagio," in insert that accompanies the compact disc *Sarajevo Belfast*. West Chester, Pa.: Appleseed.

Stevens, Edward. 1998. *Developing Moral Imagination: Case Studies in Practical Morality*. New York: Sheed and Ward.

Stroup, George W. 1997. *Promise of Narrative Theology: Recovering the Gospel in the Church*. Eugene, Oreg.: Wipf and Stock.

Tivnan, Edward. 1995. *The Moral Imagination: Confronting the Ethical Issues of Our Day*. New York: Simon and Schuster.

Varea, Roberto Gutierrez, and Peter Novak, eds. "Symposium: Artists of Resistance," *Peace Review* 15, no. 2.

Villa-Vicencio, Charles, and Wilhelm Vervoerd. 2000. *Looking Back Reaching Forward: Reflections on the Truth and Reconciliation Commission of South Africa*. Capetown, South Africa: University of Capetown Press.

Volkan, Vamik D. 1999. *Bloodlines: From Ethnic Pride to Ethnic Terrorism*. Boulder, Colo.: Westview.

Volkan, Vamik D., and Joseph V. Montville. 1991. *The Psychodynamics of International Relationships: Concepts and Theories*. Lanham, Md.: Rowman and Littlefield.

Walpole, Horace. 1754. *Letter to Horace Mann*.

Weaver, Herm. 1999a. *Travellin' Home and Back*. Singers Glen, Va.: Reardon.

———. 1999b. "Travellin' Home and Back: Exploring the Psychological Processes of Reconciliation." Ph.D. diss., Union Institute and University.

———. 2003. Personal correspondence.

Weber, Max, 1947. *The Theory of Social and Economic Organization*. New York: Oxford University Press.

Werhane, Patricia H. 1999. *Moral Imagination and Management Decision-Making*. New York: Oxford University Press.

Wezeman, Phyliss Vos. 1990. *Peacemaking Creatively through the Arts*. Prescott, Ariz.: Educational Ministries.

Wheatley, Margaret J. 1994. *Leadership and the New Sciences*. San Francisco, Calif.: Barrett-Koehler.

———. 2002. *Turning to One Another*. San Francisco, Calif.: Barrett-Koehler.

Williams, Oliver, ed. 1998. *The Moral Imagination: How Literature and Films Can*

Stimulate Ethical Reflection in the Business World. Notre Dame, Ind.: University of Notre Dame Press.

Winslade, John, and Gerald Monk. 2001. *Narrative Mediation: A New Approach to Conflict Resolution.* San Francisco, Calif.: Jossey Bass.

Yasuda, Kenneth. 2000. *The Japanese Haiku.* 14th ed. Boston, Mass.: Tuttle.

Yeats, William Butler. 1993. *Early Poems.* New York: Dover Publications.

Yeats, William Butler. 1996. *The Collected Poems of W. B. Yeats,* ed. Richard J. Finnerman. New York: Scribner.

Zehr, Howard. 2002. *The Little Book of Restorative Justice.* Intercourse, Pa.: Good Books.

Index